VARIETAL WINES
OF AUSTRALIA

VARIETAL WINES
OF AUSTRALIA

JOHN BEESTON

An imprint of HarperCollins*Publishers*

AN ANGUS & ROBERTSON BOOK
An imprint of HarperCollinsPublishers

First published in Australia in 1991 by
CollinsAngus&Robertson Publishers Australia
A division of HarperCollinsPublishers (Australia) Pty Limited
Unit 4, Eden Park, 31 Waterloo Road, North Ryde NSW 2113,
Australia

William Collins Publishers Ltd
31 View Road, Glenfield, Auckland 10, New Zealand

Angus & Robertson (UK)
77-85 Fulham Palace Road, London W6 8BJ, United Kingdom

Copyright © John Beeston 1991

This book is copyright.
Apart from any fair dealing for the purposes of private study,
research, criticism or review, as permitted under the Copyright
Act, no part may be reproduced by any process without written
permission. Inquiries should be addressed to the publishers.

National Library of Australia
Cataloguing-in-Publication data

Beeston, John.
  Varietal wines of Australia.

  Includes index.
  ISBN 0 207 16974 8.

  1. Wine and wine making—Australia. I. Title.

641.220994

Cover by Steven Bray
Typeset in Australia by Midland Typesetters
Printed in Singapore

5 4 3 2 1
95 94 93 92 91

FOREWORD

It was inevitable that John Beeston should write a wine book. After all, most of his friends have. John Beeston joins his Bulletin Place Tasting Team colleagues, including Len Evans 'The Chairman', James Halliday and Anders Ousback, who have all made their contribution to the groaning shelves of oenological literature.

Finally it is 'the General's' turn. John Beeston, like the others of the Tasting Team, has been in intensive training for the past twenty years for just this event. The thousands of sniffed, sipped, savoured, guessed at, argued about and just plain quaffed wines, which have flowed over the collective palates of the Bulletin Place Tasting Team, represent the dedicated sacrifice which makes this book possible.

The more entries in the computer, the more relevant and accurate the results of the statistical analysis. So it goes with wine with one fundamental difference—that of opinion. The descriptions of a wine by two experienced tasters should be, and normally are the same, within the bounds of the covers of a Thesaurus.

However, a decision of preference is born of a much more fickle parent, opinion. Above all else, John Beeston has written an opinionated wine book, eliminating the trivia of fashion and mere commerce, to concentrate on his preference, wines of pedigree. This book contains opinion by the *barrique* and bottle full, expressed eloquently but easily understood because of its bluntness.

To qualify for comment in this book a wine must have ancestors and the prospect of future generations of the line. It must have a pedigree based on a vineyard, region, winemaker or company and most in this book are consistent to all of these. If it qualifies, a wine is forgiven its bad vintage (the product of climatic or winemaking aberration) as long as it has shown the resilience of pedigree to return to form.

Because of John's rigorous selection of those wines which have proven their merit over time, you will find in this book the seeds of Australian regional specialisation: the Hunter for Semillon; Clare for Riesling; Coonawarra for Cabernet; and hints of other less formalised marriages of variety and region.

Technically competent, entertaining, ultimately opinionated, this book is useful. If the wine isn't in here, don't expect much unless you have made a new discovery. If it is, try it and compare your opinion of it, to that of one of the best, John Beeston.

BRIAN CROSER

PREFACE

This book is about Australian wines, in particular those made from the most important table wine varieties of this country and what to expect from them on nose and palate in their various growing regions.

It is not intended to be an exhaustive or encyclopedic work. Many wineries, both big and small, and many wines, indeed the vast majority of them, have been omitted for reasons of space or interest. The palate responsible, for better or for worse, is my own. It is a book concentrating on the top level of Australian wines, and I make no apology for that, as quality is where the future of Australian wine lies. It may annoy, it may perplex, it may even gratify, but I do hope it does not bore.

This work is intended for the serious wine consumer, who has gone beyond the wine cask, is bored by 'generics' such as 'Chablis' or Australian 'Beaujolais' and wishes to explore, for example, the intricacies of a Margaret River Cabernet–Merlot or a Yarra Chardonnay. It is, I hope, a book to help expand the palate by explaining the range of varietal wines available, the styles to be expected, and the strengths of certain varieties and varietal blends in individual areas. In that sense it promotes regionality rather than cellar brands. Yet the top cellar brands are not ignored, for Australia has become accustomed to blending wines from its many areas and is very skilled in the practice.

I trust the book is useful to many and will give as much pleasure to some as Max Lake's *Classic Wines of Australia* which was given to me many years ago.

A guide to tasting notes

Most of the wines annotated in this book have been tasted on release within the past 18 months and perhaps may still be found at quality wine merchants throughout the country. Approximate dates of tasting are also given, as are points out of 20 (15.5–16.9 a bronze medal, 17–18.4 a silver, and 18.5–20 a gold), according to the usual wine-show pointing scale, and the years when the wine in question might be drunk at its best. All wines tasted have been bottled and on sale except where otherwise noted.

The language used in these notes is typical wine judges' jargon. Words such as 'nose', 'palate', 'cut' and 'finish' are in everyday use in wine-tasting, and the English language is all about usage. I cannot therefore apologise for them. The language used in the notes also draws out smell and taste parallels with which most adults will be familiar. Ultimately, wines are like all other subjective experiences—the more harmonious they are, the better they are.

As for the selection of wines, I have consciously tried to pick those that are typical of the regional style of the particular variety or varieties while acknowledging those of individual merit which may differ in style. Both variety and varietals are to me the spice of life.

JOHN BEESTON, 1991

CONTENTS

THE WHITES

'SOFT, FRUITY AND FLINTY'
CHARDONNAY 2
SEMILLON, SAUVIGNON BLANC AND OTHERS 47

'FRAGRANT AND FLOWERY'
RHINE RIESLING, TRAMINER AND OTHER AROMATIC VARIETIES 70

THE REDS

'LIGHT AND MEDIUM-BODIED, SOFT FINISH'
PINOT NOIR 94

'MEDIUM-BODIED, FIRM FINISH'
SHIRAZ 112

'MEDIUM AND FULL-BODIED, FIRM FINISH'
CABERNET SAUVIGNON 137
CABERNET BLENDERS AND BLENDS 163
OTHER REDS 187

BOTTLE-FERMENTED
SPARKLING WINES 190

VINTAGE CHART 194
USING THE SENSES TO ASSESS WINES 201
GRAPE VARIETIES AND ACCEPTED SYNONYMS 206
GLOSSARY 207
INDEX 216

THE WHITES

SOFT, FRUITY AND FLINTY

CHARDONNAY

Chardonnay is the absolute archetype of amiability. Wherever it has travelled throughout the world, it has succeeded superbly for its versatility and charm.

Despite some winemakers' insistence on the name 'pinot chardonnay' and a similarity in leaf shape, it is not related to pinot noir; chardonnay is genetically more stable, although in the Burgundy region of France a pink version has been noted and also one with distinct muscat overtones. Like most grape varieties its origins are unknown, though there is a school of thought that connects it to the Middle East, especially Lebanon (where it is still grown, invasions permitting), and could perhaps have returned to France after those ancient Lebanese invasions, the Crusades, in the baggage of a crusader. Perhaps the village of Chardonnay, near Mâcon in Burgundy, has a claim of origin. Which did come first: the village or the variety?

On the whole, Australian viticulturists are much happier with chardonnay than with pinot noir, though research proceeds in both varieties. Physiologically chardonnay is of moderate vigour and ripens quite early in season. Like pinot noir it buds early in the spring and is therefore susceptible in the cooler and higher regions of its growth to frost damage during spring and also in exposed areas to damage by winds at the time of flowering. Though its leaves are similar in shape to pinot noir, they are smoother and less hairy on the lower surface; and as for its bunches, if an identity check is required before véraison (colour change) they are a little bigger and not as compact, carrying rounder berries.

In France there are about 13 000 hectares planted to chardonnay, almost equally divided between Champagne (6500 hectares) and Burgundy (6000 hectares). Recent increases in plantings have occurred predominantly in Champagne and Chablis, though the variety is most famous in the Côte d'Or, where alone it constitutes the noble white vineyards of Puligny-Montrachet, Chassagne-Montrachet, Meursault and Aloxe-Corton. To the south it is widely grown in the Côte Chalonnaise and also in the Mâconnais, where the villages just to the north of Beaujolais such as Pouilly-Fuissé and St Véran make excellent wine. To the north of the Côte d'Or, in Chablis, though other white varieties are authorised to be grown, it is solely responsible for that ultimately flinty dry white, true chablis; and in all classic blends of champagne it supplies that quintessence of elegant flavour, leaving to pinot noir the palate roles of length and sturdiness. By itself, of course, it is used widely in the Côte des Blancs to provide that most appetising aperitif, Champagne Blanc de Blancs.

Elsewhere in France it is seen in the Jura, sometimes blended with savagnin (synonym: traminer) to produce the sherry-like *vin jaune*; occasionally on the Loire; and quite recently in the Ardèche region where it is planted to make a varietal wine by Louis Latour—a practice seemingly tolerated (as it is largely directed at the export market) in a country where the local consumer is largely ignorant of grape varieties.

In common with other French varieties, chardonnay is now extremely popular in the north and north-east of Italy and is making inroads further south in Tuscany, Umbria and Apulia. Even in conservative Spain, innovative makers such as Torres are planting chardonnay in the Penedés area, where it is blended with local varieties. It is also extensively grown in Eastern Europe.

In the New Wine World it flourishes in California, where the world's chardonnay boom began, but is equally well known in Oregon and Washington state and is even these days planted in favourable parts of the eastern states and Canada, as well as in South America, South Africa and New Zealand.

After the 1988 vintage its area in Australia was 2978 hectares, yielding from 2344 hectares of bearing vines 20 639 tonnes (an average of 8.88 tonnes to the hectare, not a vast improvement on pinot noir).

Historically Australia owes a debt of gratitude to James Busby for the introduction of the variety, his original vines having been selected from Clos Vougeot. Thereafter chardonnay fell into oblivion for about 120 years, until clones were imported by the Western Australian government in 1957 and by Penfold's into New South Wales in 1958. Reawakening interest in the variety saw it rediscovered in Mudgee and the Hunter in the 1960s, the first chardonnays made in commercial quantities and in recognisably modern style being released by Tyrrell's in 1971. By the mid-1970s Tyrrell's Pinot Chardonnay Vat 47 was striking an exciting chord amongst consumers. Soon other Hunter producers such as Saxonvale and Richmond Grove had leapt on to the same wagon, and the chardonnay boom had begun. Away from the Hunter Valley another sizable area of chardonnay had been planted at Cowra, and it was from here that the first Petaluma chardonnay was made in 1977. In chardonnay the Hunter Valley had clearly stolen a march on South Australia which would not be made up till 1986. Chardonnay quickly became popular in Victoria also, its virtues being rapidly appreciated in both the cool and warm areas of the state.

Because of consumer response to the variety, Australia's winemakers and growers have become most enthusiastic about chardonnay. By mid-

1988 a planting boom was well under way, more than 20 per cent of all Australia's chardonnay being not then in bearing. In South Australia interest was high in the Adelaide Hills and McLaren Vale, where 22 per cent (43 hectares) were then unbearing; and those astute Barossa grape farmers, though still faithful to riesling, continued the chardonnay push (71 unbearing hectares, or 26 per cent, of the valley's chardonnay at mid-1987). South Australia's largest plantings of this variety, however, remained in the Coonawarra–Padthaway region, where there is little sign yet of enthusiasm abating. The Clare district, like the Barossa historically loyal to riesling, has also paid heed to current market trends, chardonnay plantings there at mid-1987 being 142 bearing hectares with 22 hectares yet to yield.

As is to be expected, the chardonnay styles from South Australia vary with the regions, McLaren Vale and Barossa making richer styles akin to other warm areas, whereas Coonawarra–Padthaway and the Eden Valley–Adelaide Hills areas produce austere wines and also sparkling-wine base. The Clare region pursues the middle road, climate and altitude dictating a stylistic path for chardonnay that is neither rich nor austere.

Though New South Wales vies with South Australia as the nation's largest producer in total, the Hunter Valley remains the greatest single area in extent and yield, with 494 hectares and more than 3570 tonnes in the 1987 vintage. Yet throughout New South Wales the variety is well established, notably in the Murrumbidgee Irrigation Area, Barooga, Mudgee and Cowra. All chardonnay areas in New South Wales, except the relatively new and quite small plantings at Tooma and Tumbarumba in the Snowy Mountains area (where sparkling-wine base is chardonnay's primary purpose), are warm regions in 'degree-day' terms. The result is a style of chardonnay that develops relatively quickly to the bottle, usually being quite pleasurably drinkable at 12 months of age—though to this rule, as to all rules, there are exceptions, the cool 1987 vintage producing chardonnays of great finesse in the Hunter Valley and Mudgee.

South of the Murray River in Victoria, interest in chardonnay is running high—higher even than in South Australia. Almost a quarter of the state's plantings were not yet in bearing at mid-1987. The largest areas are located in the Mildura district (Victorian Sunraysia) with nearly a third of the state's plantings, and the North-East with almost one-fifth. The chardonnay zealots, however, direct their devotions to cooler climes—to Geelong, Gippsland, Mornington, Macedon and most particularly the Yarra Valley. There the wines are often austere, even severe, when young, needing time in bottle to develop that soft fullness of flavour that is so readily apparent in wines from warmer areas. There, too, increasing amounts of chardonnay are vinified as sparkling-wine base.

More modest extents of chardonnay exist in Tasmania, but interest in sparkling wine is no less intense. At Pipers Brook, Heemskerk, spurred on by continuing Louis Roederer involvement, progresses steadily towards its first commercial 'bubbly'. Taltarni also has taken its first steps towards the production of a Tasmanian méthode champenoise by establishing 10 hectares of close-planted chardonnay, 1.5 hectares of meunier and 1 hectare of pinot noir on favourable limestone country south of Pipers Brook at Lebrina. The first commercial 'bubbly' is expected in 1994. Domaine Chandon, the Australian subsidiary of the world champagne giant, Moët, has also arranged fruit contracts with growers at Richmond, near Hobart. As for table wine, the Pipers Brook region, selected sites near the Tamar River and the suburban Moorilla vineyard near Hobart have produced chardonnays which are, as expected, very much 'cool area' in style, needing time in the bottle to develop complexity.

In Western Australia, chardonnay area is small in comparison with eastern states. Only 106 hectares were planted as at mid-1987. Yet enthusiasm remains at a high pitch. In the Mount Barker–Frankland River region, chardonnay styles reflect their cool environment (as in Tasmania) with the result that youthful local wines need time to 'fill out' in bottle. Some makers also occasionally blend local wine with richer material from the Swan Valley to produce a wine with more immediate appeal.

In the Margaret River district, climatic influences such as onshore salt-bearing winds can create severe difficulties for the variety at flowering time, though the quality of wines made by Leeuwin Estate and Moss Wood over a number of years has left no doubt as to the ultimate worth of the area for chardonnay. In the Swan Valley, climatically related to other warm areas, the wines produced are full and rich in flavour.

As 'base' for sparkling wine, chardonnay is made very simply, winemakers generally seeking high acidity, low sugar and as little varietal character as possible. 'Creaminess', as Brian Croser calls it, and finesse are its two ultimate virtues for that purpose.

As table wine, however, chardonnay presents the contemporary winemaker with such a multitude of options that it may truly be called a 'designer wine'—yet, as always, great wine does begin in the vineyard.

The winemaker must ensure that the vine is as healthy and the grapes are as ripe as possible. With this objective the vineyard must not be overcropped. Perhaps 8–9 tonnes per hectare (coincidentally the national average) is the optimum yield. A sugar content in the grape of 13° Baumé is a commonly accepted level of ripeness that maximises fruit flavours. If juice of that quality is available, the fruit should be picked at an ambient temperature as close as possible to 12°C and the fruit reduced further in temperature to 2–4°C, as anti-oxidative measures. Alternatively the fruit may be crushed immediately and the must chilled down to this temperature as quickly as possible. Thus in warmer areas, a must-chiller or an extremely effective coolroom are necessities of life to a successful chardonnay maker. Juice separation is best achieved by an airbag press, as such presses yield softer juice with greater complexity. Then the juice must be clarified. The quickest way is by centrifuge, but as centrifuges are very expensive, settling is often used, although in the absence of strict temperature control (2–4°C) there is a risk of oxidation. Therefore if a winemaker is forced to pick fruit at temperatures in excess of 12–14°C or if there is any risk of oxidation at any stage up to commencement of fermentation, he or she would be wise to use a small amount of sulphur dioxide (no more than 25 mg/L) to minimise that risk.

After the juice is clarified, comes the choice of cultured yeast. Here the winemaker is faced with several options, though R2 yeast has been popular during the 1980s, giving tropical fruit aromas to fermenting chardonnay. During fermentation also, bentonite is often added to create protein stability prior to oak maturation.

Sometimes, when fermentation is semi-complete (down to 5° Baumé), the winemaker may wish to increase complexity by running off part of the fermenting juice into new oak barrels to complete fermentation in that medium. Which oak? The winemaker may have the choice of four or five— Limousin, Troncais, Nevers, Allier, Vosges, not to mention American. Oak, like coffee, also has several levels of toasting: light, medium, or heavy. All these minute complexities will affect the flavour of the final wine.

When the barrel-fermentation is complete, the winemaker has a further choice: to clean up the wine or to leave it on lees for any length of time up to four months. (Any longer than this and the risk is that the wine will have a permanent 'lees' taste.) Some makers even stir the lees during this time. Again there are potential problems. Is malolactic fermentation desirable? Perhaps, as to a fraction of the final blend, but certainly not as to the whole, for overly soft, buttery wines do lack structure and age badly. However, in cool areas with a wine of high natural acidity it is certainly an option to be considered.

The winemaker will now have to add all these fractions together to complete the whole wine for the year. When the final blend has been assembled, the maker may or may not give the wine more time in wood. Alternatively, he or she may decide to bottle two or three different wines to emphasise various wood treatments, but after final blending and tartrate stabilisation the wine is usually bottled within a year of making.

What should now be expected of our hypothetical one-year-old chardonnay? If it has not been oxidised its colour should not be overly yellow and definitely not brown, though colour levels tend to deepen as the result of wood maturation. 'Light to medium straw' is a common Wine Show specification, though tints of green are never to be condemned. Above all it should be bright and certainly without dullness.

In bouquet, all manner of fruits, nuts, leaves and other substances have been identified. In wines from warm areas, impressions of peaches, apricots and figs have all been detected. In cool areas, grassy characters can be recognised in slightly unripe wines. In riper wines from such areas, aromas of melons, apples and tropical exotics such as guava and passionfruit are noticed. The many noses of chardonnay can also drive one 'nuts': cashews and hazelnuts. As well, 'butteriness' is a common description for wines that may have a malolactic component. All these nuances are of course both complemented and made more complex by degrees of oak maturation and 'char', which add vanillan, toast and sometimes even 'bacon' overtones to the wine.

On the palate the nuances seem easily to convert to the primary tastes of the fruits mentioned, especially the stonefruits such as peaches and apricots. With bottle age the smells and tastes will change again, as fruit and wood combine to produce an entrancing 'nuttiness'.

Such is a brief outline of the many aromas and flavours of chardonnay. But how should the palate be structured? In truth it is really quite like its Burgundian bedfellow, pinot noir, though the palate structure differs to some extent depending on the wine's warm or cool area of origin and winemaking techniques applied. In warm areas, chardonnay wines should have a soft palate entry, a full, even voluptuous, middle palate, long and persistent, which may even give the impression of nutty sweetness and then a soft dry lingering finish. It should on no account be actually sweet or alcoholically 'burning' on finish. In cool areas the palate structure should be the same, with the important exception that middle-palate fullness may not develop until after further bottle age. Yet even within those areas there remains the question of technique. Has that cool-area wine been slightly oxidised to fill out the palate? Has that warm-area wine been kept free of oxidation so that the palate remains comparatively undeveloped? Because of technique it is virtually impossible to identify chardonnays by region. Nevertheless it is the regions that the chardonnay aficionado finds so fascinating.

NEW SOUTH WALES

Without doubt the Hunter Valley is where Australian varietal chardonnay began, with the first Tyrrell's Vat 47 in 1971. This wine and its successor 1972 were made and matured in like manner to Tyrrell's semillons. Cool fermentation and maturation in large old oak vats. In 1973 came the first recognisably modern Australian chardonnay, part fermented and matured in small new Nevers oak. As a youngster this wine, which contained about 5% semillon, was extremely precocious; in middle age it built slowly upon that youthful promise and, when tasted for the purposes of this book in late 1988, was still marching on to ultimate maturity. The wine was not markedly developed in colour. True, it was mid-yellow, but there were green tints, and for a 15-year-old wine it was in magnificent condition. Hints of 'peach' intermixed with beautifully handled wood adorned the nose, while on the palate the wine was soft and finely balanced without any evidence yet of bagginess or overdevelopment. Made in an age when wine-making 'techniques' were used much more cautiously than today, it is a wine that in today's terms would be called 'simple'. Let that be no disparagement, however, for by any standards of quality it has aged marvellously and has withstood the challenge of wine's sternest critic, time. (18.5 points)

In that small but very select line of Vat 47s (1973, 1976, 1978, 1979, 1980 and 1982) there was another outstanding wine, 1979, which had developed in the 'Meursault' mould. Deeper in colour than the 1973, with typical 'noisette' on nose, its palate was well structured but, for a nine-year-old white, comparatively undeveloped. (18.5 pts) This wine and the 1973 were really the exceptions to the thesis that all Hunter chardonnays should be drunk at three years of age. Only fractionally behind 1979 were the 1980 and the 1982, both then probably drinking at their best, showing slight 'toastiness' and full flavoursome palates. Past their best were the 1978, oxidised and flabby, and the 1976, rather rich and fat and now at the drink-up stage.

Since 1982 the fame of Tyrrell's Vat 47 has continued. 1983 was a ripe and successful wine, which can still be kept (17 pts); 1984, initially thought to be flawed by vintage conditions, became, perhaps because of those self-same conditions, very much a 'Meursault' style and the winner of five trophies at Australian wine shows (18.5 pts). Then came a trio of wonderful years: 1985, very much like 1983 (17 pts); 1986, a late slow vintage with a wealth of fruit on palate (17.5 pts); and 1987, an elegant and cool year, arguably with the greatest potential of all (18.5 pts). Only 1988 (a damp vintage) might slash this ribbon of success (16.5 pts), yet, who knows, it may turn out to be another 1984.

Though the Tyrrell chardonnay techniques have changed but slightly over the years since 1973, there have been differences in fine tuning: Limousin oak in place of Nevers from 1983 onwards, an attempt to emulate the bigger, richer Californian style from 1980 to 1983 (from which the Californians themselves have now to some extent retreated), perforce changed in 1984 by a cool damp year and by a change in philosophy which favoured a lighter style with greater finesse. Tyrrell, the chardonnay pioneer, is not yet ready to yield the palm to others. (Note that Vat 47 of 1977, a famous show wine, though reputedly very good still, has not been tasted by me recently.)

Saxonvale was another early starter in the Hunter chardonnay stakes. Mark Cashmore's first vintage was in 1977. Indeed two wines were made that year, both treated identically except for German oak maturation for Bin 1. At my tasting in October 1988, Bin 1 had evolved into a full yellow colour with lovely 'toasty' aromas and a ripe, almost 'creamy' palate. This wine, though obviously mature, was showing no signs of the downhill slide and was first-equal on the day with 1986 vintage. (18.5 pts)

Of the 14 wines tasted (1977 to 1988 inclusive, with 1977 and 1978 being made in both wooded and non-wooded form), 1986 was typical of that ripe, marvellous year—full yellow in colour, almost, one might say, too advanced but colour can be misleading. On nose there was a tropical complexity of melon and guava, followed by a round, yet fresh palate with balanced acidity. (18.5 pts) It is a wine of very great potential, needing to be kept till 1991, as should its younger brothers, 1987 and 1988, both too undeveloped at the time of tasting.

Of other wines tasted, 1985 was showing a degree of volatility, which insisted to me that it should be drunk, whereas 1984 is of the intricate Burgundian mode, fascinating in its present complexity, yet still with time to develop further, as are a number of other Hunter chardonnays of that year. 1983 and 1982, on the other hand, are ready and were very good drinking in late 1988, though each is of different style, the former ripe and toasty, the latter of lighter, softer palate without toastiness. But be in no hurry for either. The rest, 1981, 1980, 1979, 1978 and the non-wooded 1977, it is now time to drink for various reasons: 1981, volatile lift on palate; 1980, German oak now starting to dominate fruit; 1979, beginning to fade; 1978s and non-wooded 1977, flabby.

Starting its experimentation first with German oak in 1977 and then Limousin oak in 1981, Saxonvale and its winemakers Mark Cashmore (1977-80) and Alasdair Sutherland (1980-89) have contributed greatly to the round soft style of Hunter chardonnay, far more greatly than sales would indicate, but then commerciality should not perhaps intrude too much into matters of palate.

At the Rothbury Estate, 100% varietal chardonnay began as late as 1982, though small areas of the grape were planted as long ago as 1972. In the 1970s those small amounts of chardonnay were either blended with semillon or made separately and sold singly in the Rothbury tasting pack. In the late 1970s, convinced that consumer enthusiasm for the variety was escalating, Rothbury greatly expanded its plantings, a decision which, though never regretted, marked the beginning of the end of semillon as its major white variety.

I tasted that initial chardonnay with its successors in September 1988.
1982 Hunter Valley Chardonnay: developed yellow colour, complex nose with lifted characters. Palate was then showing 'toasty' bottle age with volatile acidity slightly intruding. (15.5 pts) Should be drunk.
1983 Directors' Reserve Chardonnay: overwhelmed both on nose and palate by volatile acidity and a smoky wood character. Regrettably little else left to mention. (not pointed)
1984 Hunter Valley Chardonnay: full yellow colour, complex toasty nose, plus a touch of rot, very similar to a 'Meursault' of a less-than-great year. Complex stylish palate. About ready to drink. The Côte de Beaune style of this wine was shared by quite a few others in that vintage. (17.5 pts)
1985 Hunter Valley Chardonnay: mid-yellow colour, good integration of 'peaches' and wood on nose. Palate, however, was not quite complete, falling away slightly on finish. Further bottle age may correct this. (16 pts)
1986 Hunter Valley Chardonnay: full yellow colour, attractive hazelnut nose, full round harmonious palate. A very great wine in late 1988. The first of two great chardonnay years in the Hunter. (18.5 pts)
1987 Hunter Valley Chardonnay: mid-yellow colour, nose shows excellent 'peaches' and wood development. Palate was long and elegant, auguring

well for its future. A wine very much in the class of the 1986. (18.5 pts)
1988 Hunter Valley Chardonnay: pale youthful colour, nose of green peaches. Light palate, rather short, lacking the structure of the 1987. May evolve like 1984. (16 pts)

In technical matters Rothbury is thoroughly up to date. Forty per cent of the new wine is fermented in Vosges barriques from 4° Baumé to dryness and retained on lees for two to three months. Wines are strictly assessed for quality and blended in the May after vintage. Further maturation in new Vosges oak follows for two to three months, after which bottling of the various quality levels takes place. Such techniques ensure that Rothbury chardonnays are among the leading Hunter examples of the variety.

Though Tyrrell was the first runner into the chardonnay vineyard, closely pursued by Saxonvale, Hungerford Hill was not too far from the pace. Here, too, new small French oak plays its part in chardonnay wines, which are very much in the mainstream of current Hunter style. Oak from the Vosges and Allier forests predominate with a little Tronçais also used for further complexity. Though 1979 was Hungerford Hill's first chardonnay vintage, my tasting of its Merchant and Show Reserve chardonnays commenced with 1982. There are usually three chardonnays from any year:* the Ribbon sold mostly at cellar door, and very quickly; the Merchant selection, made in greater quantity and found (as the name suggests) in the trade; and Show Reserve, made in quantities sufficient for show exhibition. In July 1988 both the Merchant and Show Reserve wines were ready for drinking, and though both would hold that plateau of mature flavour for a year or more thereafter, prolonged time in the cellar would see them fatten and lose structure. As the 1983 wines had all been sold out, I could not taste them but contented myself instead with 1984, that most complex of Hunter chardonnay years. At Hungerford Hill, as elsewhere in the valley, the wines produced are of a pronounced Burgundian style. The 1984 Merchant range was yellow-gold in colour, with a developed nose of peaches, charred oak and a touch of 'noisette', the palate showing expansive peachy flavours. (16.5 pts) The chardonnay *summa cum laude* of that year, though, is the Show Reserve, medium yellow in hue, revealing a peachy generosity in bouquet, and a fairly undeveloped palate with light peach flavours that will continue to grow in bottle. (18 pts). Of the range tasted, only the 1985 Merchant wine was disappointing: hard on palate with a 'geranium' nose because of problems caused by the yeast used at fermentation. (14 pts) There were no such problems in 1986, a year renowned for opulent chardonnays. The Merchant wine is very attractive, ripe and of excellent flavour. (16.5 pts) The Show wine, however, manages to be richer in every respect, slightly fuller in colour, peachier on nose and weightier on palate. (17.5 pts)

* (That is, there were until June 1990, when Seppelts purchased Hungerford Hill.)

1987 was also magnificent for Hunter chardonnay, though more elegant and less rich than 1986. The Merchant wine was pale yellow in hue, showing a marvellously balanced bouquet of fruit and wood and long, elegant flavours on palate. (17 pts) As with the 1986, its Show Reserve brother has more size, a bigger colour, a more prominent nose and longer fruitier palate. (18 pts) The 1986 and 1987 Show wines will be hard acts to follow.

Though vintage conditions were less generous in the Hunter Valley in 1988 than in other regions, the Hunter chardonnays show typical generosity of flavour, but on a shorter palate. The 1988s will simply be ready earlier.

Lindeman's is a company with ancestral Hunter roots, a rich past and an imposing presence still in varieties such as semillon and shiraz. Paradoxically, in Hunter chardonnay it is a virtual beginner. True, some early experimental wines were made in the late 1960s, but then in the 1970s, possibly because of overly conservative management or failure to appreciate market trends, Hunter chardonnay went into limbo, an uncertain state that was reversed in the mid-1980s. From that time, Lindeman's Hunter River Winery has kept totally abreast of current developments in the variety.

Recent chardonnay vintages have been excellent and in particular 1988 Hunter River Chardonnay Bin 7282, a blend of Broke and Pokolbin fruit. At my tasting in March 1989, the wine in colour was a youthful pale yellow. On nose, there was a marvellously balanced bouquet of peaches and oak (a complex wood treatment of American, Nevers and Allier oaks). The palate was big and generous, finishing softly, though with excellently balanced acidity. (18 pts) A trophy winner at the Royal Sydney Wine Show in 1989, this wine is a forward style to be drunk in 1990-91.

Its predecessor, H.R. Chardonnay Bin 7082 of 1987, was more traditional 'chablis' in mould. Still pale yellow in hue, rather closed and a little 'melony' on nose, the wine had yet to fill out a palate, which was restrained in flavour, but with lively acidity on finish. (16.5 pts) This was a cool-year style to be drunk 1991-93.

The 1989 vintage had just been completed at the time of writing this chapter. It was indeed eminently successful for Lindeman's Hunter River Winery, and one of its highlights will be chardonnay. Though not yet in wood in March 1989, the colour of the tank sample was a fine and very pale yellow-green with nose and palate both beautifully 'peachy', all important ingredients for the future success of a Hunter chardonnay.

McWilliam's, the traditional Hunter rival of Lindeman's, came earlier to Hunter chardonnay. Since 1977 (the first commercial release) it has become a prominent contestant in the Hunter chardonnay race. Here too, as in most leading Australian wineries, there is a high level of technical competence, and again as in most wineries the oak handling of the variety has evolved from year to year according to the maker's conception of style and complexity. Thus in the 1985 vintage, the principal oaks used at McWilliam's Mount Pleasant were Limousin, American and Nevers. The following year, Limousin oak was dropped. In 1987 and 1988, a combination of Nevers Allier and Vosges was employed, then in 1989 Vosges (very subtle in its influence on chardonnay) was the major oak component. Malolactic fermentation as to part and lees contact are adopted as measures of complexity.

In March 1989, I tasted all McWilliam's Mount Pleasant chardonnays since 1985, including the exceptionally good Homestead range. Here are the highlights.

Mount Pleasant Homestead 1985: medium yellow in colour with tints of gold, this wine had a rich 'char' nose, which proved a little deceptive, as the fruit and wood flavours on palate did not quite carry the same weight as would have been anticipated. All the same, a very good wine which should fill out with further bottle age. (16.5 pts)

Mount Pleasant Homestead 1986: full yellow hues and tints of gold. A complex nose of peaches and 'char' oak foreshadows a complete well-integrated wood fruit palate, with some length and good acidity. (17.5 pts)

Mount Pleasant Homestead 1987: like all the best Hunter chardonnays of 1987, this wine on palate has elegance and subtle power. Its nose too is very attractive with a slightly understated combination of wood 'char' and tropical fruit, a highly successful liaison that will certainly develop well in bottle. (18 pts)

There is also a show wine of 1987 with all the subtlety and elegance of 1987 Homestead and a further dimension of excellence. (18.5 pts) It is certainly one of the best of that very worthy Hunter year, a year as graceful and accomplished for chardonnay as 1988 was uncertain.

Yes, at Mount Pleasant as in other wineries in the region, 1988, with its incessant showers and moody skies, came as an anticlimax. Make no mistake, the chardonnays of that year are sound and pleasant, for, as Brian Croser once said, chardonnay is an ever-forgiving variety, but following the magical performance of 1987, the 1988s were always going to have a tough act. Like tap-dancing dwarfs, they are lively but a little short. Even so, 1988 Homestead Chardonnay will be very good in a damp year. (16.5 pts)

The commercial line, Mount Pleasant Chardonnay, seems to have less emphasis on technique and wood. It is a more simple fruity wine, less complex and more appealing in price. Homestead Chardonnay will usually be worth any extra expense or even, as they say, 'a special trip'.

The largest chardonnay producer in the Hunter Valley is without doubt Wyndham Estate, which markets chardonnay under the Richmond Grove, Hollydene, Elliot, Hunter Estate and Wyndham Estate labels. It also owns Saxonvale, but because of Alasdair Sutherland's continued stewardship of that winery from 1980 to 1989, I have dealt with the chardonnay of that winery separately.

The chardonnays of the Wyndham stable are very much in the mainstream of Hunter chardonnay and are often keenly priced. The

Wyndham Hunter Chardonnay has been a definite success and as an early drinking style is generally more polished than its Hunter cousins, Richmond Grove, Hollydene, Elliot and Hunter Estate, and a cut above the other Wyndham chardonnays, Bin 222 and Oak Cask. 1987 and 1988 are both good years.

Of the old 'family' companies, only Tyrrell's and Drayton's still survive under family control, and even Drayton's has recently been 'taken over' by its winemaker, Trevor Drayton. The Drayton Family Winery was also an early starter in the chardonnay race, initiating a line of fine Hunter chardonnays with an outstanding 1979. Of more recent wines, 1988 was an undoubted success in a bedraggled year (17 pts), while 1987 was a wine of more elegant style, showing in January 1989 a developing yellow colour, a subtle nose of light tropical fruit character and a balanced palate of soft fruit and oak. (18 pts) It was quite drinkable then but did possess the reserves to develop well in bottle until 1992.

Tulloch is another old Hunter name, until 1969 family-owned. Since then it has had a procession of owners, the latest being Penfold's. In that company's favour, it might be said that it has ceased to promote Tulloch as a megastar brand and has cast it once more in the role of proficient local performer. As such, its chardonnays have typically forward Hunter style, being sometimes a little big in the girth, but always as well flavoured as the year permits and generally suitable for immediate drinking or short-term cellaring.

The Tulloch Chardonnay 1988 shows a slight predominance of wood on nose, while the palate once more relies on wood for structure. Fruit is certainly there, but it seems to be waiting rather hesitantly in the wings like a ballerina before her first solo. When tasted in April 1989 I felt that given one or two more years in cellar, the fruit would appear and make a satisfactory debut. (16 pts)

Len Evans has been instrumental in orchestrating many things to do with wine. Rothbury Estate and Petaluma are but two of the larger ventures. His own Evans Family has a line of chardonnays which, like that of Drayton, began in 1979. In a tasting in January 1989, this wine, the 1982 and the 1986 were outstanding. The 1979 was very flavoursome with the slightest touch of oxidative nuttiness, quite forgivable in a veteran. 1982 was also ready, its main feature being a long and beautifully balanced palate, while the 1986, holding a deep yellow hue, revealed a buttery peachy nose and a rich full-flavoured palate with good finishing acidity that would stand the wine in good stead until 1991. (18.5 pts)

Chardonnay is de rigueur for many other small makers in the Lower Hunter. Virtually all either grow a few hectares or have access to ever-more expensive fruit, which, combined with high production costs, means that there are rarely any chardonnay bargains, but it is always worth looking.

Of the more established smaller makers, Lake's Folly produces chardonnay, which like its cabernet cousin is obviously made for the long haul. Like a young Meursault, it is in youth sometimes dominated by oak, but usually there is fruit enough there to bring the wine back to balance in a couple of years. 1987 was such a wine. (16.5 pts)

Brokenwood also has been in chardonnay production since 1982. Its style is in the mainstream of the best Hunter chardonnays, 'peaches and cream' in warmer years and at its best when one to two years old, but more elegant in cooler vintages such as 1987 and taking just a little longer to reach its optimum. 'Graveyard' is its individual vineyard chardonnay.

Of the others, Simon Whitlam consistently makes excellent wine and certainly should continue to do so, now that a syndicate including Andrew Simon and Nicholas Whitlam and Arrowfield winemaker Simon Gilbert have purchased the Arrowfield winery.

Peterson's too have built a considerable reputation in the past five years, while newcomers Allanmere and Fraser have made very good wines in recent vintages. The rest are rather less consistent, though Terrace Vale and Sutherland often make excellent wine, contributing to that distinctive and justifiably popular Australian quality white, Hunter chardonnay, a style that wineries in cooler areas desirous of selling their own chardonnays 'ready to drink' are keen to copy.

Some critics have labelled Hunter, indeed all warm-area chardonnays, as 'peaches and cream' styles and the archetype of that style is the Roxburgh Chardonnay of Rosemount. Certainly Rosemount have a tremendous investment in Hunter chardonnay and other white varieties. The white maturation cellars at Rosemount are certainly most impressive, with a capacity of 2000 barriques and pièces all held subject to temperature control. In March 1989 I tasted all Roxburgh Chardonnays released to that date, including a tank sample of 1988 which at that time was not bottled.

The first of the line was 1983, yellow-gold in colour, showing bottle-age 'toastiness' on nose and a full, soft 'honeyed' palate. (17.5 pts) This wine was about ready to drink in 1989, though haste was not necessary.

1984 proved to be a most interesting Hunter year, with showers and rot producing chardonnays of marked Burgundian style. The Roxburgh of that year was deep yellow-gold in colour, with a particularly complex nose displaying touches of 'hazelnut' and 'old orange peel' (botrytis). The palate was full and complete, yet not heavy and quite without the oiliness that botrytis sometimes imparts. In all it was a fascinating drink and a very stylish chardonnay. (18 pts)

The following Roxburgh (1985) was the most restrained. Though full yellow in colour, the wine on nose was still slightly dominated by oak, the palate having a wood 'nuttiness' with good length without any corresponding fruit generosity. As a wine it was not nearly as complex as the 1984 nor as full-flavoured as the 1986, yet I predicted that given two more years in bottle it might well fill out. (16.5 pts)

The 1986 vintage produced Hunter chardonnays of voluminous flavour and the 1986 Roxburgh was certainly no exception to the rule. Deep yellow in colour with a complex buttery nose, it was the nose that predicted the palate, a wealth of flavour, made more intricate by a slight volatile lift. The wine was certainly ready to drink, and further bottle age would give it that 'toastiness' of ripe-year Hunters. (18 pts)

In contrast to 1986, 1987 was splendid in its finesse, especially in chardonnay. The Roxburgh is a bright green-yellow with well-integrated 'charred' oak and fruit on nose. On palate, the wine was greyhound-like, long, lean and ready to go places, but not, I hoped, in too much of a hurry. Two to three years in bottle should develop excellent palate complexity, the wine becoming in that time a most elegant Roxburgh classic. (18.5 pts)

Of all the wines, the 1988 was the lightest on palate and not only because it was the youngest. A damp 1988 vintage had seen to that. From its pronounced oak 'char' and evident 'Burgundian' sulphide on nose, I was prepared for a bigger palate, but in March 1989 this had not yet developed. It may well happen within two to three years, but the wine is certain to be controversial.

With Rosemount's enormous resources of oak and excellent Roxburgh vineyard chardonnay plus as much refrigeration as is needed, Philip Shaw looks for complexity in his chardonnay styles. He is past the stage of simple fruity wines. Malolactic fermentation, extended lees aging, at least four different types of French oak—Allier, Vosges, Tronçais and Nevers, from three different coopers—all contribute to the fascinating chardonnay canvas that Philip Shaw paints for the world gallery. The Roxburgh style, though often rich, is by no means always 'peaches and cream'. It is constantly evolving and is surely one of the world's leading 'estate' chardonnays.

Rosemount of course produces two other chardonnays, Show Reserve and a commercial 'Chardonnay'. Show Reserve is on occasions almost as opulent in some vintages as Roxburgh, but usually maintains an elegance that marks it apart. 1987 was an excellent year for this wine. (18 pts)

The only other chardonnay producer in the Upper Hunter that has from time to time impressed me is Arrowfield. Very fine wines were made in 1981 and 1984, but two changes of ownership in three years cannot have helped Arrowfield in its winemaking and marketing. Despite this the 1987 Arrowfield Reserve Selection Chardonnay (80% from the Hunter, 20% from Cowra) is a wine with a wealth of flavour and winemaking talent. (17.5 pts)

Mudgee is another region of rebirth of modern Australian chardonnay. The variety is exceptionally well made at Montrose, although in contrast to the upfront appeal that typifies the better wines of the Hunter Valley, the Montrose chardonnays are, when young, quite 'cool' in character. They are none the worse for that, but you should expect 'grapefruit' rather than 'peach' on nose and palate when tasting young Montrose chardonnays. The Montrose style is understated and requires about three years in bottle to bring it to optimal development. 1988, 1987 and 1986 are all cast in the same mould, whereas 1985 is just beginning to 'fill out', showing 'lemony' aromas and some bottle age on nose and more complete flavours on palate.

It is, however, the 1984 (tasted with the others in April 1989) that most impressed me. Medium-full yellow in colour, with a bouquet of ripe peach and also 'butter and toast', the wine has fascinating complexity on palate, showing full peachy fruit with peppery spicy wood. A chardonnay at the peak of perfect development. (18.5 pts)

Elsewhere in the district, Miramar (with modern techniques) and Huntington (with more traditional methods) produce reliable chardonnay. The newcomer Thistle Hill will certainly be worth watching in the next few years.

If there is one area in Australia whose fame is as yet based on one variety only, it is Cowra. True, other red and white varieties are grown, but chardonnay from Cowra has in the past decade become renowned as a spectacularly rich, early drinking style. Though Cowra was the source of early Petaluma Chardonnays, since 1981 when Rothbury Estate purchased a large part of the vineyard, both Cowra and Rothbury have each other to thank for what has been a liaison of great financial benefit to Rothbury and lasting viticultural kudos for Cowra.

A tasting of the whole range of Cowra chardonnays in which I took part in September 1988 confirmed my views not only of the early drinking nature of the wines but also that they do have short-term cellaring potential. Though the earliest wines (1981–83) can be dismissed as being over-developed, 1984, though ready, was holding well; it was in fact extremely attractive with its 'toasty', vanillan oak nose and full, complex palate. (17 pts) As for 1985, it too showed 'toasty' aromas on nose and a rich, complete palate. (17 pts) Cowra Chardonnay 1986, however, was outstanding—only slightly developed in colour with a deep 'peachy' stonefruit nose and a palate that can only be described as luscious. (18.5 pts) 1987 showed very elegantly with plenty of development potential ahead of it (at least two to three years). (18 pts) 1988 was clean, young and fresh, another wine to keep for three years or to enjoy when young. (17 pts)

The other vineyard in the Cowra region, producing chardonnay of quite adequate quality, is Cowra Wines. None of these wines, however, is made in Cowra. Rothbury chardonnays from this region are made at the Rothbury winery in Pokolbin, while Cowra Wines chardonnays are made at Arrowfield.

None of the chardonnays made in the Murrumbidgee Irrigation Area are of outstanding quality, but that is no hindrance to sales of bulk wine. Many cheaper branded chardonnays will obviously contain material from this area and perhaps even a few that are not so cheap. Local makers of above-average-quality chardonnay in this region are McWilliam's (Hanwood Chardonnay), Miranda and Rossetto. None should be cellared more than two years from date of vintage.

The one remaining chardonnay producer of importance elsewhere in New South Wales is Cassegrain, at Port Macquarie. There, John Cassegrain, who underwent his wine education at Roseworthy College and Tyrrell's, employs both local (Hastings Valley) fruit and Pokolbin material from his Clos Colline vineyard on Pokolbin's Marrowbone Road. Regional wines are produced from both sources, and unusually good wines they usually are. Complex French oak and rich 'peachy' flavours are the criterion of the Cassegrain Pokolbin style, while Hastings Valley chardonnay generally behaves in a lighter more elegant fashion, though oak treatment here is little different from Pokolbin chardonnay. Good Cassegrain chardonnay years have been 1984 and 1985 (Hunter) and 1986 and 1987 (both Hunter and Hastings).

AUSTRALIAN CAPITAL TERRITORY AND ENVIRONS

The ACT, once thought fit for only sheep and politicians, also has its chardonnays. The leading vineyards in the region are Doonkuna, north of Canberra, and Lark Hill north-east of the capital at Bungendore in nearby New South Wales. The chardonnays of Doonkuna I have not recently tasted, but the 1988 Chardonnay of Lark Hill was in March 1989 quite undeveloped. Very pale in hue with fresh clean melon aromas, this wine showed great elegance on palate and had the potential to develop very well in bottle over three to four years. Dr David Carpenter is now making the benchmark wines of the region. (17 pts)

VICTORIA

Chardonnay has been enthusiastically embraced everywhere in Victoria, in warm areas and cool, high in the hills and on the Sunraysia flats. Though the wines are never as varied as the locations—most Victorian makers, like their brethren elsewhere in Australia, preferring to make the 'upfront' broader-flavoured, earlier-drinking style—the much cooler southern areas of the state offer a natural home for the variety not too dissimilar to its ancestral haunts.

Pre-eminent among such areas are the famous regions of the Yarra Valley, Geelong and that new locale of great promise, the Mornington Peninsula.

John Middleton of Mount Mary and Peter McMahon of Seville Estate are elder statesmen of Yarra chardonnay, Mount Mary chardonnays having appeared since 1977 and Seville since 1976. As such, you might expect them to have conservative views about the making of Yarra chardonnay.

To a certain extent they have, but only as regards the ultimate style for the area.

John Middleton has an intense dislike for 'upfront' early-drinking chardonnay, so highly regarded by most consumers today. Attractive though it may be to some, to him it is excessive. 'Tutti frutti' and 'lychee' are his descriptions, and from his tone they are not the most favourite words in his lexicon. Yarra chardonnay should certainly not be that. To Middleton it should be reserved and elegant in youth, needing five years in bottle to show its wares and probably three to five years more to reach its peak. He does not mind oak dominance in young wines for he believes that Yarra Valley chardonnay has sufficient fruit character to catch up with any seeming imbalance of wood. The wines, he believes, are entitled to develop in the bottle, complexity and 'nuttiness' being the hallmarks of a great old Yarra chardonnay just as they are in the great white burgundies of the Côte d'Or. So it stands to reason that his own favourite wines are 1980 and 1982, though 1986 and 1987 are also held in high esteem.

As for technique, Middleton is no slavish follower of all modern trends. He does not mind if his chardonnay juice has a slight 'solids' content, but he avoids 'skin contact'. Depending on year, his fermentations, using multiple yeast cultures, may be commenced in tank for one to two days and then transferred to wood or begun and completed in wood. Nor does he experiment with malolactic fermentation, disliking its 'buttery' flavours. As for sulphur, in common with most Australian makers he keeps it low, no more than 30–40 ppm appearing in the finished wine. Yet other techniques such as lees stirring are used until the middle of July following vintage, the wine then remaining in lees contact till bottling just before the ensuing vintage. Though his favourite oak is Tronçais which he has used from the very beginning, Allier and Vosges are now also employed. With oak, however, John Middleton is a man of moderation using only about 15 per cent new wood each chardonnay vintage.

Peter McMahon at Seville Estate, that other senior winemaker of the Yarra, also feels that Yarra chardonnay should be made for bottle aging. Accordingly his wines are rather restrained when young with typical 'lemony' fragrances, subdued palates and high acidity, just the style for five years' development in cellar. He also avoids malolactic fermentation, though he does allow skin contact for some hours before pressing. Juice is cold-settled for four days before the must undergoes a two-week fermentation in stainless steel until transfer to oak at about 2° Baumé. Eight months' maturation on unstirred lees follows, the wine being bottled in November following vintage and released for sale a year later. His favourite year of older vintages was 1980, now unfortunately all consumed. Of more recent vintages he believes that 1986 and 1987 are fine examples of his style and that 1988, though riper and more forward than usual (perhaps even a little 'upfront'), will be very good also.

Of newer winemakers in the valley, new in chardonnay terms at least, his first commercial vintage being in 1986, David Lance at Diamond Valley has created a fine impression.

In its making, David certainly follows what might be called conservative Yarra technique: a cool picking day, not more than 15°C, if it can be managed, and in the Yarra it often can; skin contact for 12–18 hours; juice cold-settled for three to four days; two weeks or longer fermentation at 15°C entirely in stainless steel; low sulphurs, 35 ppm; removal from gross lees and then straight into wood, old rather than new, where the wine remains untouched on light post-fermentation lees for eight to ten months depending on time of bottling; and after bottling, three to four months' bottle maturation before release. No barrel ferment, no malolactic, no extended lees contact or stirring, none of the ultra-modernities. And the results? An extraordinarily elegant wine if the 1987 is anything to go by, though David has more than a passing regard for his 1986.

I tasted the 1987 Diamond Valley Chardonnay soon after release in August 1988. In colour the wine was extremely pale. A very youthful bouquet, underpinned by an harmonious liaison of Nevers and American oak, hinted at fig, apricot and peach, and a long but undeveloped palate, rounded off by crisp acidity, suggested similar fruit flavours. It was a classic Yarra chardonnay which needed five to six years to fill out and develop that characteristic almost Burgundian Yarra nuttiness. (17.5 pts) And age well they do, as witness David's 1984 Chardonnay, a wine made, regrettably, in minute quantity, which is now developing into a full-bodied but still elegant white of marvellous 'noisette' complexity on nose and compelling flavour on palate.

Apart from a disappointing 1986, David Fyffe at Yarra Burn has also made a substantial contribution to Yarra chardonnay style. Of recent years, 1987 holds tremendous promise. Quite austere in the manner of its vintage, it was very pale in colour with a light 'stonefruit' nose and a long though undeveloped palate. In August 1988 it was certainly a wine worth waiting for. (17 pts) At the same time, I tasted 1984. On nose it had pungent tropical fruit characters, while the palate was dominated by grapefruit flavours—a most complex wine, this product of an ultra-cool, cool-area vintage and, I felt, quite atypical even in the Yarra. The reason was not far to seek, for the R2 yeast used in fermentation and German oak employed in maturation were still showing their distinctive effect four and a half years later. It was a fascinating Yarra chardonnay still to come to maturity, whenever that will be. (16.5 pts) In 1989 vintage, David Fyffe planned to repeat the experiment.

Though James Halliday at Coldstream Hills has made a marked contribution to the sum total of knowledge of Australian pinot noir, Coldstream Hills, in its brief existence, has made some marvellous Yarra chardonnays. In no vintage was this more evident than 1987. The Four Vineyards Chardonnay of that year is marvellously constructed for aging in bottle. In early 1988 it was the palest of greens; the onset of yellow had hardly begun. Its bouquet was comparatively undeveloped, though fragrances of melon and grapefruit were starting to evolve. It was the palate that won me to the wine, long youthful flavours with almost steely (but never hard) acidity, reminding me very much of a young Puligny-Montrachet of the highest rank, and like all such wines it would have been vinocide to drink it before it was eight years old. (18.5 pts)

The 1988 Four Vineyards Chardonnay (tasted March 1989) was fuller in colour, nose and palate, perhaps reflecting the warmer vintage weather. As such it was extremely attractive at one year of age, but will it last? Most certainly, and will develop even more complexity over three or four years. (18 pts)

Halliday has a most studied approach to chardonnay. The Four Vineyards wine is precisely that, the product of four quite separate fruit sources. As such the fruit from one may be treated quite differently from others. The entire spectrum of modern techniques, which being mostly traditionally Burgundian are very old, is employed: skin contact, barrel ferments, malolactics, aging on lees, and lees stirring, as well as the more standard practices of fermentation and storage in stainless steel. These 'fractions' of different chardonnays are then melded into harmony on the blending bench. With Halliday as winemaker at Coldstream Hills, its chardonnay will never be pedestrian.

St Hubert's is an old and hallowed name in the Yarra Valley, yet here too the same modern chardonnay-making techniques are being utilised by winemaker Brian Fletcher. One of his early problems was, paradoxically, having too much chardonnay on vine, so much in fact that it was difficult to ripen properly and on occasions was afflicted by botrytis before it did ripen. This problem of vigour and overfertility is now being overcome. Like Halliday, Brian Fletcher sizes up the fruit for its positive virtues, before adopting a winemaking technique. If it is ripe and sound, Burgundian methods are followed. The must is settled but allowed some light 'solids', barrel fermentation follows, as does malolactic fermentation of some 'fractions'. Minimal sulphur dioxide is used at all times. The resultant wine usually has guava flavours and the broader diacetyl characters of malolactic fermentation. Very good material for complexity.

With other parcels of fruit, perhaps not as sound nor as ripe, he adopts more normal, in his word 'protective', measures. Protective of fruit quality and character, that is. No malolactics or barrel ferments are used, just normal white winemaking processes, although the need to be a little different may arise as it did in the case of some slightly unripe fruit in 1988, when he reduced volume and increased naturally fermentable grape sugars by freeze drying the must. As he says, the protective method usually produces the typical 'fig/melon' Yarra chardonnay. From the tank samples I have seen, 1988 will be a great year for St Hubert's chardonnay.

Another newcomer to the Yarra is Tarrawarra, presently specialising only in chardonnay and pinot noir. It is a distinctive winery set beneath the spectacular hills which tower above Yarra Glen. Regrettably, 1986, the first chardonnay of the vineyard, was not as outstanding as its vineyard setting, a wine seeming to hesitate betwixt and between classic 'cellaring' Yarra and the more buttery 'upfront' styles of warmer areas, substituting the rather mealy, broad flavours of malolactic fermentation for the more usual elegant fruit of the region.

The 1987 is much better. Tasted in May 1989, it showed youth in colour, melon and a touch of grapefruit on nose, good length, full middle-palate flavours and a firm acidity on finish. Like most of its Yarra compatriots of that year, it needed to be cellared at least five years, when patience would surely be rewarded.

At Lillydale Vineyards, Alex White and Martin Grinbergs began their chardonnay experience in 1980. They usually pick when the sugar content is between 22 and 23.5° Brix but do prefer the juice to develop the right flavours within this range of potential alcohol. Their chardonnay technique is quite standard for the valley, though there are a few variations. Chilling reduces the must temperature to 5–6°C, after which a period of 12–16 hours skin contact follows. The juice is then pressed and cool-settled for three days. Fermentation in stainless steel proceeds on minimum 'solids' until dryness, when the wine on light lees is transferred for maturation into stainless steel and Allier, Vosges and Nevers oak, about a third of which is new each year. Malolactic fermentation, though not actively sought, sometimes occurs in a few of the casks in warmer weather and occasionally the lees are stirred, but Alex White tries to do without sulphur dioxide. Bottling takes place after six to nine months' barrel maturation.

As for the wines, they age extremely well, coming to their peak of palatability eight to nine years after vintage, when they develop those nutty, toasty flavours so typical of the region. The best years in White's opinion have been 1982, 1984 and 1986, with 1987 showing great elegance and long-term potential in February 1989. My notes at that time were most enthusiastic about the 'creaminess' of its nose and great length of palate, which would fill out over the next four to five years. (17 pts)

Elsewhere in the Yarra Valley—and it is only fair to say that as a vineyard area it has Australia's most exciting prospects as the 1990s are upon us—there are many other makers whose chardonnays will in this decade be justly famous. Long Gully and Yarra Ridge are two of the newer names. Chateau Yarrinya, under new ownership since 1987, may well join the list, while the chardonnay of Yeringberg, though produced in tiny quantity, is always worthy of respect.

Another region of intriguing chardonnay interest is the Mornington Peninsula, in national vineyard terms quite Lilliputian, but like those impressive midgets capable of a performance far outstripping its size. Few vineyards yet produce a thousand cases in all, let alone of chardonnay, so the wines are as yet hardly plentiful in quantity.

The chardonnay styles are typically cool-area, with hints of melon, grapefruit and occasionally peach on nose, showing on palate rather undeveloped grapefruit flavours and a counterpoint of new oak. There are of course other variations on those simple themes, as makers seek to add the complexities of barrel ferment and malolactic fermentation. There is no reason whatever why the Mornington chardonnays should not show similar aging characteristics to the Yarras.

Names to seek out are Dromana Estate (particularly), Elgee Park, the pioneer of the area, Main Ridge Estate and Stonier's Merricks.

Typical of Mornington in a fine year was Elgee Park Chardonnay 1988. Tasted in March 1989, it was very pale in hue and understated on nose with oak dominant at that time. On palate, the wine was fine and delicate with a good backbone for further cellaring. (17 pts) Drink in 1992-94.

Challenging the Yarra in pinot noir is Geelong, with Bannockburn (as befits its name) keeping the standard high, but is there the same threat in chardonnay?

Certainly Garry Farr's Bannockburn chardonnay style seems to change from vintage to vintage. The 1986 wine was distinctly herbaceous on nose with a soft riper palate that seemed to belie the nose. Did it lack structure or was it simply in need of bottle aging? In April 1988 it was a wine at the crossroads. (16.5 pts)

The 1987 Bannockburn chardonnay was a much more technical wine. On nose there was melon, grapefruit and barrel ferment characters which made for a great deal of complexity. A youthful palate, quite undeveloped and rather lean in February 1989, showed excellent spicy wood but did need five years more in bottle. The 1987 was definitely the more impressive wine. But it is not I suppose consistency of style that counts, so much as versatility in response to differing vintage conditions, and this Garry Farr has in abundance. (18 pts)

South-east of Geelong, and indeed, across the Port Phillip Heads, a comparatively short crow's flight or car-ferry ride from Mornington, is the Bellarine Peninsula.

There, Hickinbotham Winemakers, which is an incorporation of the many winegrowing and winemaking talents of the Hickinbotham family (now sadly without the winemaking mainspring of the family, Stephen, tragically killed in an aircraft accident in 1986), have encouraged many winegrowers by their advice and, more practically, by the purchase of their crops.

In addition to the outstanding Geelong Pinot Noir 1988, Hickinbotham have produced a very modern chardonnay from the Coghill vineyard close to Port Phillip Bay. Mostly barrel-fermented with a small portion undergoing malolactic fermentation, the wine matured on unstirred lees in a mixture of Tronçais, Allier and Vosges oak until bottling in December 1988. In

February 1989 this complex wine revealed quite a big, buttery nose and an appealingly deep peachy palate. In contrast to many cool-area styles, it was very definitely 'upfront', showing all the technical prowess that had gone into its making. Warmer-area wines made in such a way become big and blousy within three to four years. However, I feel that this wine may just have the stamina to last at least six or seven years. It promises much for the future of Geelong chardonnay. (18 pts)

Far to the east of Melbourne, Gippsland is certainly cool and one of the most remote vineyard areas in Victoria. At Nicholson River winery, Ken Eckersley makes chardonnay of high quality in very small quantity. Though 1986 was a very good wine, 1987 certainly excelled. The quality of Nicholson River chardonnay is without doubt, but can Eckersley increase production sufficiently to make East Gippsland a viticultural name of the importance that it deserves?

The large expanse of undistinguished countryside that surrounds Melbourne Airport masks an historic viticultural area once more rising to prominence. A few minutes' drive past the airport is the cool, often windswept locality of Sunbury, where 120 years ago Craiglee was a famous winery indeed. Though, in common with many other cool-area Victorian wineries, it fell to grazing in the 1920s and gradually faded from the viticultural scene, it was restored by the Carmody family in the mid-1970s. The 1987 Chardonnay that I tasted in May 1988 was light, rather subdued in fruit and needed three to four years' bottle development. (16 pts)

Also in the Sunbury area is Goonawarra, not a comical misnomer of the South Australian viticultural region, but in fact, as a vineyard site about 30 years older. It too died as a vineyard during the first 80 years of the twentieth century, but was revived in 1982. I have not tasted its chardonnay, but on the strength of its wine consultant appointed for 1989 vintage, John Ellis, it should not be less than very good.

That same Sunbury road leads on to Bendigo and beyond, but before then the Mount Macedon area deserves attention, if only for the great promise shown by the Romsey Vineyards of Cope-Williams. Here the winemaking is certainly of the more conservative school, if the 1987 Chardonnay, tasted in May 1988, is typical. That wine was restrained both in colour and nose, but did have the fine 'melon' fruit and low-profile wood of good cool-area chardonnay. It was a cellaring style that could be laid down with confidence for five years. (17 pts)

Close by and within sight of its monolithic namesake is the Hanging Rock winery of John Ellis. The surrounding vineyards are planted primarily to chardonnay and pinot noir, and though there have been as yet no releases of chardonnay, one feels compelled to adopt the slogan of the advertising man: 'watch this space'.

North of the Mount Macedon region and on a rather more circuitous route to Bendigo is Heathcote. In the heart of town is the aptly named Heathcote Winery. Earlier chardonnays (the first appeared in 1981) were a little inconsistent up to 1984, a trophy winner and very highly regarded indeed. Vintage 1985 continued the fickleness of the line, being rather lean and austere, whereas 1986 returned Heathcote to top chardonnay form with a fine wine of grapefruit and melon aromas with good length on palate and excellent cellar potential. (17.5 pts) Though I have not tasted it, 1987 is reputed to be a generous style showing some intensity of tropical fruit and oak on nose and palate.

Chardonnay of course has always been said to be the red-wine drinker's white. So it is only proper that the most famous chardonnays of Bendigo, which even in its twentieth century renaissance has remained predominantly a red wine area, are those made by Stuart Anderson, the region's restorer and best winemaker. Though Balgownie is now owned by Mildara, he toes no corporate lines, and like all his Balgownie-grown wines, his chardonnays make a very individual statement about his winemaking credo.

He picks ripe, 12.5° Baumé, though not superripe. Fruit is field-crushed and held under inert gas, drained overnight and cold-settled; it is a handling method that results in quite a lot of 'solids'. About 40 per cent of the wine is fermented in barrel, where it remains on stirred lees. The rest, fermented in stainless steel, is racked off lees and spends the next eight months in new oak. Anderson's preferred oak is from the forest of Bertranges in Central France. After bottling before Christmas, the wine is allowed to rest for a further ten months before release.

Anderson loves the complexity of chardonnay and aims in style for the sumptuous intricacy of Meursault. As might be expected, his chardonnays are on release quite generously but not excessively flavoured wines, midway in style between the austerity of cool-area and lavishness of warm-area chardonnays. His favourites of recent years have been 1984, 1985, 1987 (a little austere), 1988 (generous) and 1989, which he describes as a 'ripper'.

In May 1989 I tasted four Balgownie chardonnays, 1984 to 1987 inclusive. Of them all, 1984 was the most complex and appealing. A developing yellow in colour, the wine showed aromas of peach and 'Burgundian' sulphide on nose, the typical 'noisette' of aging white Burgundies. On palate there were nicely compact but intricate flavours of butter and oak. It was all very 'Meursault' and proved an excellent accompaniment to pork fillet with a sauce of reduced cream, Dijon mustard and green peppercorns. (18 pts) Of the rest, 1986 was rich and ripe with nutty wood on nose and palate, reminding me very much of some Corton-Charlemagnes of the ripe Burgundian year of 1976. (17 pts) The ensuing wine, 1987, was then very young, revealing grapefruit and oak char on nose and a palate which, though slightly hollow and reserved, might, given time, turn out like 1984. (16.5 pts) Only 1985 was a trifle disappointing on the day, having a phenolic nose and a sturdy four-square palate, with some bitterness on finish. (15 pts)

Stuart Anderson is very much his own winemaker, yielding to noone in his concept of style. His Balgownie chardonnays are hand-crafted wines, individual in style and hardly ever showing the boring upfront sameness of most chardonnays in this modern wine world. Like most of the chardonnays from the Yarra Valley, they are always worth trying. More strength to his winemaking elbow!

South-west of Bendigo are the neighbouring areas of Avoca–Moonambel (the Pyrenees) and Great Western. The Australian Pyrenees, unlike their European counterpart, are a series of wooded hills which protect the region from the excesses of the prevailing south-west weather pattern. As a result, the region receives sufficient but not generous rainfall and may experience extremely cool vintages. In general it is warmer than the more southerly Victorian areas. The district's chardonnays behave accordingly, being usually fuller in youth than their southern cousins, but retaining some of their elegance.

The chardonnay style of this region is epitomised for me by the wines of Dalwhinnie. 1987 reflects its cool vintage, showing delicate fruit and beautiful oak handling both on nose and palate. It is a clean, crisp wine which should age well in bottle over a short to medium term. (17 pts)

Similarly 1988 echoes the warmer riper conditions of the vintage. It was a bigger, more forward wine, ripe and buttery on nose and palate and extremely pleasant drinking in February 1989, with nonetheless good short-term cellaring prospects. (17.5 pts)

Another reliable maker of chardonnay in that region is Mount Avoca.

To Viv Thomson at Best's in Great Western, the flavour of chardonnay is a much more important consideration than ripeness. Not that ripeness is in any way discounted, it is just that after certain levels of ripeness have been reached, usually 12° Baumé, flavour becomes the most important criterion in picking.

The fruit is lightly sulphured and treated with enzymes on crushing, drained, pressed and cold-settled for two days before fermentation at 14°C until the must is reduced to 3–4° Baumé, when it is transferred to oak, about 30 per cent of which is new, to complete its fermentation. The new wine remains on unstirred lees for three to four months, when it is cleaned up and put back into barrel. Malolactic fermentation is not presently employed, but Thomson has no philosophical objection and will experiment with it in future vintages.

As for oaks, in common with many other Australian winemakers, he has great confidence in that old favourite, Nevers, though Allier and Vosges are playing an increasing part of the 'mix'. After bottling no later than January, the new chardonnay is rested for about six months and released in the following July. Best's best recent years (no pun intended) have been 1984, 1987 and 1988.

As in most vineyard areas in south-eastern Australia, 1988 was quite a ripe year in Great Western. The Best's Chardonnay of that year, tasted in June 1989, is no exception to its vintage conditions. Though it has an undeveloped 'grapefruit' nose with slight floral complexities, its palate is rich, ripe and soft. (17.5 pts) It is a forward style which will be nicely accessible by 1991.

By contrast, the older yet more typical 1987 was at the same time more austere, revealing melon/grapefruit aromas on nose and a light- to medium-bodied palate, needing at least two more years in bottle. (17 pts) Drink in 1991–92.

The oldest wine of the trio, 1984, showing grapefruit, wood char and a little bottle age on nose, with fig and peach flavours on a generous palate, was my favourite. How good the 1984 chardonnays from southern Australia were, five years on! By no means had this wine yet reached its peak. Indeed in two to three years it would be even more complex. Certainly cellaring cool-area chardonnays has its rewards. (18 pts) Drink in 1991–92.

Trevor Mast is also an experienced chardonnay hand at Great Western. His Mount Chalambar estate, though small, produces excellent chardonnay, which before 1988 was used entirely for sparkling-wine base. In 1988 Trevor made his first Mount Chalambar chardonnay table wine. He is another maker who picks on flavour; and flavoursome, Mount Chalambar chardonnay most certainly is. He is strongly of the opinion that chardonnay fruit flavours should always dominate those of wood, and with this in mind only about 20 per cent of his chardonnay is barrel-fermented, the balance being fermented in stainless steel. Nor does malolactic fermentation play any role, for it too detracts from fruit. Oak of course is not totally ignored, Tronçais, Allier Vosges and Nevers all participating in wood maturation which lasts till the following October. Naturally, 1988, the only Mount Chalambar Chardonnay released at time of writing, is Trevor's favourite. It is a wine very much in the modern tropical fruit mode. Very pale and young in hue, with high-toned aromas of passionfruit, the wine shows great depth of fruit flavour and very little oak. If there are criticisms to be made, they are of degree. Perhaps the wine should have a little less fruit and a little more oak, but certainly it is a very promising start for chardonnay table wine at Mount Chalambar. (17.5 pts)

Trevor Mast is also consultant winemaker for the Fratin Brothers at Mount Langi Ghiran, whose first chardonnay was made in 1989 vintage. If the quality of the chardonnays to come from Mount Langi Ghiran in any way matches that of the shiraz wines, already made, there are many treats in store.

Most chardonnay from the Great Western vineyards of Seppelt goes into one or more of the premium sparkling wines of that company. Sometimes, however, there is sufficient fruit for both sparkling and still wines. 1986 was one of those years, in which both a superb sparkler (the Charles Pierlot Blanc de Blancs) and a very fine single-vineyard chardonnay were made.

In colour the 1986 Great Western Chardonnay is quite brilliant, in both senses of that word. Not only is it extremely good, but it also shines. A scintillating green-yellow hue preceded a complex modern nose of tropical fruit, charred oak and barrel ferment characters. On palate, there were well-integrated grapefruit and oak char flavours and a crisp acid finish. (17.5 pts) A wine with three to four years' good cellaring life ahead of it (tasted June 1989).

Other chardonnay makers in the area are Cathcart Ridge and Montara.

That Central Victorian arc of hills constituting the Great Divide is usually thought to separate not only north from south but also warm from cool. That may be true of the plains vineyards of the north-east and the Murray River banks, but these days the general rule in Victorian chardonnay viticulture seems to be, subject to one notable exception, to rise above the excessive heat of the plains and cultivate the cooler hillsides and hilltops above the valleys of the Goulburn, Ovens and King Rivers. Thus the Mount Helen Vineyard of Tisdall stares north from the very top of the Strathbogie Ranges, the Delatite Vineyard of the Ritchie family can almost see the skiers on Mount Buller, and the new plantings of Brown Brothers peer north from the 800-metre high Whitlands plateau. Spectacular views! Spectacular chardonnays? On the whole, yes.

On the Whitlands plateau, chardonnay has been an instant success, if the 1987 Brown Brothers wine is a reliable guide and I am sure that it is. Mid-yellow in colour this wine was, in January 1989, very much state-of-the-art, carrying attractive melon/grapefruit aromas, nicely integrated with new oak. The palate was typical of cool-area chardonnay, being comparatively austere at that stage, but with the latent fruit to develop well in bottle and be at its peak by 1992. (17.5 pts) Its successor, 1988, though a little riper on palate because of its year, should be just as good with same optimal development. (17.5 pts) As pioneers of cool-area viticulture in north-east Victoria, Brown Brothers will release some exciting Whitlands chardonnays in years to come.

John Ellis, already mentioned briefly as a notable winemaking inhabitant of the Macedon region, came to Tisdall's Mount Helen in 1979 and found 16 hectares of very cool-area chardonnay ready and waiting for direction. His first Mount Helen Chardonnay, vintaged in that cool year, was made very much in accordance with the standard Australian white-wine textbook of the time: chilled must, free of solids, fermented cool in stainless steel for two weeks or so, taken off lees, cleaned up, and left to mature in a mixture of new and old oak and stainless steel for several months.

Ellis describes that first wine as 'riesling-like' and not only because of the method of making. The flavours also were not too different. But the learning-curve had begun. 1980 was a perfect year for the new chardonnay maker at Mount Helen. Ripe but not overripe fruit, marvellously flavoured juice, nature and John Ellis succeeded admirably. This wine, I recall, had intense fruit and lovely balanced acidity, which very early on marked it out for long-term development. 1981, was a trophy winner at Brisbane Wine Show; and 1982, late-picked in a cool year, had its followers. Ellis, however, continued to strive for more complexity.

While in Burgundy for the 1982 vintage, he satisfied himself as to the essentials of Burgundian chardonnay making at that time (and it is very much the same today), solids, musts, barrel-fermentation and wild yeasts. This information he put to use in the ensuing 1983 vintage at Mount Helen, making in that very hot year a conventional wine and a Winemaker's Reserve, embodying those three Burgundian precepts. The wine was introduced to a technical seminar in Perth later in 1983, where he suffered some trenchant criticism. It quite frankly caused a furore.

His last chardonnay vintage at Mount Helen was 1984, an extremely cool year, in which he once more employed his Burgundian techniques. The resultant wine received great acclaim. I remember it still, dominated on nose and palate by almost penetrating aromas and flavours of grapefruit, very youthful and totally different from the run o' the mill wines fermented in stainless steel, which were the accepted wisdom of that age.

In June 1989 I came back to it. It had of course developed markedly in the meantime. A mature yellow-gold in shade, the wine showed toasty buttery aromas on nose with hints of ripe peach and varnishy oak, very complex and quite advanced. I tasted similar butter, peach and nutty oak flavours in a nicely integrated palate with a long aftertaste. The wine had come of age but was not fat or overblown, just full-bodied, dry and reminiscent of a rich Meursault in a ripe Burgundian year. Really, I suppose, what Ellis set out to achieve. (17.5 pts)

Having completed six years at Tisdall and having established their Mount Helen winery as a leader in contemporary chardonnay style, Ellis left Tisdall in November 1984. He was succeeded as winemaker by Jeff Clarke, his assistant for the two prior vintages. The approach to chardonnay remains basically as Ellis left it. In June 1989 I tasted the Tisdall Mount Helen Chardonnay 1988. Medium yellow-gold in hue, this wine initially showed very slight solids on nose, which after further aeration developed nuances of peach and charred oak. In all quite complex and reminiscent of a ripe Burgundian year. The palate was rich and flavoursome with a touch of sweet oak and residual sugar to complete a soft finish. Though the wine was not then quite ready to drink, it was not a style suitable for lengthy cellaring. (16 pts) Drink by 1992.

The third of the trio of mountain chardonnays is Delatite, more famous in the past for elegant rieslings and gewurztraminers which certainly suit the Alpine scenery. 1988 was Delatite's second only chardonnay vintage.

In line with its youth it is very pale in colour, revealing grapefruit and a touch of oak-char on nose. On palate, there are similar youthful traits, grapefruit-citrus flavours and a lack of middle palate in June 1989, all of which, colour, nose and palate, should develop well given three to four more years in bottle. (16 pts)

Earlier I mentioned Brown Brothers and Whitlands, their inspired contribution to north-east Victorian viticulture. There are many other Brown Brothers chardonnays released from time to time: Koombahla and King Valley are two more that are never less than very good, and the 1987 vintage of each of these wines does not disappoint, though each will need time in bottle. An optimum drinking year for each is 1992. (16.5 pts) Other richer styles are Brown Brothers Victorian, made from divers Victorian fruit sources; and Family Reserve, the 1986 of which was (in January 1989) ripe, full and peachy on nose with a dash of 'cream' on palate for good measure, a truly sumptuous wine. (17.5 pts)

If ever a vineyard area had a natural propensity to produce reds and fortifieds of high alcohols and extract, it is Victoria's North-East. Hubert de Castella made this point a century ago. What of chardonnay here?

Roland Kaval at St Leonards on the very banks of the Murray near Wahgunyah makes a delicate wine for that area, but the technical assistance afforded by a large modern winery (Brown Brothers of Milawa own St Leonards) is undoubted. In January 1989 St Leonards Chardonnay 1987 was pale yellow in hue with a lightly spicy nose and quite a long well-balanced palate. It was certainly a wine that would improve in cellar for at least two more years. 1987 was of course a cool year, and there is no doubt that in this area chardonnay does best in such years. (17.5 pts) At the same time I tasted the 1984 (another very cool year). This was a marvellous wine with aromas and flavours of peach and melon, very elegant and in need of about two more years to reach its peak. (18 pts)

Chris Pfeiffer (formerly of Lindeman's now defunct Corowa winery) practises his craft these days not far away in Wahgunyah. Here, too, chardonnay is important and usually extremely well made. Pfeiffer Chardonnay 1988 (tasted March 1989) was delicate in all its modes, very pale in colour, rather herbal and nutty on nose and lightly fruity-spicy on palate. (17 pts) It was a wine that needed bottle development, two years at least from time of tasting to come to a very harmonious fruition.

Some paragraphs earlier I wrote of an exception to the seemingly obvious Victorian rule that the further north you plant chardonnay, the more you must climb. Though the Warby Ranges have a respectable altitude (400 metres above sea level) they in no way rival the Himalayas.

It was perhaps surprising then that Harry Tinson on his departure from Bailey's should have planted his own vineyard not on the top of the Warbys but on the adjacent flatter country to the south-west. Its advantage is its microclimate, a proximity to water, Lake Mokoan, which gives a beneficial local humidity to an otherwise extremely hot region. 1984 was a great year in Victoria especially for chardonnay and nowhere better than HJT Vineyards at Glenrowan. This surely should not be chardonnay country, but in that year, Harry Tinson produced arguably the best in the land. Certainly on the judging bench at the 1986 National Show in Canberra, where it secured a gold medal (it ultimately finished second in the Farmer Brothers Trophy, unfortunately I was in a minority), it was extraordinarily impressive. Though lacking a seductive upfront nose (it showed in November 1986 rather quiescent Puligny–Montrachet aromas, just a touch of nuttiness and the beginnings of 'noisette'), it had a remarkable palate, long almost steely, yet refined and elegant with a firm acidity that acted like a rein on the palate, letting it out ever so gently. It was a palate that you could return to time and again and still find nuances not there moments before. (19 pts) Its successors, 1985 and 1986, were also very good.

Though in most ways Tinson's chardonnay technique is quite simple, in one way it is unique. Whole bunches are picked and kept under a carbon dioxide 'blanket' for up to two days before processing. By this maceration technique, the grape skins soak in their own juice. The bunches, stalks and all, are crushed in a basket press again under CO_2, the juice settled and fermentation proceeds subject to gentle temperature control until the must reaches 2°C when it is removed to French oak for its completion. Like all modern makers, Tinson uses low free-sulphur levels.

Like the Browns in the King Valley and at Whitlands, Rick Kinzbrunner has also chosen altitude. His Giaconda vineyard site is high in the hills near Beechworth due east of Wangaratta. Giaconda Chardonnay 1989, tasted in late January 1990, was of delicate pale yellow hue, with light melon aromas and a slight yeasty lift. There was excellent fruit on palate, and the whole wine was so clean and refreshingly pebbly on finish that it reminded me of a Premier Cru Chablis, so distinct was it from the usual hyper-sophisticated barrel-fermented style. (17.5 pts) Drink in 1990–93. Giaconda is very much a name to watch.

The remainder of Victorian chardonnay belongs to the tortuous banks of the Murray River. Echuca and its irrigated Rosbercon vineyard are represented by the Tisdall label, a cousin of course to the more famous Mount Helen wines and made in the same winery. Usually quite good value, but lighter and a lesser wine generally than Mount Helen. Closer to Shepparton is Monichino, by repute a name of reliability, whose wines have unfortunately never come my way.

Another vineyard of importance in this general area and the source of excellent chardonnay is Barooga, owned by Seppelt, though it is rarely seen as a single estate wine.

Further west near Mildura are the bigger batallions, Lindeman's and Mildara, whose local chardonnays are usually good value at their price.

That is Victoria and its chardonnay, certainly a land of promise, if not the promised land, for the variety, where there are wines of both warm- and cool-area definition with a multiplicity of quality, as may be expected in any of the chardonnay-producing regions of Australia. By and large, though, the standards are improving rapidly, and the creators of chardonnay standards in other Australian states need to keep a wary eye on the cooler areas especially.

SOUTH AUSTRALIA

One gets the distinct impression when talking to older makers in the traditional white winemaking areas of South Australia such as Clare and the Barossa Valley that they are waiting patiently for that far-off day when chardonnay will topple from its popularity pedestal and rhine riesling will resume its 'rightful' place. They may have an extremely long time to wait.

Though the cooler south-eastern regions, Padthaway especially, grow sizeable amounts of riesling (over 12 200 tonnes in 1987 vintage), it is the exciting chardonnays of the area that have captured the consumer's imagination in recent times.

Arguably the highest chardonnay profile in the Coonawarra is that of Wynn's, two of whose more recent wines I tasted in April 1989. Consistent with present-day practice, Wynn's use the usual mixture of modern techniques, barrel-fermentation, malolactics, lees contact and of course maturation in new, small oak barrels. Here they differ quite markedly from other makers, for at time of writing no French oak was employed, only German and American.

The Wynn's Coonawarra Estate Chardonnay 1988 already had a medium yellow colour at time of release, evidence no doubt of new small oak fermentation and maturation. On nose, American oak was dominant, but there were also the ripe stonefruit aromas of a warm year. At that time, the palate rather belied the nose, being subdued and 'holey', finishing with a distinct acidity that seems typical of young Coonawarra chardonnays. That did not alarm me unduly, for given two to three years in cellar it would fill out and display the customary fullness of its predecessors. (17 pts)

This conclusion was totally vindicated a few hours later when I tasted the 1985, then only slightly more developed in colour, with an attractive buttery, peachy nose and well-integrated oak. The palate had filled out well, displaying similar flavours to nose and being one to two years from full maturity. (18 pts)

Curiously, Lindeman's Coonawarra chardonnays are marketed under its Rouge Homme label—curiously, I say, not because wines sold under that label are in any whit inferior, but because that label has been very much middle market in Lindeman's scheme of things, always coming after more prestigious names such as St George, Limestone Ridge and more lately Pyrus. Now I realise that these vineyards are planted to red grapes, but one would have thought that space would have been found and plantings made to establish a top-label chardonnay from Coonawarra as well as from Padthaway. Perhaps the idea has been considered and abandoned or perhaps not at all. Either way the consumer benefits, for Rouge Homme Chardonnay is usually an extremely reliable wine at a keener mid-market price.

The usual modern chardonnay-making techniques are employed, but as opposed to Padthaway wines, those from Coonawarra seem to have less youthful fruitiness and more initial acidity.

The 1988 Rouge Homme Chardonnay is riper than the norm, with an interesting mint and spice nose though without obviously identifiable fruit such as melon or peach. On palate the wine is quite accessible revealing long fruit flavours and good balance that will ensure a harmonious drinking wine by 1991. (16 pts)

Katnook also produces chardonnay of consistent quality in the Coonawarra. Of other area chardonnays tasted in June 1989, smaller makers Brand and Hollick seem to be developing more complexity in their wines, a factor that should guarantee their place in the mainstream of Coonawarra chardonnay.

Further north in Padthaway, Lindeman's has been master of the local chardonnay universe for some years, but it is a dominance that may be coming to an end, as Hardy's make ever better wines from chardonnay in that region.

In March 1989 I tasted six Lindeman Padthaway Chardonnays from 1983 to 1988. My favourites were the coolest of those years, 1984 and 1987.

Lindeman's Padthaway Chardonnay 1984: an enticing bright yellow hue with a green wash, this wine revealed on nose complex, toasty, peach aromas, now aging very satisfactorily. On palate, the wine is equally impressive with long peachy flavours, good finishing acidity and lovely balance. Though the wine has entered its midlife, no crises need be expected for some time yet. (18.5 pts) 1992 appears to be the optimal drinking year for this wine.

Its younger brother, 1987, was also a wine of harmony, unfolding, at time of tasting, a tropical fruit nose and a *sotto voce* palate, then of austere melon character, which needed to deepen in flavour. (17.5 pts) Four more years in cellar should do the trick.

Also at a cocoon stage was 1986, wood char and grapefruit still dominating nose and a palate again needing time to fill out. (17 pts)

I have mentioned Hardy's but briefly, and this curt mention needs to be enlarged if only for the fine chardonnays released under the Collection and Eileen Hardy premium labels. An outstanding Eileen Hardy Chardonnay is the 1987. In June 1989 this wine was pale to medium yellow in tone with tints of gold. A clean, attractive nose revealed aromas of peach and spicy oak, while on palate the wine showed initially subdued melon fruit which lengthened to mirror the nose—lovely peach and spice. (18.5 pts) This was a marvellous chardonnay which needed to fill out on middle palate just a little more to be set fair for drinking in 1993.

Due, I suppose, to the disastrous frost that savaged Padthaway in late 1987, the 1988 Collection Chardonnay was a blend of Padthaway and Clare material. This wine too was evolving well in bottle, with soft round fig flavours (perhaps the Clare influence) dominating palate. (17 pts) The 1989 vintage saw a return to 100% Padthaway provenance, but at time of writing this wine had not been tasted.

Seppelt also is a major grower of Padthaway chardonnay, which is utilised by that company in both its sparkling and still wine ranges. To date, it has not bottled a chardonnay totally from that area.

Despite the presence of Hardy's, one of Australia's wine giants, at Chateau Reynella, it is fair to say that the Southern Vales region of South Australia is more and more the stomping ground of good small- to medium-sized winemakers. In fact, McLaren Vale, of all South Australian regions, came earliest to chardonnay, perhaps because the white variety it came to supplant at the top of the market, rhine riesling, was never at its elegant best in that region.

In style, McLaren Vale chardonnays especially from its lower areas are not unlike those of the Hunter Valley: rich and full-bodied, fairly early maturing (two years in bottle will usually see them at their best), peach flavoured and very satisfying for consumer and maker alike.

Early names coming to prominence in McLaren Vale included Pirramimma and Wirra Wirra. Planting the first chardonnay vineyard in the district in 1977, Pirramimma certainly led the chardonnay charge in McLaren Vale, though in winemaking terms the region owes a great debt of gratitude to the chardonnay pioneering of Brian Croser at nearby Petaluma.

Though Pirramimma chardonnays were the epitome of regional style during the early 1980s, technical developments in chardonnay making and local competition have certainly caught up with Pirramimma. The result is simply that Pirramimma chardonnays though soundly made no longer have the excitement of a few years ago.

Wirra Wirra, however, has maintained most of the magic that kept it in the top flight of the region's chardonnays during the 1980s. Its 1988 McLaren Vale Chardonnay was, in August 1989, pale yellow in colour with complex aromas of grapefruit and toasty oak. Its palate though initially full-flavoured was well balanced and was by no means fully developed, clean acidity on finish auguring well for two to three years more in bottle. (17 pts)

Other McLaren Vale names that starred in the 1988 chardonnay vintage were Hugo and Scarpantoni. The Hugo wine showed typical barrel-ferment 'grapefruit' aromas and nicely integrated toasted oak characters, while on palate the wine was round and well structured, revealing rich peachy flavours. (17.5 pts) Like most of its regional cousins it would be at its best by 1991.

The Scarpantoni Chardonnay 1988 was pale in colour in June 1989, showing a fascinating nose of cloves and vanilla. Its palate was slightly dominated by wood, but there was also rich underlying fruit which would balance that oak given two to three more years in bottle. (17 pts)

Ryecroft is another famous McLaren Vale name, renowned for reds in the 1960s and subsequently taken over by a large brewing conglomerate and tried as a national 'brand' during the 1970s. Back now in more private hands, it has added a McLaren Vale chardonnay to its wine portfolio. The two wines I tasted in the middle of 1989 were 1988 and 1986 (a show reserve wine). The 1988 Chardonnay was massively constructed with lashings of toast and honey on nose and ripe buttery and char oak flavours on palate. Though a huge wine it was not built for the long haul and would be at its peak about 1991. (17.5 pts) Similarly the 1986 had reached its peak in mid-1989, drinking quite well at that time but without any cellaring future. (17 pts)

Geoff Merrill is one of those knockabout characters who make winemaking such a pleasure to write about. His wines never detract from that pleasure. The Geoff Merrill McLaren Vale Chardonnay 1987 is an exception to the generally ripe and forward McLaren Vale style. In August 1989 it was medium yellow in colour, revealing a beautifully balanced peach and charred oak nose and a palate still needing one or two years to integrate its component parts. By 1991, this should have been achieved and an attractive full-flavoured chardonnay will certainly be the result. (17.5 pts)

The oldest resident of the region is of course Chateau Reynella, now owned by Hardy's. It too produces a McLaren Vale Chardonnay. In August 1989 I tasted Chateau Reynella Chardonnay 1988. Despite the ripeness of that year which led some makers of the region to make wines of huge dimensions, this wine was elegantly handled. There were pleasant aromas of honeysuckle and vanillan oak on nose, while honeysuckle and passionfruit flavours formed quite a complex palate. (16.5 pts) Chateau Reynella usually produces reliable if not spectacular chardonnays.

Clarendon is in the foothills of the Mount Lofty Ranges to the northeast of McLaren Vale. There on the scenic return route to Adelaide or to the Adelaide Hills is Norman's winery quite grandly called Chais Clarendon. The Chais Clarendon Chardonnay 1987 was quite typical of the bigger wines of the area: lots of smoky oak and butterscotch on nose and a ripe but complex palate, quite the antithesis of the Chateau Reynella wine. It was a wine of excellent technique lacking, in all that complexity, a little fruit on palate. (17 pts) Nonetheless in this age of technical prowess, a very acceptable wine, ready to drink, in mid-1989.

As one of Australia's leading chardonnay areas, McLaren Vale is home to many other wineries, producing very good chardonnays from time to time. Such wineries are Beresford, Coriole, Currency Creek, Daringa, Ingoldby, Thomas Fernhill and Woodstock.

The Adelaide Hills is one of the most recent and exciting wine regions in Australia—that is, if you are talking about the extremely cool Piccadilly area below Mt Lofty. In a sense, the whole area has been the inspiration of one man, Brian Croser, who has seen the district turn from cauliflowers to chardonnay (and pinot noir). If it ever reverts to its market gardening past, it will not be for Croser's lack of effort. Yet it is only at the time of writing that Adelaide Hills fruit is beginning to be utilised in his Petaluma Chardonnay, although in fairness it must be pointed out that Croser's Piccadilly priorities have been concentrated hitherto on his sparkling wine 'Croser'.

So Petaluma Chardonnay has evolved as a 'cellar style' up to the present time, Brian Croser choosing the best available chardonnay from his vineyard resources in any given vintage. Thus Petaluma chardonnay grapes have been sourced from places as far apart as Cowra, Clare and Coonawarra. Only in 1985 was there sufficient Piccadilly chardonnay (10 per cent of the final blend) for the Petaluma wine of that year.

Though Brian Croser believes that the Hills chardonnay will ultimately be superior to fruit from any other source and that the chardonnay content of Petaluma from Piccadilly and associated vineyards will undoubtedly increase from year to year, he is not committed to the 'estate' concept for Petaluma Chardonnay, preferring to keep his options open, just in case there is a new fruit source that might add some further excellence to his wine.

In mid-1989 I tasted all Petaluma Chardonnays from 1977 (the first vintage) to 1987. My notes follow.

1977: an amazing wine this one, seemingly set in a time warp, as it refuses to show its years. Still only medium yellow in shade, showing a very pleasant balance of developed fruit and nutty oak on nose, the wine is quite mature but certainly not overdeveloped. Though it certainly can be drunk now with great enjoyment, it seems capable of holding its pleasant plateau indefinitely. All the same it is always wise to check old wines every six months. 100% Cowra. Nevers oak. (17.5 pts)

1978: a developing yellow in colour, this wine also shows a rather full and aging nose. On palate, where there were rich toasty flavours, the wine is beginning to fade. However, still quite enjoyable. 100% Cowra. Nevers and American oak. (16 pts)

1979: then past its best with lifted characters on nose and a wood dominant palate. 100% Cowra. Nevers and Limousin oak. (15 pts)

1980: good drinking in June 1989. An elegant style with good fruit-wood balance on palate, though starting to show some volatility on finish. 50% Cowra, 50% Coonawarra. Limousin oak. (16.5 pts)

1981: medium to deep yellow in hue, this wine was rather diminished in nose, showing bottle age and a little oak. On palate, there were full ripe peachy flavours of mature chardonnay, with a slightly lifted finish. A good wine to drink at that time. 50% Cowra, 50% Coonawarra. Limousin and Nevers oak. (16.5 pts)

1982: an outstanding wine, just beginning to drink at its best at time of tasting, though doubtless it would hold at least until 1993 before beginning its downhill run. A full, brilliant yellow green in colour, it revealed a marvellously complex nose of tropical fruit and Burgundian 'noisette'. Its palate also was ripe without being overblown, full without obesity; in short it was a beautifully made soft and rich chardonnay at the top of its form. 70% Coonawarra, 30% Cowra. Limousin oak. (18.5 pts)

1983: a difficult if not controversial year for Petaluma, with serious discussion at one stage whether there should be a Petaluma Chardonnay at all. However, there was and it has not turned out badly. At time of tasting, it was full yellow in colour, ripe and straightforward on nose and rich but lacking complexity on palate. A fairly simple style for Petaluma without fault to be drunk no later than 1991. A very good wine, however, bearing in mind the considerable botrytis problems in Coonawarra that year. 80% Coonawarra, 20% Clare. Limousin oak. (16 pts)

1984: though perhaps not the year of the century that it was thought to be at the time, most 1984s have developed very well. The Petaluma Chardonnay of that year was medium yellow in shade, lightly peachy on nose with long, clean, lightly buttery flavours on palate. Seemingly and perhaps deceptively light, it may yet turn out extremely well. 50% Coonawarra, 50% Clare. Limousin oak. (17 pts)

1985: pale to medium yellow in colour, with delightful fruit aromas, this wine also showed excellently balanced fruit and oak on palate. A baby at time of tasting, all it needed was three to four more years in bottle. 45% Coonawarra, 45% Clare, 10% Piccadilly. Limousin and Vosges oak. (17.5 pts)

1986: still quite pale in colour, this wine revealed lovely vanillan oak aromas on nose. Its palate, superbly balanced, showed rich and complex fruit beautifully integrated with that vanillan oak. It was a marvellous wine to taste in June 1989 and should age very gracefully in bottle until 1994 at least. Akin to 1982 in quality. 40% Coonawarra, 40% Clare, 20% Piccadilly. Limousin and Vosges oak. (19 pts)

1987: very pale and youthful in colour this wine had a slightly lifted nose, with some grapefruit and char oak traits. The palate then needed three to four years to fill out but doubtless would be first class by 1993. 50% Clare, 50% Piccadilly. Vosges oak. (18 pts)

1988: delightfully youthful and bright in its yellow-green raiment when 18 months old, this wine revealed ripe sherbety aromas on nose and, for Petaluma wines of this age, quite a rich palate. It was a palate that was well balanced in its fruit and oak components, showing soft fruit, very harmonious wood and good acidity so that, although it may seem forward, there is very good potential for cellar development over the next four years. 50% Piccadilly, 50% Clare. Vosges oak. (18 pts) (Tasted May 1990.)

Thus it is easy to see wine and fruit evolution at work, a continuous progress from the warmth of Cowra to the cooler climes of Coonawarra and Clare and the coolness, if not the downright chill, of Piccadilly. There is also a continuing experimentation with oak, from Nevers to Limousin to Vosges and who yet knows where else. One thing is certain. The pioneering drive, the care and skill that Brian Croser has lavished upon chardonnay will continue, for he has not yet made the perfect wine, at least not in his eyes.

Though Petaluma has arguably the highest chardonnay profile in the nation, its comparative neighbour, Stafford Ridge, is relatively unknown. This vine-child of Hardy's chief winemaker Geoff Weaver yielded about 5 tonnes of chardonnay in 1988 vintage, producing a wine of typical cool-area melon character, which, when tasted in October 1989, needed at least three to four more years to achieve full maturity. (16.5 pts) By 1994 we should have some idea of the full chardonnay potential of the southern Adelaide Hills, and it may just be that the Stafford Ridge vineyard will prove one of the benchmarks.

About 50 kilometres to the north is the high country claimed both by the proponents of the Adelaide Hills region and by the much longer established Barossa Valley. Certainly this region, situated between Mount Pleasant and Keyneton, and traditionally the source of most of Australia's finest rieslings when judged in terms of climate and soil, has more in common with its southern tip than the Barossa Valley floor.

There are several important estates in pursuit of chardonnay excellence in this region. Perhaps the most impressive chardonnays at the present time are to be found at Henschke, whose 1987 Eden Valley Chardonnay, tasted in May 1988, was marvellously complex, uniting the elegance of cool-area fruit with top technical standards and producing a wine that will mature well until the mid-1990s. (18 pts)

The quality of Henschke and Eden Valley as Stephen Henschke's chardonnay vignoble was confirmed by the marvellous 1988, tasted in late 1989. Medium yellow in colour, with most attractive aromas of ripening peach and toasty oak, this one showed deliciously long peach flavours on palate, which were not at all fat or overblown. Though it was almost ready to drink at time of tasting, it would still develop very harmoniously, reaching its peak about 1992. (17.5 pts) It was certainly the best chardonnay of that vintage tasted from the Barossa Valley and its environs.

Others makers are also names to be reckoned with. Karl Seppelt at Grand Cru makes reliable chardonnay. Adam Wynn at Mountadam has his own individual style reminiscent often of Meursault in its broader palate.

Two bigger 'boutique' vineyards in this region are Hill-Smith Estate and Heggies, both offshoots of the Yalumba company and both with some years experience of chardonnay. Both are made in the same modern, rather technical style with barrel-ferment and malolactic characters evident on nose and palate.

The Heggies Chardonnay 1987 tasted in September 1989 was already deep yellow gold in hue, revealing an attractive nose of peaches and coconut oak. Though the same peach and coconut flavours were carried on to palate, here the wine was a little fat and short in fruit. This was a wine that promised on nose more than it delivered on palate, which is sometimes a side-effect of malolactic fermentation, indicating soft, forward development. (16 pts) The 1986 and 1985 Heggies Chardonnays tasted with the 1987 were similarly forward.

The chardonnays of the Barossa Valley floor have very much the fuller ripe-peach aromas and flavours of other warm-area wines and are generally far removed from the more elegant wines of the Eden Valley and the more southerly Adelaide Hills, though the warm 1988 vintage did bring these regional styles rather closer together than usual. However, the Barossa wines are none the worse for that. Notable Barossa 1988s came from St Hallett (a lovely fuller style), Peter Lehmann and Kies Estate (a big, muscular wine), while Basedow and Lakewood also produce reliable local chardonnays.

The giants of the valley, the Penfold's group*—Penfold's, Tollana, Killawarra and Leo Buring (Kaiser Stuhl is also part, but I have never tasted a chardonnay from it), Orlando, Wolf Blass and Yalumba—rarely release local chardonnays, preferring instead anonymous multi-regional cellar styles mostly of excellent quality and some aging potential. A notable recent success has been the Penfold's 1988 Chardonnay, reasonably priced, of excellent nose and palate complexity, and finely balanced. Definitely a wine that could be drunk at 18 months of age (tasted August 1989) or kept two more years. Knowing the boundless skill and the years of experience of Penfold's in the use of small new oak, I can predict with confidence that Penfold's Chardonnay will become as famous in its style in the next decade as Penfold's cellar-style reds have become in the past two. (18.5 pts)

Similarly Penfold's Chardonnay 1989 is of gold medal quality. Tasted in April 1990, it held a medium straw-yellow hue with attractive hints of green. On nose the wine was most complex, showing aromas of peachy fruit and biscuity oak with creamy malolactic characters adding a further delightful dimension, while palate offered a very harmonious union of peach, toast and cream flavours. A wine both elegant and powerful. (18.5 pts) Drink in 1990–92.

Wolf Blass Chardonnays have also shown good aging potential, the 1984 wine on the market in the latter half of 1989 being a remarkable older wine toasty, soft-flavoured and alluring at that time and vindicating

---

* Penfold's purchased the Lindeman's group (including Leo Buring) in January 1990 and was itself purchased by S.A. Brewing Holdings Ltd (owners of Seppelt) in November 1990.

the great reputation of vintage 1984 throughout South Australia. (18.5 pts)

That other longtime resident of the Barossa, Seppelt, is mentioned here only to point out that its chardonnays also are virtually all cellar-blends, but are made at its Great Western winery, while those of Orlando (RF, Gramp's and St Hilary) are also usually of excellent quality but made from chardonnay fruit sourced from many areas. Of the rest, Yalumba relies on its Heggies and Hill-Smith Estates in the hills above the Barossa for individual vineyard releases, its worthwhile Signature and Gourmet Series brands being blended from various regions; and medium-sized Krondorf (a subsidiary of Mildara) also uses cellar-blends as its Show Reserve and ordinary Chardonnays.

A good deal of chardonnay also wends its way west to the Barossa from the vineyards of the Riverland. A good deal more remains on site, to be made locally into attractive and usually light drinking of excellent value for money. The two heavyweights here are Angove's (year in, year out consistently good-value, honest if never very exciting chardonnays) and the huge Berri-Renmano co-operative group, whose chardonnays are marketed under several labels: Renmano (its Chairman's Selection Bin 104 1988 winning the Tucker Trophy as Best Wine of Show at the 1989 Royal Sydney Wine Show, a chardonnay of hugely ripe dimensions), Berri, Barossa Valley Estates and Lauriston, the last two brands being also made at the co-operative's other winery, Lauriston at Angle Vale north of Adelaide close to the Main North Road to Clare.

In this same Adelaide Plains area is Primo Estate owned by Joe Grilli, a talented winemaker whose chardonnays match the high quality of his colombard, cabernet and auslese styles, while a little way off at Hope Valley, now a north-eastern suburb of Adelaide, is Douglas A. Tolley Pty Ltd whose excellent chardonnay fruit, sourced from the Barossa Valley, produced a very fine 1988 vintage.

Of all areas invaded during the past decade by chardonnay, Clare seems most determined to resist its inroads. Rhine riesling is still the king of Clare, most certainly in planted area and, one suspects, just as surely in the sentiment of local growers and winemakers. Nonetheless the chardonnay area is slowly increasing. Importantly, the area now has the attention of several winemakers of national and international repute, whereas at the start of the 1980s only Stanley Wine Co. (now part of Hardy's) and to a lesser extent Taylor's had any claims to national clout. Thus both Penfold's and Wolf Blass now have extensive vineyards in the Polish Hill River area, both with substantial chardonnay plantings, while Stanley (purchased in late 1987 by Thomas Hardy) is a key source of chardonnay for that company. Taylor's also is important in mid-market chardonnay, and at the very top of the chardonnay market, let us not forget that Clare content of Petaluma in vintages 1983 to 1988.

But what is the chardonnay style of Clare? In essence, it is midway between the wealth of early-maturing aromas and flavours of warmer areas and the subdued austerity of those that are cooler. In cooler years, such as 1987, they may be slightly grassy; in warmer years such as 1988, ripe and full. It is a region with many similarities to Eden Valley, but on the whole a little riper and more straightforward in chardonnay.

Given the extensive experience of Tim Knappstein with most varieties in that region, his chardonnays are a fair reflection of the region's capabilities and its vintage variations since 1986.

1989 (tank sample): pale yellow in hue with a typical barrel-ferment nose of grapefruit and charred oak and a palate of similar tropical/citrus flavours, this was long on palate with excellent finishing acidity. (17 pts) Good prospects over four to five years more, but see again when in bottle.

1988 (tasted June 1989): for a comparatively ripe year, this wine is not at all forward, its subdued nose showing just a little oak and herbaceousness while palate offered slightly appley flavours. (17 pts) This needs two to three more years to fill out.

1987: medium yellow colour with a green wash, this one also had a fairly subdued nose, cool-area melon and grapefruit aromas predominating and no obvious oak. On palate, there was also a certain lack of development. Again melon flavours with some citrus overtones dominated palate. (17.5 pts) Keep two to three more years.

1986: a medium to full yellow in shade, this wine revealed ripe, cashew aromas on nose again with citrusy overlays. Medium-weight palate long and flavoursome now starting to mature. Can be drunk or kept one to two years more. (17.5 pts) (All these wines were tasted in August 1989, with the exception of the 1988.)

As Tim Knappstein makes his chardonnays 'straight down the line'—that is, without overmuch technical bravura—they can be said to be typical of the variety in the Clare region, and if it is at all valid to draw conclusions, they would appear to require three years in bottle in most years and probably longer in cooler years.

The Clare Estate Chardonnay of Penfold's is the only single-vineyard white wine released by that company. Beginning with 1986 these wines are excellent examples not only of that company's expertise with oak, but also how essentially complementary oak and chardonnay are. Both 1986 and 1987 Clare Estate Chardonnays are most harmonious, 1986 being ready to drink in mid-1989 (17.5 pts), whereas 1987 needed two more years at least, the 'cool' of that year showing in the comparative lack of development of palate. (17 pts)

Stanley Wine Co. also produces very good Clare chardonnay under its Leasingham label, 1987 being a case in point. This wine had in July 1989 a smoky oak dominant barrel-ferment nose with cool-area melon fruit evident on a long palate. (17 pts) Just the wine to cellar until 1992.

At the southern end of the Clare Valley near Auburn, Taylor's also produce a substantial amount of good-quality chardonnay at a reasonable price, winning a trophy at the Royal Sydney Wine Show in 1988 for its 1986 wine.

As for smaller makers in the region, Jeffrey Grosset has since the 1983 vintage built up a sizeable reputation for quality chardonnay, and Pike's at Polish Hill River are also producing a very good forward-drinking style of which 1989 is a typical example.

What else may be said of South Australian chardonnay? Though it still is regarded as somewhat of an interloper and an eastern states fad, the Wine State has accepted it, to the great benefit of all Australian chardonnay lovers.

TASMANIA

Together with Queensland, Tasmania runs a very close race for the title of Australia's smallest chardonnay producer. It so happened that in 1987 Tasmania was only just ahead, though in years to come it is likely to increase its lead, so great is the interest in it and its cool-area confrere, pinot noir. Nevertheless with a 1987 vintage of about 43 tonnes it is scarcely ever likely to be the flavour on everyone's palate.

The state's senior chardonnay makers are the neighbouring Pipers Brook producers, Heemskerk and Pipers Brook Vineyard. Though close in proximity, their chardonnay styles are kilometres apart, Pipers Brook being a modern, technically charismatic wine, sometimes seemingly 'warm-area' in style with the concomitant peachiness and spicy wood on nose and palate, whereas Heemskerk usually makes a more reserved chardonnay often needing two to three years in bottle to develop subdued aromatic elements and to fill out its palate. The other old hand in Tasmanian chardonnay is Moorilla, whose wines are of excellent standard despite winemaker Julian Alcorso's preference for pinot noir.

Tasmanian names for its chardonnay will undoubtedly include Freycinet, away from the mainstream of Tasmanian viticulture on the spectacularly beautiful east coast, Marion's Vineyard, 25 kilometres north of Launceston, and St Matthias at Rosevears, also close to Launceston.

QUEENSLAND

Though plantings of the variety are increasing in the Granite Belt, centred around Stanthorpe in Queensland, its chardonnay quality in general does not yet reflect that increased interest. Nonetheless there are wineries and skill enough in the region to remedy what must be a very temporary situation.

WESTERN AUSTRALIA

With a crop of only 419 tonnes in 1987 vintage, Western Australia runs a distant fourth to the major eastern states in amount of chardonnay produced. Quantity of course isn't everything, but in the winemaker's mind it would help to satisfy a growing interest in the wines of the West; and as chardonnay continues to intrigue the palates of consumers in the eastern states, so plantings of chardonnay continue to increase in the west.

It is of course a truism to say that the Swan Valley is one of Australia's warmest grapegrowing areas. As such, its chardonnays fall quite naturally into the earlier-maturing ripe peach and peppery wood style, which is always most appealing to consumers.

Typical of this Swan Valley style are the chardonnays of Jane Brook. Its 1989, a tank sample tasted in July 1989 and a bottle tasted six weeks later, was peachy on nose, soft and ripe on palate and a little hot on finish. (16 pts) A forward style, it will be at its peak in late 1990.

Houghton is the giant of the Swan Valley, but its local chardonnays are in no way gigantic. The 1987 Gold Reserve Chardonnay was still comparatively subdued and youthful in July 1989. Pale-medium yellow in hue with hints of green, it showed an atypical lemony nose, with restrained but long melon flavours on palate. (16 pts) This was certainly a wine to remain in cellar for one or two more years.

Houghton's other brand is Moondah Brook, its extensive vineyard north of the Swan at Gin Gin. Moondah Brook Chardonnay 1988 shows quite pungent 'grapefruit' barrel-ferment aromas on nose and a marked degree of charred oak flavour on palate. (17 pts) Its palate does have fruit, but it needs cellar time (two to three years) to develop.

Chittering Estate cannot be said to be in the Swan Valley, rather it belongs to the Darling Ranges (also called 'the Perth Hills'). Its winemaker, Steven Shapira, makes quite a different chardonnay style. Without the technical bravura of other wines, the Chittering Estate Chardonnay 1987 in July 1989 showed herbaceous aromas and slightly 'mealy' oak characters on nose. On palate the wine revealed a firm acid backbone and a 'pebbly', rather neutral flavour that set it firmly in the mould of 'chablis' rather than the more generous styles of the warmer Swan. (15.5 pts)

Other producers of quality chardonnays in the Swan Valley and surrounding areas are Olive Farm and Westfield (both Swan-based), and Paul Conti at Wanneroo in the tuart sand country that borders the coast from north of Perth south almost to Busselton.

That same tuart sand also carries Leschenault, Dr Barry Killerby's estate south of Bunbury. The Leschenault Chardonnay 1988 was, at time of tasting in July 1989, quite pale in hue, offering a lemon citrus nose with a touch of sawdusty oak and a long full palate of excellent fruit and oak balance, my only note of criticism being that the wine lacked a little complexity. (16.5 pts)

Further south towards Busselton is Capel Vale, whose vineyard is sited on some of the rare alluvial loam in this region, though on a limestone base similar to neighbouring lands. Capel Vale Chardonnay usually has a very high profile, 1988 being no exception to the rule. This wine is pale to medium yellow in tone, showing beautiful peach and melon fruit and spicy new oak aromas on nose, all in restraint and not overdone. On palate there are long peachy fruit flavours, skilfully imprinted oak and a crisp acid finish (tasted August 1989). (18 pts) This is certainly a wine of complexity to age in cellar for at least three to four years.

Another producer of medium size just south of Perth, near Mandurah, is Peel Estate, which also produces chardonnay. Its 1989 chardonnay, tasted in August 1990, was pale in colour, showing light melony aromas and flavours, lacking somewhat in complexity but clean and fruity. (15.5 pts) Drink in 1991.

Strangely for such a versatile winegrowing region, Margaret River has had great difficulty with chardonnay. The chief problems are wind-derived, not only because of spring gales but also because of salt sprays driven inland by the full force of the onshore winds of the Indian Ocean, just a few kilometres away, which attack the flowering chardonnay bunches, causing floral abortion and a severe diminution of crop. Birds, too, do more than their fair share of damage especially in years when the native gums fail to flower before the early-maturing vines (chardonnay being amongst them) ripen. By planting windbreaks and by establishing vineyards on the reverse sides of hills in that undulating region, winegrowers are overcoming their earlier chardonnay misfortunes.

Problems aside, there is no doubt that Margaret River chardonnays are amongst the best in Australia. From its earliest days, Leeuwin Estate has matched the beauty of its setting by the standard of its chardonnays. Though expensive and delightfully labelled, the attraction of Leeuwin Chardonnays is very much within the bottle, and what is more, to justify that often-criticised price, they are always offered with about four years of bottle age on first release.

There have been and will be some great wines of the 1980s. 1980 and 1982 are but two. The current release is 1985, which I tasted in November 1989. Medium straw-yellow with a green wash this was a chardonnay offering an intense nose of pineapple and honey aromas with touches of malolactic butteriness. Its palate was tight in structure and for its age quite undeveloped, but there was length, very good balance, sufficient depth of peachy flavour and acidity enough on finish to indicate that the wine would not reach its peak of maturity until 1993. (18 pts) Though I have not yet tasted it, I am informed that 1987 was also a superb year for Leeuwin Chardonnay.

Mosswood follows Leeuwin only alphabetically, most assuredly not in degree of wine quality, its chardonnays always being of superlative standard, though released, unlike those of Leeuwin, comparatively young. Just be patient and those Mosswood Chardonnays will be most rewarding. Of earlier vintages, 1980 was superb. Of later years, 1988 promises much. When tasted in August 1989 this wine was medium yellow in hue with those touches of green that usually point to a great year. On nose there were hints of melon and herbaceousness, while its finely balanced palate had not then fully evolved, but there was depth enough of melon flavour to forecast a certain progress to a graceful maturity by 1994. (18 pts)

Arguably the most technically proficient maker of chardonnay in

Margaret River is Mike Peterkin at Pierro, and if my description in any way sounds as if this winemaker might incline towards expediency, the wines most certainly do not indicate it. 1986, 1987 and 1988 are a marvellously consistent trio of high-quality chardonnays. Tasted in July 1989 the 1986 vintage was still quite pale in colour. On nose the wine offered complex aromatics of 'peach' and 'butter', while palate transposed similar tastes on to the tongue. This wine was just starting to develop a ripe satisfying fullness of flavour and will continue to mature well for two to three years more. (18 pts) Drink in 1993.

The Pierro 1987 is perhaps the 'sleeper' of the trio, if such an attractive wine may be so described. Very pale in colour, it showed on nose the typical grapefruit and oak char characters of barrel fermentation. Its palate at that stage needed to fill out, which it undoubtedly would, given two to three years, but it was well balanced requiring only cellaring patience for a delightful maturity. (17.5 pts)

In some ways the 1988 was akin to the 1986. Though pale in hue, this wine already offered ripe peach and char oak on nose and a full soft complex palate. This was an open wine of generous flavour and seemed much more forward than the 1987. (18 pts) Drink in 1992.

Though all the Pierro Chardonnays are exceptional, the 1989, tasted in August 1990, is the best yet. With its 'peachy', 'nutty' aromas, it is delicious to sniff, while its palate is long, lingering and beautifully balanced in its peach and spice flavours. (18.5 pts) Drink 1992 onwards.

Perhaps the most individual (even 'French') style of chardonnay made in the region is that of Cullen. The 1988 Cullen Chardonnay owes much more to the wines of the Côte d'Or than to current Australian style. This may well have been intended, as Diana and Vanya Cullen are no slavish followers of wine fashion.

Tasted in November 1989 this wine was most complex on nose, with vanilla, butterscotch and malty aromas pointing up the barrel and malolactic fermentation techniques used in its making. Its palate was full with lots of distinctively malolactic 'buttery' flavours and a lively acidity. Time will tell whether it will evolve into a Meursault lookalike, but it is a fascinating chardonnay. (17.5 pts)

More classically Australian 'cool area' in character are the Margaret River Chardonnays of Evans & Tate. 1987 showed lovely melon fruit, a touch of wood char and lees character also in a most complex nose. On palate the wine showed lots of undeveloped fruit and a deft touch of oak. This would be a superb wine to consume in 1992. (18 pts) Its 1988 counterpart is also a chardonnay of excellent standard, though slightly fuller than its older brother when tasted in May 1989. (17.5 pts) This wine also will cellar well to 1992–93.

The Evans & Tate Chardonnay 1989 tasted in April 1990 may well be the best of the line to date. This held a pale to medium yellow hue and showed a deep and complex nose of guava and melon aromas with nuances of butter and cream (malolactic fermentation of part). On palate, elegant fruit, a touch of chardonnay cream and soft acidity made this chardonnay a marvellous mouthful. A delicious wine. (18.5 pts) Drink in 1992-93.

Very new to the Margaret River chardonnay scene, but a very famous and experienced winemaker in the area is Cape Mentelle, whose 1988 Chardonnay is only the second such wine of that winery. When tasted in July 1989, it was pale to medium yellow in hue and possessed of a most attractive peachy nose. Its palate was full and complex, showing ripe peach-vanilla flavours and a soft lingering finish. (17 pts) Even at that youthful age it was very accessible and virtually drinkable, but it may well last two to three years more.

Other makers of chardonnay in the district are Erland Happ (whose 1989 was very pleasant but light), Fermoy, a new vineyard which first came into production in 1988, Freycinet, a maker of good sauvignon blanc and whose chardonnays I have not tasted, Chateau Xanadu and Ashbrook.

The other cool Western Australian region of tremendous quality is Mount Barker-Frankland River located in the Lower Great Southern region. The most senior winery of the district is Plantagenet, which may justifiably be called its Alma Mater, for a number of the area's wines are made there by winemaker John Wade on a contractual basis. Chardonnay is a relative newcomer here, although by the early 1990s there should be supply enough, as approximately 200 hectares should be in bearing. The Plantagenet Chardonnays that I have tasted from vintages 1987 and 1988 have been either wines made from local fruit blended with material from the Darling Ranges (1987) or from 100% Swan Valley fruit, forward styles both and therefore impossible to assess as local wine. But knowing John Wade's skill and experience with the variety at Wynn's in Coonawarra, it is hard to imagine that a 100% Mount Barker chardonnay from Plantagenet would be anything but superior.

Arguably the most successful chardonnay produced in the region (again made by John Wade) is that of Wignall. In August 1989 the 1988 wine was still very pale in hue, showing very harmonious melon fruit and toasty oak aromas, excellent wood-fruit balance on palate and a long lingering finish. This was an exceptionally good wine. (18 pts) Cellar till 1994 to reap the benefits of cool-area chardonnay at its best.

Established in Denmark (a picturesque village to the south-west of Mount Barker) since 1971 and builders in 1989 of the newest winery in the Mount Barker area on their substantial Langton Estate, Mike and Alison Goundrey can properly be called veterans of the region. Though chardonnay is a comparative newcomer to their portfolio of wines, it will during the 1990s play an increasingly important part. Goundrey Chardonnay 1989, tasted August 1990, was a typical cool-area wine. Pale yellow in colour, offering a subdued melony nose, this wine needed time to develop on palate though all the portents were there for excellent aging in bottle. (16.5 pts) Drink 1993 onwards. 1988, a more forward, riper style, was also very good.

The Forest Hill Vineyard, the oldest in the Mount Barker region, was sold in early 1989 to interests associated with the late Robert Holmes á Court. From time to time chardonnays of high quality have been released from the Forest Hill Vineyard but none from recent vintages. No doubt under the new ownership and from the Vasse Felix winery at Margaret River, Forest Hill Chardonnay will again emerge in due course.

Frankland River is some distance even from Mount Barker, and Alkoomi further still, but distances seem not to matter very much when the wine is good, as it usually is at Alkoomi. Its first chardonnay, 1989, tasted in August 1989 when just bottled, was a very pale yellow in colour. On nose, however, it was more forward, revealing most complex peachy woody barrel-ferment aromas. Its palate also was predominantly peachy in flavour, again seeming slightly precocious, but nonetheless with good length. (16.5 pts) This is a wine to keep in cellar until 1991, to reassess and then if necessary to drink up.

The giant of Frankland River, growing still, is Houghton, whose Netley Brook Vineyard was saved in 1989 from severe salination by the construction of an extensive new drainage system. This problem, endemic to the area because of a high brackish water table, has been exacerbated by extensive tree clearance and the use of irrigation and has caused Houghton to show interest in other Western Australian cool areas, notably Pemberton, a high-rainfall region with excellent drainage, situated midway between Frankland River and the Margaret River area, while remaining guardedly optimistic about Netley Brook. The Houghton Show Reserve Chardonnay 1984 (100% Frankland River in origin) had acquired a marvellous green-gold hue when tasted in June 1989. Aromas were rich and toasty made even more complex by a slight smokiness that suggested ham sausage. On palate, light flavours were again dominated by a toasty character, the wine finishing with a crisp acidity. (17 pts) This was a wine of indeterminate potential, perhaps to be drunk but if kept in cellar to be examined carefully every six months.

No chapter on chardonnay can be fully complete without a few words on cellar style, which was briefly mentioned when the Barossa Valley was discussed. Penfold's in particular after a late start has made excellent multi-area wines since 1986. Both Wolf Blass and Orlando are also very consistent, but for unvarying value and excellence it is very difficult to surpass Seppelt Gold Label Chardonnay 1988. Because of its widespread chardonnay resources (good vineyards of excellent quality and, importantly for price, quantity) in Padthaway, Barooga, Great Western, Partalunga and Qualco, areas so far apart that one natural disaster could scarcely affect all of them, Seppelt is admirably equipped to make outstanding chardonnay at most price levels. Even Woodley Queen Adelaide Chardonnay (marketed independently but from the same Seppelt resources), which sees little oak, is an extremely good wine at its price. My notes of Seppelt Gold Label Chardonnay 1988, written for *Wine & Spirit* September 1989, read: 'An artist's delight in hue, very pale yellow with a delicate green wash. On nose, the wine shows elegant melon fruit with excellent understated oak, a very fine liaison of fruit and wood. On palate the wine is very long on fruit, with oak again playing an harmonious counterpoint. This wine is not a blockbuster, but a beautifully made chardonnay to cellar for two to three years more.' (18.5 pts) Seppelt also market a multi-area Black Label Chardonnay and a Premier Vineyard Show Chardonnay at the top of the range.

Australian chardonnay has reached the crossroads. More and more is it becoming a creature of techniques well known throughout the wine industry which are obscuring the regional differences, still apparent in other varieties. The day may regrettably arrive when Margaret River will be indistinguishable from Hunter, and Yarra Valley identical to Barossa. It will be a boring day indeed. Let us hope that there are enough winemakers sufficiently proud of their chardonnays and their region to continue to make individual wines of quality, which are totally representative of that region, for the enjoyment of the chardonnay consumer.

SEMILLON, SAUVIGNON BLANC AND OTHERS

Semillon

It was fashionable in Australia a few years ago to pooh-pooh semillon as being excessively boring, an attitude as unreasonable as it is unreasoning, but indicative, I suppose, of the soaring popularity of chardonnay which caused all other white varieties to mark time while it encroached upon their markets. A pity, but such is faddism. Semillon is well worthy of respect, for, unlike modern riesling which does not tolerate oak maturation at all well and equally unlike chardonnay which is hard-pressed to produce a satisfactory botrytised sweet wine, semillon can be made in as many complex ways as chardonnay (barrel ferment, oak maturation, malolactic, etc.) or very simply like dry riesling and, left to botrytise on the vine, to produce a wine as complex and luscious as a trockenbeerenauslese riesling. It is then as worthy and noble a variety as either of the other two.

Its home is the Bordeaux region of France, some experts even localising its origin to Sauternes itself. In Bordeaux it is the major variety, making notable contributions in conjunction with sauvignon blanc and muscadelle to the luscious botrytised whites of the region—Sauternes, Barsac Cadillac, Loupiac, etc.—and to the excellent, newly emerging, wood-fermented and matured, white Graves.

From Bordeaux it has spread in small quantity to northern Italy, Yugoslavia, Hungary, Rumania and the Soviet Union, while elsewhere in the world it has taken root in California (to a small extent), Chile (to a much larger), Argentina, South Africa, New Zealand and of course Australia. It was almost certainly brought here as part of James Busby's collection in 1832 and is now grown in all Australian states, except Tasmania.

As at mid-year 1988 semillon accounted for 2447 hectares of the Australian vineyard, yielding 37 004 tonnes of winemaking grapes. It is most important in New South Wales where the Murrumbidgee Irrigation Area and the Hunter Valley together produce about three-quarters of Australian semillon. Elsewhere it is held in high esteem in Western Australia's Margaret River region, but is not so highly regarded in Victoria where it is little grown anyway, or in South Australia where it is sometimes genericised as 'white burgundy', though making eminently satisfactory wines.

As I have mentioned, it may be made by any modern white winemaking technique. When fermented in barrel or made subject to malolactic fermentation it can show similar characteristics to chardonnay, and like chardonnays made in that manner it shows complexity but is inclined to be forward in maturity. When fermented in stainless steel at a controlled temperature, it reveals lemony straw aromas and fairly neutral flavours when young, but takes well to new oak maturation, especially American. Even if it is not so matured, Hunter Valley experience has shown that the variety there grows in complexity in bottle often for a decade or more, producing a honeyed wine, not unlike rhine rieslings of similar age from the Clare or Eden Valleys and sometimes with age developing a 'wood-matured' palate, even though the wine had never even seen an oak chip, let alone a barrel.

It can be favourably or extremely unfavourably attacked by botrytis, more often than not unfavourably in the Hunter Valley, where in the humid warmth of late February, botrytis can run riot in a few days, creating great grey-green balls of mould spores that were once semillon bunches. Elsewhere in more favourable climatic conditions, botrytis, like an alchemist of old, can turn wine into gold, a burnished yellow, orange-fragrant, luscious nectar to which no words do justice.

Hunter semillon is idiosyncratic also in that it often develops well after years which in other areas would be called mediocre, years when the weather leading to and during vintage is damp and humid, years when the sun sullenly retires behind a curtain of clouds and ripening stops at 10.5° Baumé, years when there is seemingly little varietal flavour and quite high acidity, in short a fairly typical Lower Hunter vintage.

Some say that this cloud curtain is the saviour of the region as a quality viticultural area, otherwise it would be too hot, but certainly semillon picked in such vintages often ages extremely well in bottle and this directly contrary to the mainstream of Australian viticultural thought which insists that grapes for table wine should be ripened optimally (ie the best balance of sugar and acid should be obtained, for both flavour and longevity). Has semillon some other answer?

NEW SOUTH WALES

It is only fitting therefore to begin this survey of semillon in its Australian place of origin, the Lower Hunter Valley, lamenting just a little the Hunter's inability to produce great botrytised sweet white in all but the most exceptional years.

Though some might press the claims of wineries such as Mount Pleasant, Rothbury or Tyrrell's to pre-eminence in Hunter semillon, and each of those wineries has made semillons from time to time totally typical of the best the region has to offer, it is to Lindeman we must turn for superb semillon quality in the past 30 years and to the two Lindeman winemakers responsible for those glorious wines, Karl Stockhausen and Gerry Sissingh.

The great series of Lindeman semillons virtually corresponded with Karl's first tenure as winemaker at Pokolbin (1960–80), beginning with wines such as Bin 1616 of 1960, then of course called 'Hunter River Riesling', a synonym for semillon still used in the Hunter and in other parts of Australia, which is now (happily in the cause of accuracy) beginning to die out.

A great wine came from the old Lindeman Sunshine Vineyard in the hot drought-stricken year of 1965, the Sunshine Riesling (semillon) Bin 2760, and more top wines from 1967 and 1968. Arguably, Lindeman's most successful semillon year has been 1970, a Hunter vintage unremarkable in all other aspects. All three of the Lindeman semillons of that year, 'Chablis' Bin 3875, 'White Burgundy' Bin 3870 and Hunter River 'Riesling' Bin 3855 have been covered in wine show glory, especially the last, still being shown at time of writing, 20 years old and the most decorated white wine in show history with 10 trophies and 33 gold medals in a distinguished career. In May 1988 I was fortunate enough to taste both the 'Chablis' and the 'Riesling' together. My notes read:

Chablis Bin 3875: lovely colour, still green, vanillan oak nose but no oak used in maturation, brilliant, elegant palate with some austerity. Will it just gradually fade away? (18.5 pts)

Hunter River Riesling Bin 3855: slightly deeper in colour than 3875, nose more developed (toasty), very good developed palate, still with some flesh. (18.5 pts)

Almost two years later in February 1990 Bin 3855, in receipt of one more trophy, was still showing its seemingly ageless Peter Pan palate. What could be the *raison d'être* for the youth of this wine, 20 years on? Philip John, Lindeman's chief oenologist, says that the wine has always had a higher than usual residual sugar content, being made at a time when winemakers tended to rely more on palate than laboratory analysis and, being ever so slightly sweet because of that residual sugar, has lived on it ever since. The theory has much to commend it, especially when one recalls the longevity of the intensely sweet Sauternes of Bordeaux, which are made primarily from semillon.

Since that marvellous 1970 vintage, no Hunter semillons of Lindeman seem to have made such incisive marks upon the show scene, but certainly the basic quality remains and Lindeman's Hunter semillons are always worth trying, be they labelled 'Chablis', 'White Burgundy' or merely 'Semillon'. Indeed one is tempted, probably quite mistakenly, to lament the passing of the old Ben Ean Vineyard, the Sunshine Vineyard (nematode-infested though it was) and the advent of stricter laboratory regimes, which measure everything about grape must and even about young wine, except its ability to age, which of course must still be gauged for better or for worse by palate.

I have mentioned the generally unfavourable influence of botrytis upon semillon in the Lower Hunter Valley. Only in rare years such as 1983 and 1986 have conditions been forgiving enough to allow a trickle of sweet botrytised white to be produced in that area, yet the Hunter has for many years made sweet table white of excellent quality from semillon by the *mistelle* method. This method involves the blending back of semillon juice concentrate into very ripe semillon, the addition of sulphur dioxide to restrict any tendency to referment, and the maturation of such wine in new small oak for several years. Though the resultant wines live for many years and many fine examples such as Lindeman's Porphyries of 1949 and 1956 spring to mind, only exceptional examples of such wines can match the intense complexity of the luscious botrytised semillons of the Murrumbidgee Irrigation Area, the mistelle semillons seeming too neutral and austere for too long. Perhaps my own impatience is to blame.

The other notables of dry Hunter semillon are McWilliam's at Mount Pleasant, Rothbury, and Tyrrell.

Since the mid-1970s McWilliam's at Mount Pleasant have made Hunter semillon of very good quality. 'Elizabeth Riesling', now simply 'Elizabeth' but still made of semillon, was a consistent white of good quality, which one looked for on restaurant lists if there was nothing else to excite the tastebuds. Since 1981 vintage the quality of 'Elizabeth' has increased markedly, so much so that they are regular trophy winners at wine shows throughout Australia and, marketed as they are with five to six years' bottle age, are true examples of the virtues of semillon and the benefits of bottle age. In October 1989 I tasted Elizabeth 1983: medium to full yellow in hue with complex lemon and toast fragrances and a slight lift that made for an attractive aged nose. Palate showing lemon and honey flavours on entry and middle and finishing with crisp acid. Will age further for one to two years. (18 pts) Drink in 1990–91.

'Anne Riesling' used to be the seldom-seen sister of the more gregarious

'Elizabeth', but that shyness ultimately proved her undoing as she lost her identity in the late 1980s, becoming simply 'Mount Pleasant Semillon'. The high quality, however, has remained, as has the Mount Pleasant policy of aging such wines beyond what might reasonably be termed the norm.

The Rothbury Estate produced some superb semillons in the 1970s when Gerry Sissingh was winemaker. Mention must be made of vintages 1972, 1974, 1976 and 1979. Since the early 1980s the company, quite justifiably from a commercial viewpoint, has come to rely more and more upon chardonnay. Excellent though that chardonnay is, and I have been a member of the Rothbury Tasting Committee since 1982, having had more than a passing acquaintance with it for all that time, it seems now to dominate the Rothbury scheme of things to such an extent that the semillon of the 1980s, though of excellent quality, seems to be very much a second son, well respected but not quite the heir to the title. Good years for Rothbury semillon during the decade were 1983, 1986, 1987 and 1989.

In April 1990, however, I was reminded very much of the Sissingh style when I tasted the Rothbury Estate Wood Matured Semillon 1979. This wine showed a seemingly ageless medium yellow colour, its nose pointing to slightly greater maturity with classical aromas of toast and honey. Its palate was long, toasty in flavour and beautifully balanced with an elegant drying finish. (18.5 pts) A classic Hunter style, delicious on palate, but which could still be kept, though it is recommended to 'look at' such wines every six to twelve months.

That bastion of tradition, Tyrrell's, makes up the quartet of quality in what might be termed the orthodox Hunter semillon style. Here Vat 1 'Hunter River Riesling' (the old synonym still remains*) signifies the pick of the Tyrrell semillon crop in any given year, and marvellous wines they have been, most aging superbly over a decade to show the classic lemon–toast aroma and long persistence on palate that typify the very best of the breed.

Older and more established Lower Hunter semillon names also worthy of mention are Saxonvale (a great Bin 1 Semillon in 1987), Drayton (often 'appley' on nose and palate), Hungerford Hill, Tulloch (marketed as 'Chablis') and limited releases from Wyndham.

Despite the inroads of chardonnay, amongst the smaller Hunter makers semillon is definitely alive and well. A distinct departure from tradition was made in 1983 at Brokenwood when winemaker Iain Riggs, recognising the great quality of the intense fruit of that year, made a zestier, more youthful semillon than was the norm. This style certainly proved more than acceptable in the marketplace and has continued since. Its features are a lively herbaceousness on nose and palate and a zingy acid finish, markedly different from the traditionally more neutral lemony style and, as the older wines are nearing the end of their first decade, maturing quite

---

* (Or rather did, until the 1990 vintage, when the label was changed to 'Vat 1 Semillon'.)

well in bottle, though not perhaps with the ultimate longevity of the classical style.

Though Brokenwood has explored the frontiers of Hunter semillon, most other smaller makers continue the traditional style. Makers to note are Allandale, Allanmere, Calais Estate, Chateau François (old-style wines, which accept bottle age very graciously), Fraser, Little's, Marsh Estate, Oakvale, Peterson, Simon Whitlam, Sutherland, Tamburlaine and Terrace Vale.

In the Upper Hunter, semillon is also widely planted. Here, small oak and malolactic fermentation play a significant part in the semillon styles of both Mount Arrow (formerly Arrowfield) and Rosemount, with the result that semillon seems destined to become a chardonnay look-alike.

Complex though such wines are there is little point in aging the Mount Arrow 1987 Reserve Selection Semillon (noted in July 1989 as having an excellent union of fruit and oak on nose and palate, a very good wine, marked at 16.5 pts, but ready to drink), nor for the same reasons the Rosemount styles which are similarly made. Complexity alone is no guarantee of ability to age.

Other local producers of good semillon are Reynolds Yarraman, Horseshoe Vineyard and a relative newcomer, Serenella Estate.

Mudgee also grows substantial quantities of semillon, though the variety here rarely shows the distinction and aging ability exhibited in the Lower Hunter Valley. Nevertheless good wines are made by Montrose and Miramar, while Huntington Estate occasionally makes an outstanding wine.

The largest producing area of semillon in Australia is the MIA (Murrumbidgee Irrigation Area). Here for many years, semillon was merely a slightly better variety than many others, making, if carefully handled, clean dry white for fairly immediate consumption. McWilliam's, the largest winery in the area (in fact the company has three wineries), makes typically clean semillon under its Hillside (cask) and Inheritance (bottle) labels.

Yet the starring role of semillon in this area has not been in dry table wines at all; it has been in lusciously sweet botrytised styles. Here de Bortoli led the way in the mid-1980s with magnificent botrytised semillon 'sauternes' from 1982, 1983 and 1984, all vintages that have received Australian and world acclaim.

In October 1989 I tasted de Bortoli Semillon Sauternes 1985. Full gold in colour, showing toast, raisin and orange-peel fragrances on nose, this wine offered luscious toffee, malt and honey flavours on palate, balanced by excellent acidity. Marked at 17.5 pts because of a slight hessian-oak flavour, giving an impression of heaviness.

McWilliam's also make excellent sweet semillon from MIA botrytised fruit. In July 1989 I saw McWilliam's Botrytis Semillon 1987, noting a medium yellow hue with clean orange-peel aromas, a lovely full soft palate, good sweetness and balance, and a cellaring potential of three to four years. (17 pts)

Dry semillon whites of superior quality for the MIA region are also featured under the Wyangan Estate label of Miranda and the Mount Bingar label of Rossetto.

The only remaining mention of semillon in New South Wales should be of Cassegrain, the Port Macquarie winery with considerable areas of vineyards close to the town and a substantial Pokolbin estate, renamed Clos de Colline, formerly the Hillside vineyard on the Marrowbone Road.

As a consequence of his training at Tyrrell's, John Cassegrain makes Pokolbin semillon very much in the traditional mould and releases his wines with some bottle age (two years at least). As a result his earlier releases (1984, 1985 and 1986) are now beginning to show the honey and lemon characteristics of good Hunter semillon on both nose and palate.

VICTORIA

As a semillon-producing state, Victoria need not detain us very long, the variety being only nominally represented there. Though the plantings are small, the quality is high in its few planting locales, especially in the Yarra Valley, where Coldstream Hills made an excellent wood-matured wine in 1988. Without the influence of oak, the variety seems to behave in typical cool-area mode, exhibiting herbaceous aromas and tangy grassy flavours on palate.

It is a little broader and more traditional, however, in the warmer areas of the state, such as the Goulburn Valley, where it is grown at Chateau Tahbilk and Mitchelton and Bendigo (Chateau Le Amon).

SOUTH AUSTRALIA

In South Australia, in the Barossa Valley, semillon is particularly versatile, accepting American oak maturation very favourably in whites such as Basedow's White Burgundy (the 1987, 1988 and 1989 vintages were all very good); luscious botrytis influence in that consistently good 'sticky', Peter Lehmann Semillon Sauternes; and blending with sauvignon blanc in wines such as St Hallett Semillon Sauvignon Blanc.

Tasted in December 1989, the St Hallett Semillon Sauvignon Blanc 1989 was a pale to medium green-yellow in hue, offering lemon straw aromas with a hint of herbaceousness, while palate revealed quite full lemony/grassy flavours most characteristic of the blend. (17.5 pts) Drink in 1990–91.

Yet without such assistance in its Barossa home environment, it is a rather plain white wine with no great capacity to age. Further mention must be made of the wooded style, for it is here that Barossa semillon will surely come into its own, if the wines of Basedow and Grant Burge are any guide. Both made excellent 1989s. My notes follow.

Grant Burge Semillon 1989:   a medium yellow in hue, showing clean lemony aromas on nose. Palate was well balanced offering fresh lemon and vanilla flavours and a crisp acid finish. (17.5 pts) Quite a complex young wine, which may be kept two years more. (Tasted January 1990.)

Basedow's White Burgundy (Semillon) 1989: a most attractive mid yellow-green in colour with vanillan-lemon aromas on nose, slightly wood-dominant. Palate was full and soft, revealing excellent harmony of wood and fruit. A successful wine without the weight of the Grant Burge. (17 pts) May be kept one or two years. (Tasted December 1989.)

Other Barossa makers of semillon relevance are D. A. Tolley with its winery in the north-eastern suburbs of Adelaide and its vineyards in the Barossa, Wolf Blass with its winery in the Barossa and contributing vineyards in most South Australian areas, Henschke and Hill-Smith Estate, both in the ranges high above the Barossa Valley.

In most respects, dry semillon in McLaren Vale is a mirror image of the variety in the Barossa, ripening readily in the warmth of the Southern Vales, responding well to barrel fermentation and American oak maturation and also to blending with varieties such as sauvignon blanc and chardonnay.

Ryecroft usually makes a very good wood-matured style. Its 1989 was no exception. Tasted in October 1989, the wine showed medium yellow in hue with tropical fruit fragrances and grassy overtones. Its palate was long and full with lemony/grassy flavours and a hint of cashew-nut oak. (17 pts) A harmonious style to be drunk in 1991–92.

Another semillon-dominant wine of top quality originating in this area is Geoff Merrill Semillon-Chardonnay, a wine far removed from the standards of commercial expediency usually exhibited by such blends.

Blewitt Springs is a new name in the region, rapidly gaining a fine reputation for both quality and value in semillon. The 1989 Blewitt Springs Semillon tasted in January 1989 was pale to medium yellow in colour, showing most attractive lemony, leafy aromas on nose, while its full-bodied palate offered a smooth liaison of tropical fruit and spicy oak flavours making for an easy-drinking style to be consumed in 1990–92. (16.5 pts)

Southern Vales, whose brand 'The Wattles' recalls the first name of this near-century-old winery, also produced an excellent semillon in 1989. Tasted in October 1989, this wine revealed youthful yellow-green tints, herbaceous citrusy almost riesling-like aromas and a rich palate with lingering lemony flavours. (17.5 pts) Drink in 1990–92.

The final McLaren Vale winery whose competence with semillon has impressed me over the years is Wirra Wirra, which prefers to blend some fresh zingy sauvignon blanc into its semillon. The resultant wine, one of the first of its blend in Australia and still among the best, is always pleasant drinking and complements shellfish particularly well.

More so than McLaren Vale, the Clare Valley has had a substantial association with semillon for many years mainly through those veteran wineries of the district, Quelltaler (now renamed Eaglehawk Estate) and Leasingham, formerly Stanley (now the Clare branch of the worldwide Hardy tree).

At Eaglehawk, semillon is made both dry and sweet, but either is subjected to considerable oak complexity, derived both from barrel fermentation and maturation.

Wolf Blass–Quelltaler Clare Valley Semillon 1987, tasted October 1989, was a deep yellow in hue with lemon–grass aromas marvellously enhanced by nutty, toasty oak. Palate offered a long smooth integration of lemon citrus and toasty flavours. (18 pts) Drink now to 1993.

I tasted the sweet style, Noble Gold 1988, in September 1989. Medium yellow in shade, this one offered lifted lemon-citrus aromas with orange-peel overtones on nose, and sweet honeyed flavours and a citrusy tang within a rich palate. A fetching dessert style with short-term cellaring prospects. (16 pts) Drink 1991.

The Leasingham Semillon 1989, tasted in February 1990, showed delightful lemon–vanilla aromas on nose, long, lemony flavours and a fine fruit–oak–acid balance on palate. (16.5 pts) Could develop well in cellar; drink in 1991-93.

Another Clare maker who obviously delights in the complementation of semillon and oak is former Stanley maker, Tim Adams. His 1989 Clare Valley Semillon was deep yellow-gold in hue with rich vanilla wood on nose, big vanilla–lemon-spice flavours and a crisp acid finish. (17 pts) Drink in 1991-92.

WESTERN AUSTRALIA

If winemaking techniques such as barrel and malolactic fermentation and small oak maturation are the forces that drive semillon in South Australia, it is certainly fruit quality that makes the variety exciting in Western Australia's Margaret River and Mount Barker.

In Margaret River, the variety is made straight and also blended with sauvignon blanc. In addition, makers such as Moss Wood employ both barrel and malolactic fermentation techniques to increase the complexity of what is in Margaret River a tangy, fresh, fruity variety at times difficult to distinguish from sauvignon blanc.

Of the straight varietal semillons made in Margaret River, Moss Wood has always been tremendously impressive. Its Wood Matured Semillon 1988, tasted in July 1989, was a lovely medium yellow-green colour, offering grassy, asparagus aromas with just a trace of subtle French oak. Palate was long and smooth, again intermingling asparagus and vanillan oak flavours most harmoniously. (18 pts) Drink in 1990-93.

In contrast with the suave ripeness of 1988, the 1989 Moss Wood Semillon, tasted late August 1989, was very pale in hue, showing a fresh grassy nose and crisp herbaceous flavours on palate. Lean and tight with little wood influence, but very clean and alive in the mouth. A lighter style. (17 pts) Drink in 1990-92.

Chateau Xanadu, exotic though it may sound, makes excellent semillon in most years. Its 1989 Semillon, very youthful in colour, held attractive appley, lemony aromas on nose, while a light but balanced palate showed good potential for bottle development. (16.5 pts) Drink in 1990-93. (Tasted December 1989.)

Another maker of archetypal Margaret River semillon is Ribbon Vale. Its 1988 showed the 'cut grass' aromas and fresh herbaceous palate, quite usual for the variety. (17 pts) Drink in 1990-91. (Tasted August 1989.)

I have left the best Margaret River semillon made in 1989 till last. That is indisputably the marvellously elegant wine of Evans & Tate. Tasted in late 1989, this was of pale to medium yellow with strong green tones, and complex aromas of lemon/grapefruit and smoky oak. On palate there were long lemon/grapefruit flavours with a delicious counterpoint of vanillan oak. A wine of perfect balance which avoids grassiness and rivals any semillon made in Australia that year. (19 pts) Drink in 1990-95.

As for the semillon blends with other varieties, these too are usually of high quality. Chief 'blender' is sauvignon blanc, but chenin blanc is also used to good effect and sometimes both varieties are employed. My longest acquaintanceship is with Cape Mentelle Semillon Sauvignon Blanc. Its 1989 was very youthful in colour, showing lightly herbaceous aromas on nose with a nice touch of spicy oak, while palate was long flavoured, zesty and fresh. (17 pts) Drink in 1990-92. (Tasted August 1989.)

Other typically fresh blends of semillon and sauvignon blanc are made by Cape Clairault, Freycinet and Ribbon Vale.

As would be expected in the cool climes of Mount Barker, semillon tends to herbaceousness both on nose and palate. At the time of writing, Alkoomi is the sole outpost of semillon here. Tasted in July 1989, its 1989 Semillon was a bright pale yellow in hue with 'cut-grass' aromas on nose, palate showing lemony/grapefruit barrel-ferment flavours and a keen acid finish. (16.5 pts) A fresh style suitable as an accompaniment to shellfish, it might also be worth two years' cellaring.

Semillon is also grown on the tuart sand country at Leschenault, near Bunbury. Here because of its maritime proximity and sandy soils, semillon is usually a supple easy-drinking style, but retaining just a touch of herbaceousness on nose and palate. The Leschenault Semillon 1989, when tasted in August 1989, showed subtle lemony/grassy aromas and a pleasant forward flavoursome palate, which was certainly ready to drink, but could be kept a year or two more. (16.5 pts) Drink in 1990-92.

QUEENSLAND

The Granite Belt in southern Queensland is our last stop on the semillon route. There the variety is grown quite widely, considering that Queensland as a whole produced less than 400 tonnes of wine grapes in 1987 vintage.

Makers producing semillon are Ballandean Estate, Kominos, Rumbalara and Winewood.

Ballandean Estate Semillon 1988 is the only area wine known to me. Tasted in July 1989, that wine held an excellent pale yellow-green colour. On nose it unfolded delicate lemon-straw aromas typical of the variety, while palate revealed crisp clean lemon-grass flavours and fresh finishing acidity. (17.5 pts) Drink in 1990-93.

Sauvignon blanc

Sauvignon blanc is a variety that admits of no compromise. It is loved or hated, but it is never ignored. Its home, like that of semillon, is the Bordeaux region of France, where it adds complexity, though little lusciousness to the sweet whites of the region and grassy vegetative characters and zesty acidity to the dry whites. Solo, it is accountable for most of the best white wines of the Eastern Loire, being responsible for Pouilly Fumé and Sancerre as well as the lesser-known Quincy, Reuilly and Menetou-Salon.

In this century it has spread to Poitou, Chablis and other parts of France. Elsewhere in Europe it is quite well known in Northern Italy and also in Eastern Europe. In the New World it is widely grown in California (where Robert Mondavi rescued it from oblivion in the 1960s and 1970s by 'smoking' it in new oak, the resultant fumé blanc taking California by storm), Argentina and Chile. In the Antipodes it shows its distinct personality very explicitly in New Zealand and in the coolest areas of Australia, where it arrived as part of James Busby's collection in 1832.

Though it is grown in all states of Australia, nowhere has it been taken thoroughly to heart, as has chardonnay in most states. Perhaps the reason is sauvignon's distinct personality, that love-me-or-leave-me nose, termed 'gooseberry' by its admirers, 'grassy' by its apathists (very few), 'tom-cat' by its detractors and 'methoxypyrazine' by oenologists, or its quite individual palate, once described to me as 'steely acid, like sucking ballbearings'.

Though sauvignon is quite high in acidity, its cellaring life is not thereby prolonged. Most sauvignons are ready to drink when a year old and, though quite fresh drinking at that stage, unlike semillon, do not improve in bottle past three years and are usually very tired at five. The same comments apply also to the better sauvignon-based fumé blancs.

As at mid-year 1988, Australia had 730 hectares of the variety, about a quarter of which were still to bear—obviously enough a sign of a growing enthusiasm if not a fervour. Virtually half of those hectares were in South Australia, most in the warmer McLaren Vale and Barossa districts—just a little odd for an early-ripening variety accustomed to cooler climates, which may account partly for the rather bland nature of most of Australia's sauvignons and the need to boost the complexity of the variety by barrel fermentation and new small oak maturation. Yet in moderate to cool Australian areas such as Padthaway, Coonawarra, western Victoria and the higher parts of central and north-east Victoria, not to mention Margaret River and Mount Barker in Western Australia, the variety has produced wines of authentic gooseberry grassy aromas and balanced spicy palates in which small oak, if used at all, is a partner not a dictator and which, importantly, are good with food.

But what of the grape itself? It is a vigorous upright grower with rough three- to five-lobed leaves of a bright green shade; and small, cylindrical, tight, at times winged bunches, close to the cane and difficult to pick, with oval yellow-green berries that ripen early in the season.

In winemaking techniques, makers have not yet been as adventurous as with chardonnay. Minimal skin contact, solids-free juice and long cool fermentation in temperature-controlled stainless steel tanks—in short the standard approach to Australian white wine making remains the accepted wisdom, though barrel fermentation in part is sometimes used for greater complexity.

What of the wine styles? Let us first make mention of that peculiar phenomenon, Fumé Blanc (smoked white), presumably derived from the French synonym for sauvignon, *blanc fumé*. Though our better examples such as Lindeman's Padthaway, Taltarni, Tisdall Mount Helen and Tim Knappstein are made purely from sauvignon blanc (that is, 80% minimum, in accordance with the law), many others, by and large much cheaper, see no sauvignon at all with the result that Australian wine marketers have created yet another meaningless generic to rank in originality with 'Chablis' or that latest steal 'Australian Beaujolais'. Surely the time has come to codify fumé, to insist that it contain a minimum amount of sauvignon (say, 50%), the balance being provided by naturally affinitive varieties such as semillon, colombard and chenin.

SOUTH AUSTRALIA

Of the better examples of fumé mentioned above, Lindeman's Padthaway wines have enjoyed spectacular and well-justified show success.

Lindeman's Padthaway Fumé Blanc 1987: I mentioned above that sauvignon blanc or, for that matter, fumé does not improve in bottle beyond three years. This wine is an exception to the rule. Tasted in April 1990 this was pale to medium yellow-green in shade, offering delightfully ripe and full gooseberry fragrances on nose, and showing on palate very rich spicy gooseberry flavours and well-balanced acidity. A wine of sheer class. (18.5 pts) Drink in 1990–92.

Lindeman's Padthaway Fumé Blanc 1988: a year of much-reduced quantity because of a devastating spring frost, which did not affect quality. Medium yellow with green tints, this wine showed excellent charred oak and a slightly subdued herbaceousness on nose, while palate harmonised ripe gooseberry fruit and beautifully handled spicy oak to excellent effect (17.5 pts) Drink in 1990–92. (Tasted at the same time.)

Lindeman's Padthaway Sauvignon Blanc Bin 7498 1989: pale to medium yellow in colour with an excellent bouquet of lantana-gooseberry and vanillan oak aromas, this wine presented quite a fresh palate showing a very pleasing harmony of grassy gooseberry, nutty oak flavours and balanced acidity. A fine example of arguably Australia's best made and most consistent sauvignon blanc style. (18 pts) Drink in 1990–93. (Tasted April 1990.)

Hardy's also source sauvignon blanc from Padthaway, calling it Fumé Blanc. The Hardy Collection Fumé Blanc 1988, tasted in December 1989, was pale to medium yellow in hue, highlighted in bouquet by an excellent integration of gooseberry and charred oak aromas. On palate there were rich broader flavours quite in keeping with the ripe 1988 year, but still elegant and fruity and beautifully combined with smoky oak. (17 pts) Drink in 1990–91.

Few sauvignons blancs are made in Coonawarra, but one of consistency is Katnook. Its 1989 Sauvignon Blanc, tasted March 1990, was a delightful pale yellow-green in hue, offering typical gooseberry aromas on nose, and showing on palate long but controlled grassy flavours of great impact but without coarseness. (17.5 pts) Drink in 1990–92.

Though McLaren Vale is certainly a warm area, this warmth often endows the variety with most pleasing soft and spicy characters, while the distinctively grassy traits remain.

From the mid-1980s, Wirra Wirra has made consistently successful sauvignon blanc. The wines of 1988 and 1989 are no exception to the rule.

1988: pale yellow-green in hue, lifted smoky grassy and gooseberry aromas in a most complex nose, having a medium-bodied well-balanced gooseberry-flavoured palate, soft and rich yet not heavy. (17.5 pts) Drink in 1990–91. (Tasted March 1989.)

1989: very pale yellow in tone. Fresh, grassy aromas. Long palate showing herbaceous flavours with a touch of spice. Dry and refreshing finish. Forward. (16.5 pts) Drink in 1990–91. (Tasted December 1989.)

If its 1989 Sauvignon Blanc is any sure guide, Currency Creek is also in the top league of McLaren Vale makers of the variety. Tasted in March 1990, that wine was a pale to medium yellow-green in tone, offering grassy gooseberry aromas and a subtle touch of smoky wood on nose. Its palate also was gooseberry flavoured, with excellent acidity and charred oak in good balance. (17.5 pts) Drink in 1990–92.

Like Currency Creek, Scarpantoni Estates is another excellent small winery in McLaren Vale. It too makes fine sauvignon blanc. Tasted in December 1989, Scarpantoni Estates Sauvignon Blanc 1989 showed a youthful pale yellow colour, green gooseberry aromas, with similar flavours on a dry crisp-finishing palate. (16.5 pts) Drink in 1990–91.

Mount Hurtle, the beautifully restored winery where Geoff Merrill also produces 'Geoff Merrill', makes excellent sauvignons and sauvignon blends from time to time. The Mount Hurtle Sauvignon Blanc Semillon 1989, tasted December 1989, offered a complex bouquet of lemon-citrus and herbaceous aromas with fresh herbaceous flavours softened somewhat by the fuller lemony character of the semillon. (16.5 pts) Drink in 1990–91.

Other McLaren Vale wineries making a softer richer sauvignon style are Beresford, Daringa, Ingoldby, Ryecroft, Thomas Fernhill and Woodstock.

In the Southern Adelaide Hills, vine-planting in the 1980s concentrated chiefly on chardonnay and pinot noir, though a little sauvignon blanc has been planted in small vineyards such as Stafford Ridge, where the variety is showing great promise.

Further north in the Barossa ranges, the variety is represented at Hill-Smith Estate, which makes a sauvignon-based Fumé of good style. The 1988 Hill-Smith Estate Fumé Blanc, tasted late 1989, was medium yellow in colour, showing barrel-ferment, malolactic and charred oak aromas in a complex nose, while palate was long and well balanced revealing gooseberry, buttery and smoky wood flavours. (16 pts) Drink in 1990–91.

In the Barossa Valley, Grant Burge is a winemaker who has had wide experience with all varieties. The Grant Burge Sauvignon Blanc 1989, tasted in December of that year, showed very complex herbaceous, citrusy, vanillan aromas in a fascinating nose. On palate the flavours were rich and toasty with lively acidity providing a fresh finish. (17.5 pts) Drink in 1990–92.

By acquiring Tollana, Penfold's have added yet another resilient string to an immensely strong bow. The Tollana Barossa Valley Sauvignon Blanc 1988 is typical of the consistent quality of the Tollana range. Pale to medium yellow in hue, this wine offered a spicy grassy slightly oak-dominant nose, with palate showing long spicy flavours and a crisp finish. (16 pts) Drink 1990–91. (Tasted December 1989.)

Other makers of Barossa sauvignon of solid quality are Tolley's Pedare, who also offer a reasonable fumé style; and nearby, but outside the valley proper, Primo Estate at Virginia, north of Adelaide.

In the Riverland, sauvignon blanc also flourishes. The style here is lighter and more tamed than dryland sauvignon and usually very good value, as exemplified by Renmano Chairman's Selection Sauvignon Blanc 1989. When tasted in late 1989 this was pale yellow in hue, with a gooseberry nose and a 'tamed' palate showing soft smooth fruit on palate, which lacked the aggressively vegetative characters often seen in the variety. (16 pts)

If sauvignon can be said to be experiencing a surge in popularity, Tim Knappstein at Clare must be given a lot of the credit, for it was his pioneering work with the variety in the mid-1970s that created Australia's first Fumé Blanc in 1978. Though fumé may have gone off the gold standard in some quarters since then, the Tim Knappstein Fumé Blancs are of high quality with a quite-justified popularity. The 1989 marque, tasted in March 1989, held an excellent green-yellow hue, with smoky wood, mint and gooseberry aromas all playing their parts in a complex bouquet, while a well-balanced palate showed generous depths of spicy, gooseberry flavours. An excellent fumé with short-term cellaring potential. (17.5 pts) Drink in 1990–93.

Bridgewater Mill Sauvignon Blanc 1989, a 50:50 blend of Clare and Coonawarra fruit, is an excellent wine. Delicate pale yellow in hue with estery capsicum characters on nose, the wine shows a long elegant palate with great depth of rich fruit. (17.5 pts) Drink in 1990–92.

As a natural complement to their excellent rhine riesling and chardonnay, Neil and Andrew Pike also produce a very trustworthy sauvignon blanc. The 1989 vintage, tasted in August 1989, was pale yellow in colour, nicely grassy on nose, showing grassy flavours also on a well-balanced palate. A civilised wine without any hypervegetative aggression. (16.5 pts) Drink in 1990–92.

Reliable sauvignons from the Clare region are also made by Jim Barry Wines and Neil Paulett.

VICTORIA

Sauvignon blanc is also grown quite widely in the cooler regions of Victoria, though in common with its representation in the rest of vinous Australia, nowhere does it dominate.

Generally such Victorian sauvignons are of the distinctively grassy style without that overtly vegetative aggression that sometimes repels the nose and palate. They do, however, have the fruit weight on palate to carry the oak necessary to create a quality fumé blanc. A prime example of such a wine is Taltarni Fumé Blanc, consistently one of the best of its genre in Australia. Its 1989 is conspicuously successful: pale yellow in colour, with classic gooseberry aromas on nose, fresh but not aggressive, having a long clean gooseberry-flavoured palate with excellent acid balance. (18 pts) Drink in 1990–92.

In the Pyrenees area also, Mount Avoca produces good sauvignon blanc.

The other high-profile fumé blanc style to emerge from Victoria has been that of Mount Helen, high above the Goulburn Valley. Tasted in December 1989, the Mount Helen Fumé Blanc of that year was a delicate yellow-green in hue. Its nose carried grassy smoky aromas of good depth, palate also showing complex spicy grassy flavours with good oak characters and balance. (17 pts) Drink in 1990–92.

Further north but also in the mountain country, above the King River, Brown Brothers employ Koombahla fruit to produce a sauvignon blanc, which I have always found to be very true to variety and consistently well made. The Brown Brothers Koombahla Sauvignon Blanc 1989, tasted late 1989, was youthful both in its pale straw colour and its herbaceous nose. Palate showed delicate grassy-gooseberry flavours, good fruit-acid balance and a crisp finish. (16.5 pts) Drink in 1990-91.

In the same general area, Bailey's of Glenrowan, recently equipped with new refrigeration much to the delight of winemaker Steve Goodwin, produced a commendable 1989 Sauvignon Blanc, which though a little high in residual sugar had pleasing gooseberry aromas and flavours. (16 pts) Drink in 1990-91.

Based on its performance in the Yarra Valley during the late 1980s, sauvignon has found a natural home there and in other cool areas such as Geelong and in all probability the Mornington Peninsula. As yet sauvignons from Mornington are hard to come by, but those from Geelong, where Bannockburn makes a consistently good wine, show that Geelong is eminently suited to the variety.

In the Yarra Valley, the Yarra Ridge Sauvignon Blanc 1989 swept all before it late in that year. A beautifully made wine. I tasted it in December 1989, noting: a pale yellow hue, delicate capsicum aromas with hint of fresh-ground white pepper and fine-boned capsicum and spice flavours in an intensely fruity palate. Should develop well in bottle for one to two years. (17 pts) Drink in 1990-92.

Elsewhere in the Yarra, sauvignon blanc has been blended with semillon to make a fumé style at Coldstream Hills, and a fresh zingy dry white at Yarra Burn, as well as being a partner with semillon in the richer Dry White No. 1 style of Yarra Yering.

NEW SOUTH WALES

In New South Wales, the variety has never been completely at home in the Hunter Valley, though in cooler years it sometimes makes a satisfactory junior partner to semillon in semillon-sauvignon blends or plays a supporting role in a commercial fumé.

In Mudgee, Amberton and Montrose each have made good sauvignons in cool years.

In the MIA, de Bortoli made an excellent 1989 Sauvignon Blanc. Tasted in late 1989, the wine offered authentic gooseberry characters on nose and palate, with a touch of residual sugar on palate and fresh clean acid on finish. (16 pts) Drink in 1991.

In New South Wales Sunraysia, at Wentworth, the Trentham Estate also makes very complex and interesting sauvignons, while John Cassegrain in his Hastings Valley winery, near Port Macquarie, uses both local and Stanthorpe-grown sauvignon to good effect.

WESTERN AUSTRALIA

I have written above of semillon and its similarity to sauvignon blanc in Margaret River. There are differences of course. Though often noticeably grassy, semillon can rise to heights of elegance—as witness the 1989 Evans & Tate Margaret River Semillon—whereas the gooseberry flavours of sauvignon, though honest and perfectly palatable, are usually more simple and one-dimensional. If complexity is required, then it is up to the winemaker to provide it by making an appropriate selection from his or her technical repertoire, a touch of barrel-ferment, perhaps, or a special choice of oak.

I must say that I find Cullen's Sauvignon Blanc to be amongst the most interesting and complex of the region. Certainly 1988 lived up to my expectation. That wine, tasted in both July and August 1989, was pale yellow in hue, offering spicy vanillan oak and 'tamed' herbaceous aromas. Palate was full and soft, spicily oaky at first, then ripe and fruity, a wine in need of two years in bottle to fulfil the promise of the palate. (18 pts) Drink in 1991–93.

Another specialist in the techniques of sauvignon blanc is Bob Cartwright at Leeuwin Estate. The 1988 Leeuwin Estate Sauvignon Blanc tasted April 1990 was pale to medium yellow in tone with tints of green. On nose, the wine revealed intense gooseberry varietal aromas, while palate was surprisingly soft and deep, though still showing authentic gooseberry flavour and cleansing acidity on finish, all the result of 50 per cent barrel fermentation with three months' lees contact and maturation in mainly one-year-old oak. Arguably the richest of the Margaret River sauvignons. (17.5 pts) Drink in 1990–93.

The other Margaret River style is straightforward, though it remains a refreshingly zingy white, most suitable for serving with shellfish. The chief exponents of this style are Cape Clairault, Redgate and Ribbon Vale Estate.

Cape Clairault Sauvignon Blanc 1989: pale yellow in hue with capsicum–gooseberry characters on nose, this wine showed quite long grassy herbaceous flavours on palate, with balance and importantly without any excess varietal aggression. (17 pts) Drink in 1990–92.

Redgate Sauvignon Blanc 1988: pale to medium yellow with green tints, offering on nose fresh grassy aromas, this wine on palate mirrors the nose, continuing crisp herbal flavours. Clean acid cut on finish. (16.5 pts) Drink in 1990–91. (Both wines were tasted in December 1989.)

Ribbon Vale Sauvignon Blanc 1989: pale yellow in colour, revealing grassy herbal aromas on nose, this one showed light clean gooseberry–herbal flavours on palate, which had good short-term cellaring prospects. (17 pts) Drink in 1990–92. (Tasted August 1989.)

Freycinet also produces sauvignon blanc in a similar fresh style. Pierro blends sauvignon blanc, semillon and chardonnay to create a zesty current-drinking white of some style.

At Capel Vale, Dr Peter Pratten prefers to blend a lesser proportion of semillon into his sauvignon blanc, usually producing a lively spicy white. The 1989, typical of the style, was of a pale yellow tone, showing intensely grassy sauvignon aromas and crisp, spicy flavours cut by fresh finishing acidity. (16.5 pts) Drink in 1990–92.

In the Mount Barker–Frankland River region, Alkoomi has long made a fresh true-to-variety sauvignon blanc style, vintage 1989 being no exception. Pale yellow in hue, this wine showed controlled gooseberry–grassy aromas on nose, with palate also offering similar flavours and a clean acid cut on finish. No technical bravura here, just excellence of fruit. (17.5 pts) Drink in 1990–92. (Tasted August 1989.)

Closer to Albany, Wignall's King River grow superb chardonnay and pinot noir. Sauvignon blanc completes this trio of excellence.
Wignall's King River Sauvignon Blanc 1989: a very pale yellow-green in colour, this wine showed grassy, green peach aromas (a touch of barrel-ferment?) on nose. On palate, light tropical fruit–capsicum flavours are very pleasing and lightly elegant. Fresh acid finish in good balance. (17 pts) (Tasted August 1989.)

The brand new Goundrey Langton winery near Mount Barker is also a sauvignon blanc specialist. Goundrey Windy Hill Sauvignon Blanc 1989, tasted in July 1989, was a very youthful straw-yellow in shade. On nose, aromas were typically grassy but not overdone, while similar grassy flavours of some length were evident in the mouth, a slight mid-palate hollowness intervening before a clean acid finish. Should fill out in bottle (16.5 pts) Drink in 1990–92. (Tasted July 1989.)
Goundrey Windy Hill Sauvignon Blanc 1988: pale yellow in colour, showing smoky wood and grassy aromas on nose, this wine offered restrained asparagus and smoky–spicy oak flavours on a crisp well-balanced palate. (17 pts) Drink in 1990–92.

Sauvignon blanc should not be allowed to indulge in the wilder excesses of its fruit potential, but civilised or 'tamed' (a word I have occasionally used in these notes) it becomes a much more reliable, though never boring, white wine worthy of any serious wine consumer's attention.

Chenin blanc

Chenin blanc is a variety of considerable importance in Australia, though seemingly it remains at the crossroads of the Australian wine market. It suffers a similar crisis of personality in its French home, the central Loire valley, where it jumps like a jack-of-all-trades from sparkling to dry to semi- and fully sweet whites, depending on season and, one suspects, the market's whim.

Plantings of 517 hectares (458 hectares in bearing) existed in Australia at mid-year 1988—growers' interest, like that for sauvignon blanc, increasing but not passionate. In Australia, its main use is for dry white, though it may double as sparkling-wine base from time to time; and there is no reason whatever to suppose that it would not botrytise as well as any area in the Loire to produce marvellous sticky wine, given the right Australian location.

Though nearly half Australia's plantings occur in South Australia, the winemakers there are remarkably shy in identifying it varietally on their labels, with the result that most of it would find its way into generically labelled bottles such as 'White Burgundy' or 'Chablis' or as a perfectly legal addition to chardonnay, a variety with which I think it has many palate affinities.

In most Australian locations, except parts of Victoria and Western Australia, it makes an average soft white of generous but eminently forgettable flavour.

The chief exceptions to this rule in the West are, quite surprisingly (given their notorious heat), the Swan Valley and its neighbour, Gin Gin. Both areas are dominated by Houghton, by far the largest producer in Western Australia and the maker of its best chenins blancs, some of which most advantageously find their way into the West's best-known white, Houghton White Burgundy.

1989 (50% chenin blanc, 32% muscadelle, 18% chardonnay): pale yellow against a green wash, green peach and melon aromas on nose, long palate with soft chenin flavours well complemented by chardonnay with well-balanced acid. (17.5 pts) Always one of Australia's better generics and often worth cellaring for two to three years. Drink in 1990–93.

By contrast, on the same evening in July 1989, I tasted the 1983 (60% chenin blanc, 30% muscadelle, 10% other varieties): developing yellow-gold in hue, classic toast and honey aromas on nose, full soft developing well-integrated palate with honeyed flavours and hints of lemon. (18 pts) Drink in 1990–91.

Moondah Brook Chenin Blanc is also made by Houghton. The 1987 was medium yellow in tone, just starting to develop. On nose the wine offered incipient honeyed aromas, another sign of bottle development, while palate also showed soft honeyed flavours and soft finishing acidity. A more forward style. (16 pts) Drink in 1991. (Tasted July 1989.)

Another Swan producer whose chenin blanc is well worth seeking out is Jane Brook Estate. Its 1988 Chenin Blanc was pale yellow in hue, with tropical fruit aromas on nose, and a ripe soft palate with an almost tangy citrus acidity on finish. (16 pts) Drink in 1990–91.

Though not strictly in the Swan Valley, Paul Conti at Wanneroo to the north of Perth certainly makes chenin blanc of consistent quality from Swan Valley fruit. The Paul Conti Chenin Blanc 1988, tasted July 1989, was of medium yellow colour with a soft fruit salad nose and a touch of spicy oak. Palate was clean, round and soft-finishing. (15.5 pts) Drink in 1991.

In Victoria, chenin blanc is made into an altogether crisper and more acidic style. The Heathcote Winery, south-west of Bendigo, has made very good chenin blanc in this style in the past few years—wines when young easily mistaken for cool-area chardonnay. Regrettably none has come my way recently.

Even in the warmth of the Swan Hill region, Best's make a very consistent chenin blanc. Best's Victorian Chenin Blanc 1989, tasted December 1989, was a very pale yellow in colour, offering on nose lightly herbaceous aromas with similar flavours and a touch of residual sugar on palate. Acidity is well balanced, keeping the wine fresh in the mouth. (16 pts) Drink in 1990–91.

Verdelho

From the statistics, verdelho seems of little importance: only 99 hectares in the whole of Australia in mid-year 1988, half of which were in Western Australia and the balance divided almost equally between the Hunter Valley and South Australia. Yet in its contribution to the quality of Australian white wines it seems to deserve a much broader area.

In the Hunter Valley until quite recently the variety has been cast in a supporting role to give additional flesh and softness to semillon. Traditionally Lindeman's and Tulloch have used it in this way: Lindeman's in its four-figure Hunter River 'White Burgundy' series; and Tulloch in similarly styled whites. Though both styles are intended to be soft, they usually manage up to ten years in bottle with comparative ease, and fifteen years from exceptional vintages.

In 1989 Wyndham introduced a 100% verdelho to its top range. Tasted in January 1990, the Wyndham Estate Verdelho 1989 was pale to medium yellow in colour, showing light varietal sherbet aromas and a touch of herbaceousness on nose, while palate offered spicy sherbety flavours of good depth and balance. An interesting wine to cellar for two years. (16.5 pts) Drink in 1990–92.

Lindeman's, Tulloch and Drayton's have all produced verdelhos of good quality in recent vintages.

Of the area of verdelho in South Australia, most is planted at Padthaway, where Lindeman's have from time to time produced a straight varietal, which in recent times seems to have gone into recess and now possibly finds its way anonymously into generic blends. Elsewhere in South Australia there is little emphasis on verdelho.

All of which leads to verdelho in its most important state: Western Australia. There its comparatively few hectares are scattered throughout all its wine-producing regions, where it is made both into table- and dessert-wine styles.

Houghton, as befits its size and the skill of its winemaking, is the state's most important producer. Its verdelho fruit comes from the Swan Valley, Gin Gin and its Frankland River vineyard. Two verdelhos of fine quality were tasted in July 1989:

Houghton Gold Reserve Verdelho 1987:   pale yellow in tone with pineapple and sherbet aromas on nose, this wine revealed on palate a good depth of ripe tropical fruit flavours, some bottle development and well-balanced acidity. (16.5 pts) Drink in 1990–91.

Moondah Brook Verdelho 1989:   very pale yellow in shade, this one showed a most complex nose in which sherbety/grassy aromas combined to excellent effect. On a beautifully balanced palate, tropical fruit and sherbet flavours offered zesty, mouth-filling flavours. Should hold its freshness for one or two years more. (17 pts) Drink in 1990–91.

Sandalford, the other large Swan Valley resident, looks to the Swan and Margaret River for its verdelho fruit. Though few tank samples have been reviewed for the purposes of this book (because the trip from tank to bottle is sometimes hazardous), the tank sample of Sandalford Margaret River Verdelho 1989 was outstanding: pale yellow-green in hue, attractive sherbety nose of great depth, with a palate of powerful tropical fruit flavours and excellent balance. Lovely wine of great potential. If in bottle, it would have been pointed at 18, with good cellaring prospects for two to three years. (Tasted July 1989.)

Impressive too was the Willespie Margaret River Verdelho 1989. Very pale and youthful in its yellow hue, this wine showed typical sherbety–grassy aromas on nose, palate offering crisp clean fruit with excellent acid balance. (17 pts) Drink in 1990–92.

Marsanne

While verdelho is a variety destined to grow in area Australia-wide, marsanne is that rarity amongst Australian wine varieties: a grape of one area which it seemingly prefers to all others.

The area in question is the Nagambie region of central Victoria, where marsanne, a fairly rare grape even in its Rhône Valley habitat, has made its Australian home. In Australian vine statistics, marsanne is not recorded separately, though it is thought that about 50 hectares are cultivated, primarily in the Nagambie region but with scattered plantings in north-east Victoria and in New South Wales.

Marsanne's chief protagonists are Chateau Tahbilk and Mitchelton, whose styles could not be more different. Like semillon, marsanne can be made in what is now the traditional manner for Australian white wines, clean juice cool-fermented over some 10–14 days at 12–14° Baumé in a stainless steel tank. Or it may be subjected, like chardonnay, to all manner of permutations and combinations of skin contact, tank and barrel fermentation, malolactic fermentation, lees contact, and many oak variants in maturation.

Mitchelton has basically chosen the chardonnay path for its marsanne, attempting to place as much complexity as possible into the bottle. The Mitchelton Marsanne 1987, tasted January 1990, was full yellow in colour, offering honeysuckle aging into honeyed aromas and slightly lifted oak. On palate, honey and oak flavours were well integrated and the acid well balanced. A complex wine to be drunk within two years. (16.5 pts) Drink in 1991-92.

Chateau Tahbilk Marsanne 1989, tasted July 1990, was a classic cellaring white. Pale yellow in colour and showing distinctive honeysuckle aromas on nose, it offered clean and crisp fruit flavours and fresh acid on finish with no evidence of new wood used in maturation. An outstanding wine that will build in flavour in bottle. (17.5 pts) Drink in 1992-96.

Made either way, marsanne with three to four years' bottle age is often a very interesting substitute for older semillons or chardonnays.

Viognier

Brief mention must also be made of viognier, a native of the Northern Rhône area of Condrieu and its exclusive enclave, Chateau Grillet. As yet it is grown in Australia in only extremely small, mostly experimental plots in cooler regions of Victoria. I have tasted only one Australian viognier, from Elgee Park in Mornington. I have not reviewed it because of the obviously minute amount of production, but it does augur well for the future of this variety in cooler regions. Its jujube, honey and herbaceous characters recalled both marsanne and verdelho, with a palate structure not unlike chardonnay, and it should prove an interesting alternative for any of our softer-finishing varieties.

Colombard

In total contrast to marsanne, verdelho or viognier for that matter, colombard (or French colombard, as it is sometimes seen on Australian labels) is grown for its zingy acidity which gives it wonderful freshness in warmer areas if handled correctly, for it is terribly prone to oxidation. It hails from western France, where its acidity is put to good use in the making of base wine for the distillation of cognac. It has been well received if not well marketed in Australia, for at mid-year 1988, 612 hectares were in cultivation, more than 90% in bearing. Chiefly its use so far has been to add acidity and herbaceous flavour to blander and more neutral whites destined for the generic 'Chablis' tag, but on its own, made carefully, it is well worth scrutiny as a fresh summer luncheon drink, its zesty flavours complementing seafood and shellfish particularly well.

It is almost equally distributed between New South Wales, Victoria and South Australia; and there mostly found in the irrigation areas of the MIA, Sunraysia and the Riverland.

Makers of reliable colombard are Angove's in Renmark, St Hallett in the Barossa Valley, and Primo Estate in the Adelaide Plains north of Adelaide.

Primo Estate Colombard 1989: the palest of yellow-green hues, this wine offered attractive estery grassy aromas in a delightfully fresh nose. Palate was also fresh and zesty with herbaceous flavours and a zingy acid finish. A delightful summer wine. (17 pts) Drink in 1991–92.

Muscadelle

A grape, whose origins may be in Bordeaux where it is used in the sweet whites of the region, and whose very subtle muscat aromas betray its family origins, this varietal is used chiefly in Australia to 'soften' white table wines, which are then mostly genericised as 'white burgundy'. Grown chiefly in the Barossa Valley, where there were, as at mid-year 1988, 219 hectares in production. Most famous in North East Victoria, where, as 'Tokay' it is fortified, and becomes with age, a glorious nectar.

There are many other white varieties used anonymously for sparkling and table wine, muscat gordo blanco and the humble sultana being the two biggest quantity producers in 1988 vintage. Unless you are addicted to muscat flavour (which I confess is not one of my favourite tastes) or little flavour at all, you will not find such bulk wines particularly enticing, nor are the old sherry varieties, palomino or pedro, or other neutrals such as trebbiano or doradillo.

The decades of the 1970s and 1980s have been eras of varietal trial, with resultant tribulation for some wine varieties and triumph for others. As larger areas of more popular wine varieties are planted in more suitable areas, the 1990s should see the bulk varieties phased out by the simple laws of supply and demand, a vast improvement of quality in the lower and middle sectors of the market and, hopefully, in all sectors a greater price stability.

FRAGRANT AND FLOWERY

RHINE RIESLING, TRAMINER AND OTHER AROMATIC VARIETIES

Rhine riesling

It has been customary in the past few years to label riesling (or as it is called throughout Australia, rhine riesling) passé, a discarded child of a bygone fashion or a symbol of the pre-chardonnay era. Riesling remains vigorously alive, however, and merely awaits its next event in the wine fashion Olympics.

Its home is, as it has always been, Germany, where it is the second most widely grown variety after muller-thurgau. On its native heath its greatest wines are undoubtedly sweet, ranging from the off-dry Kabinetts through the lightly sweet Spätlese, semi-luscious Auslese and Beerenauslese to that elysian nectar, Trockenbeerenauslese. Its difficulty there has always been its place at table, where it is suitable for little else other than dessert. But when confronted by a riesling of a great year such as 1976, from a great area such as the Rheingau or the Mosel, who cares about its place at table? It can be drunk with equal pleasure on its own under an appletree at eleven o'clock in the morning.

In a sense also, riesling marks the sphere of German influence, being grown in most places where the vine can thrive and where German has been the language of authority or the local patois. Thus did it spread to Alsace, its expansion thereafter being stoutly and quite successfully resisted by French nationalism. Thus is it grown to a greater or lesser extent in central and eastern Europe and even northern Italy. The Hapsburgs and Hohenzollerns used their ploughshares as well as their swords. And thus, perhaps, did it come to South Australia with the Silesian migrations of the 1830s and 1840s, even though Sir William Macarthur is credited with its introduction to New South Wales in 1838.

Outside Europe riesling has spread to all the countries of the New Wine World, the eastern and western United States, to South America, South Africa and New Zealand.

From time to time it has been so popular that its name has inspired that most sincere form of flattery, imitation, as well as numerous synonyms for the true variety. Thus we have the synonyms Rhein riesling (Austrian), weisser riesling (German), Renski rizling (Yugoslavian) and J.R. himself, Johannisberg riesling (Californian), while on the more imaginative side even in our own fairly small (by world standards) wineland, there are Shepherd's riesling (semillon), Hunter Valley riesling (semillon, again) and Clare riesling (crouchen). Add to these the many other 'rieslings' of Europe, and you will readily appreciate how popular riesling once was.

In cool climates it is vigorous and very hardy, reportedly resisting temperatures as low as $-20°C$. In warm climates it is not as vigorous or for that matter as productive, though this may be a question more of clonal selection than climate.

It is described by the late Allan Antcliff in his book *Major Grape Varieties of Australia* as having 'rough, dark green leaves, entire to three-lobed with a few tufted hairs on the lower surface. Leaf stalks usually show some red coloration which may continue into the base of the veins. The bunches are small and compact with short and often woody stalks. The berries are small and round, gold where exposed to the sun and irregularly marked with brown spots, and juicy with a tough skin.'

Riesling ripens mid to late season and given appropriate weather conditions produces marvellously sweet botrytised wine, as well as dry or off-dry white of floral lime-citrus aromas and lime and spice flavours.

In Australia during the past decade, rhine riesling has retreated somewhat in the face of a stern attack from chardonnay, declining from 4250 hectares as at mid-year 1986 to 3658 hectares as at mid-year 1988—chardonnay rising from 1967 hectares to 2344 hectares as at the same dates. However, for winemaking riesling remains our most widely used white grape of quality.

SOUTH AUSTRALIA

As the greatest quantity of quality rhine riesling is produced in South Australia, it seems only logical to begin any discussion on Australian riesling there.

It is widely grown in the south-eastern wine regions of the state, both in Padthaway and in Coonawarra; and, averaging between 12 and 13 tonnes per hectare as it does, it may be justifiably described as a grower's joy, though it is very susceptible to outbreaks of botrytis in Coonawarra and therefore requires a stringent spray program and suitable ripening conditions to perform at its best in that area.

Of the larger makers in Coonawarra, Wynn's possibly combines both value and quality to best effect in its Coonawarra Estate Rhine Riesling, and though the vast majority of that wine sold is probably drunk within days or perhaps hours of its purchase, a tasting I attended in late October

1989 of all vintages from 1982 to 1989 showed that even bargain-priced rhines from Coonawarra do have cellaring capacity. The best of that range were 1989, 1987 and 1984.

Wynn's Coonawarra Estate Rhine Riesling 1989: very pale yellow in hue with a light green wash, very clean and light floral nose, lovely intense lime flavours; hint of residual sugar, and a touch of botrytis complexity adds richness to palate. (17 pts) Drink in 1990–94.

Wynn's Coonawarra Estate Rhine Riesling 1987: pale yellow still with green tints, light lime-citrus aromas on nose with a hint of toast (nose has a way to go yet), palate just starting to develop but has most attractive lime-citrus flavours, length, balance and acidity. (17.5 pts) Drink in 1990–93.

Wynn's Coonawarra Estate Rhine Riesling 1984: developing mid to full yellow colour, developing citrusy aromas on nose with some toastiness, full citrusy toasty flavours on a beautifully balanced palate with soft pleasant acidity. A lovely drinking style in late 1989. (18.5 pts) Drink in 1991.

Other larger producers of rhine riesling in Coonawarra are Lindeman's and Mildara.

Lindeman had mixed marketing fortunes with its individual vineyard 'Nursery' rhine riesling before withdrawing the label from the market after 1985 vintage. Top Coonawarra rhines now occasionally appear under the arguably more famous label (for riesling), Leo Buring. A recent Buring Coonawarra release of good quality was Rhine Riesling DWQ 19 1987.

Mildara seems to confine its Coonawarra riesling activity to the middle market where its wines are usually good value at their price.

The Coonawarra Machinery Company is also a substantial producer of rhine riesling in the area, selling its wines under the prestigious Katnook label and a second label, Riddoch Estate. These wines also are in the general run of good-quality Coonawarra rhines.

Very few Coonawarra rhines, except those that are botrytised and quite sweet, justify more than a 'good average quality' rating. Somehow, that 'star factor' of varietal intensity, which bigger producers pull out of the hat with odd batches of rhine riesling elsewhere even in poor years, seems missing in Coonawarra and in such vintages the result is usually a hard, ungenerous wine. Perhaps the whole area is unsuited to rhine or rather is much better suited to red.

Most of the smaller Coonawarra makers include a rhine riesling in their portfolio of wines. Of these, recent Hollick Rhine Rieslings have been quite impressive and, with the arrival in 1989 of Pat Tocaciu, formerly of Tollana, as partner-winemaker, coming vintages should be outstanding. These will be awaited with impatience, but in the meantime the 1989 Hollick Rhine, the product of an uncertain year in Coonawarra for both riesling and shiraz, can be drunk with pleasure.

Hollick Coonawarra Rhine Riesling 1989: pale yellow with a green wash, subtle lime-citrus aromas in an harmonious nose, quite long lime flavours on a medium-bodied well-balanced palate. (17 pts) Drink in 1990–92.

Bowen, Brand, Hungerford Hill* and Zema Estate are all smaller to medium-sized Coonawarra makers from whom good rhine rieslings can be expected in reasonable years.

In all, Coonawarra rhine rieslings pale in significance beside the monumental reds of the area, which are an awesome act either to precede or to follow. Indeed, rarely are they, when seen in the whole fabric of Australian rhine riesling, convincing enough to be called classic, lacking in most years the depth of nose, the intensity of flavour and the palate structure of the more proven northern areas of Clare and Eden Valley. The great virtue of rhine riesling in Coonawarra lies in its ability in some years to produce magnificent botrytised wines, mostly lusciously sweet, but very occasionally dry, such as the marvellous Hungerford Hill 1983.

So far, Petaluma has made most of the running in the ultra-sweet botrytised riesling styles of the Coonawarra region. The Petaluma style began, albeit not under that label, in 1981 with the release of the Evans Family Botrytis Riesling. Releases under the Petaluma label followed in 1982, 1984, 1985 and 1988. In January 1990 I tasted Petaluma Botrytis Riesling 1988: medium yellow-gold in colour, this wine showed very clean and deep aromas of dried apricot. Its youthful, slightly viscous palate was fully sweet, but did not cloy, revealing rich apricot and ripe peach flavours and very well-balanced acid freshness on finish. An opulent style with a bottle development potential of at least five years. (18.5 pts) Drink not before 1995, if this wine is to be seen at its best. Petaluma Rhine Riesling, a dry spatlese style, is made from fruit grown at the company's Clare vineyard and will be discussed below.

Much the same comment may be made of Padthaway rhine riesling as of Coonawarra: wine of good quality, leading the second rank. Always interesting but never compelling, rhine riesling from Padthaway plays a major part in many excellent multi-area rhine blends.

From Padthaway Hardy's have in the past produced both a dry rhine riesling and an often outstanding botrytised rhine of auslese sweetness or greater.

Seppelt, that other long-term resident of the region, rarely releases a 100% Padthaway rhine, but does from time to time make a wonderful auslese style, the last such wine being 1985 vintage. Padthaway rhine, however, looms large in content in the excellent multi-area Black Label and Gold Label ranges.

Hardy's also use a great deal of Padthaway riesling in their various commercial ranges, principally in the very reliable Siegersdorf and Old Castle ranges, and formerly in the Collection Series (dry rhine riesling has been discontinued in the latter series). Fortunately Collection Series will still feature a sweeter Padthaway botrytis rhine from time to time

---

* Hungerford Hill was purchased by Seppelt in June 1990. Any future Coonawarra Rhine Riesling releases may be under the Seppelt label.

as quality permits, the most recent classic Padthaway sweet rhine in that line being Hardy Collection Padthaway Beerenauslese Rhine Riesling 1987, which I tasted in July 1989: medium yellow in hue with distinct orange-peel and apricot aromas on nose, long sweet palate with a lime tang which prevented any cloying in the mouth. Finely balanced. (17 pts) Drink in 1993–95.

Rhine riesling is certainly grown in Langhorne Creek and no doubt sold to the multi-area winemakers of the Barossa and elsewhere. Local makers are Bleasdale and Bremer Wines, whose rhine rieslings rarely come my way.

McLaren Vale still produces a substantial amount of the variety, often making a fuller style akin to that of the Barossa Valley floor, though certain makers such as Wirra Wirra manage a delicacy and style in rhine riesling that would be creditable even in Eden Valley. The Wirra Wirra Hand-picked Rhine Riesling 1989, tasted late January 1990, was then pale yellow in hue, showing light clean floral aromas on nose and a palate of delicate lime-citrus character and crisp acidity on finish. (16.5 pts) Though it was fresh and young when tasted, it should, given one or two years in cellar, fill out more. Drink in 1990–92.

Most of the numerous small makers of McLaren Vale offer rhine riesling on their lists. Amongst the most consistent makers are Norman's and its second label, Coolawin, Hugo, Pirramimma, Scarpantoni and Thomas Fernhill—though it must be added that rhines from this area are often blends of fruit from several areas. Two of the giants of the area are Seaview and Thomas Hardy, both famous in years gone by for McLaren Vale riesling and both making rieslings of very high quality these days mostly from fruit of other areas, such as Padthaway and Clare.

While rhine riesling is not of major importance in the yields of the South Australian Riverland, it is most assuredly present in the wines of the region. Angove's and Berri–Renmano are the two leading producers, both usually offering very good value for money.

Rhine riesling in the southern Adelaide Hills is centred on Lenswood where Geoff Weaver, Tim Knappstein and Stephen Henschke all have vineyards containing plantings of this variety. Though Stephen Henschke is satisfied with the performance of his fruit so far (bearing in mind the youth of the vines), the first wines, which have been rather herbaceous in character, bear only a passing resemblance to the fuller, more lime-citrus style of the warmer Eden Valley. The very coolness of this area suggests that rhine riesling may experience ripening problems in all but the more favourable years.

Even the more northerly parts of those Hills and Eden Valley itself do imbue riesling with grassy flavours in extremely cool seasons.

In more normal conditions, Eden Valley is for riesling what Coonawarra is for cabernet sauvignon, a most perfect environment. Here, 500 metres above sea-level, rhine riesling reaches elysian heights of aroma and flavour. High tropical lime and pineapple aromas are typical of young wines, while palate flavours show a lime-citrus intensity, steely acidity and aging capacity unmatched usually by any other Australian rieslings.

The company that traditionally has set all the standards of high-quality rhine riesling making with Eden Valley fruit is Leo Buring and its winemaker emeritus, John Vickery. Except for a period of nine years at Coonawarra, Vickery has superintended virtually every riesling vintage at Chateau Leonay for close to a generation, having joined Leo Buring in 1955. Though the changes in white wine making practice during that time would merit a book by themselves, rhine riesling making in particular changed dramatically. The period 1950–65 saw the change from open fermentation to pressure tanks and later, because of the availability of refrigeration, to controlled fermentation at cool temperatures and much more attention paid to anti-oxidative handling of fruit and must.

Though some of the rhines made at Leo Buring during the 1960s were classics by any standards, John Vickery is convinced that riesling quality improved dramatically during the 1970s, showing greater body and substance. Because of more careful handling and sterile filtration, the wines not only exhibited greater freshness and aromaticity but also could contain sufficient residual sugar to fill out the middle palate without risk of refermentation in bottle. And though various companies produced wines that were too high in residual sugar and therefore rather mawkishly sweet, the resulting switch in public taste led to a surge in popularity in rhine riesling in the mid-1970s, which brought an end to the red wine boom that had commenced about eight years earlier.

But what is the magic of Eden Valley rhine that has given rise to so much justified praise over the years? Comparisons with fruit from the Watervale vineyard owned by Lindeman's until a few years ago are inevitable, and Karl Stockhausen, the vastly experienced former Lindeman's winemaker who in 1981–82 was in charge of Chateau Leonay, feels that Eden Valley riesling develops more slowly in bottle than its Watervale counterpart perhaps because of cooler ripening and higher acidity which give young Eden Valley rhines a steely structure not unlike some of the drier wines of Schloss Vollrads in the Rheingau, whereas the rhines of Watervale have more forward flavours and less immediately noticeable acidity, but retain a marvellous ability to age long term as gracefully as do those of Eden Valley. Good balance of fruit and acidity is crucial to quality in rhine riesling, more than in any other white variety—the truth of this statement being nowhere plainer than in the old Eden Valley rhines of Leo Buring reviewed below.

Leo Buring Eden Valley Rhine Riesling DWC 17 1973 (tasted June 1988): a bright medium yellow in hue, this marvellous old wine revealed the typically honeyed aromas of old Eden Valley rhine. Flavours also showed unmistakeable 'honey' (without any sign of the 'kerosene' oiliness that in moderation is not unattractive in old rieslings), while palate was long, well structured and finished with lively acidity. (18.5 pts) Has reached a plateau, will not improve, but is quite typical of top years of Eden Valley. Do be wary, however, for bottles of any wine as old will vary.

Leo Buring Eden Valley Rhine Riesling DWE 17 1975 (tasted June 1988): mid-yellow and green tinged in colour, this wine was amazingly undeveloped for its age, showing delicate floral aromas and incipient honey flavours. Thirteen years of age when tasted, this wine seemed no more than five. Though it is of course drinkable at the present time, there is lots of life left in it. (18.5 pts)

Leo Buring Eden Valley Rhine Riesling DWI 16 1979 (tasted June 1988 and again December 1989): deep yellow-green in colour, showing slightly lifted 'kerosene' aromas on nose, this wine was the most advanced of this trio on palate, offering rich soft citrusy flavours and a drying finish. Albeit still a good wine, it needs to be drunk. (17 pts)

Though it fell into disuse in the 1920s because of economic conditions, Pewsey Vale was the pioneer vineyard of the Eden Valley area. About 114 years after those initial plantings by Joseph Gilbert in 1847, Yalumba reincarnated Pewsey Vale, planting rhine riesling as a matter of course. Pewsey Vale rhines are picked quite ripe these days with more varietal flavour, but a high acid level in the grape is usually regarded as a good indicator of potential quality. Alan Hoey, Yalumba's chief winemaker, sees Pewsey Vale rhines as having more tropical fruit flavours than that other local Yalumba vineyard in his charge, Heggies, which exemplifies the classic lime-citrus characteristics of the variety in this region. Lower levels of grape acidity may also, according to Alan Hoey, play a significant part in the early development of 'kerosene' flavours in rhine riesling.

The best years in the modern rhine riesling era of Pewsey Vale have been 1969, 1973, 1979, 1984, 1986 and 1987, while the cream of the Heggies Rhine Riesling vintages have been 1979 (the first), 1982, 1984 and 1986.

Though Heggies Rhine Rieslings are held in cellar for a year or two before release, those of Pewsey Vale are released in year of vintage. In October 1989, I tasted Pewsey Vale Rhine Riesling 1989, noticing a bright pale yellow colour in the glass, delicate passionfruit floral aromas and a palate of good structure and balance, but a little subdued in flavour intensity at that time. (16.5 pts) Drink in 1990–93.

Heggies Rhine Riesling 1987, tasted in September 1988, was pale yellow in hue, showing typical lime-citrus aromas in a fairly undeveloped nose. Palate flavours were reticent but palate was well balanced. Should age well. (16.5 pts) Drink in 1990–95.

There is a reverse side to the riesling coin in Eden Valley, and that is botrytis, which in most seasons has a marvellously beneficial effect.

1987 was also extremely good for the sweet botrytised riesling wines of the area, amongst the best of which was Tollana Eden Valley Botrytis Rhine Riesling 1987. When last tasted in October 1989, this was a deep amber-gold in hue with most alluring aromas of honeysuckle and orange blossom. Its palate was a triumph of lusciousness, revealing rich flavours of honey, vanilla, orange peel and glacé fruit and an enlivening acidity which refreshed the mouth. (19 pts) An Australian classic.

Other Eden Valley botrytised rieslings of quality made in the 1987 vintage but not quite reaching the celestial heights of the Tollana were Pewsey Vale, Heggies and Henschke.

One of the most spectacular vineyards in this entire area—proving that large companies sometimes prefer corporate idiosyncracy to hardnosed economics—is Orlando's Steingarten. Planted entirely to rhine riesling on a hillside literally hewn out of rock as the name implies, this small estate with its close-planted vines would not be out of place in the Mosel or any craggy valley in Germany.

Whereas 1988 had been a relatively warm and easy vintage, 1989 was not without its difficulties. These are reflected to some extent in the Steingarten Rhine Riesling of that year, which in May 1990 held a delicate green-tinted pale yellow hue. On nose it showed light floral lime aromas with a most intriguing hint of green apple. This nuance of green apple was also part of a dry and predominantly lime-citrus flavoured palate, which was a touch short on finish. This was a very good rhine, obviously made in difficult ripening conditions. (16 pts) Drink in 1991-92.

By contrast, in February 1989 I tasted Steingarten Rhine Riesling 1988. This was pale yellow in hue with a light green wash. Its nose showed deep, almost Germanic lime-juice aromas, but its palate was quite austere, leaving an imprint of acidity rather than fruit. Despite this the wine gave the distinct impression that it would fill out given three to five years' patient cellaring and then might hold that palate plateau for many years. (18 pts) Drink 1993 onwards.

At the same time, I tasted a relic from Orlando's past, the first wine of the vineyard, 1966. This was then a very developed yellow-gold in colour with distinct browns. Its nose was old, honeyed and slightly maderised, but its palate was still just together, though a touch bitter on finish. (15 pts) A memento of bygone technique yet a privilege to taste, this wine had been made in one of the old 'cookers', the German pressure fermenters imported by Orlando in 1952. Another extremely reliable, keenly priced and sometimes stunning white made by Orlando from Eden Valley fruit is St Helga Rhine Riesling.

Numbers of other winemakers, domiciled both locally and in the Barossa Valley, offer rhine riesling of reliable to excellent quality from year to year. Names to remember are Henschke, Karl Seppelt, Mountadam and Craneford (all local producers) and Stafford Ridge, further south near Lenswood.

In the Barossa Valley proper, many makers produce an Eden Valley Rhine, Tollana from its Woodbury vineyard arguably the best of them. Others rating a very honourable mention are Grant Burge, well in control of his new venture after his departure from Krondorf, Krondorf itself, Rockford, and Seppelt, whose Partalunga vineyard will certainly create some riesling masterpieces in the future.

The lower slopes of the Barossa and the valley floor make a distinctly different style of rhine riesling from that of Eden Valley. It is fair to say that it is usually more obviously floral in aroma, while on palate it is broader and more generous in flavour and definitely softer, earlier maturing and at its peak sometimes after one to two years. Its aromas and flavours with age tend to coarsen, becoming oily and thick. The term 'keroseny' aptly describes the nose and palate of such wines. Fortunately, modern cool-fermentation techniques retain freshness as much in young Barossa rieslings as in other varieties, and the result is usually a first-quality young wine, which should be drunk as it is made—fresh and young.

Makers of good local rhine riesling are Leo Buring, Krondorf (its Lyndoch Estate 1989 being especially good), Elderton, Basedow, St Hallett and Tolley's Pedare.

As with their reds, the Barossa winemakers utilise a good deal of Barossa riesling in big multi-area blends, rhines of excellent standard that are 'commercial' only in the keenly priced sense of the word. Wolf Blass Yellow Label and Orlando Jacob's Creek are probably best known, but a favourite of mine is Kaiser Stuhl Green Ribbon, often a cut above these.

It is a matter of friendly dispute among lovers of great rhine rieslings whether the Eden Valley or the Clare Valley produces Australia's finest rhines. Certainly great rieslings have been made by each in the past generation, though the pleasant dilemma falls to the consumer to choose between the slightly earlier palate accessibility of Clare and the steely backbone and great aging potential of Eden.

Geologically, the soils of the two areas are quite different. Eden Valley has thin podsolised acid soils, which produce rieslings of correspondingly low pH and high acidity, wines that are often leaner, lighter and of greater delicacy than those of Clare. However, the Clare rieslings certainly do not lack delicacy, but coming as they do from richer, brown earth soils, sometimes limestone based and of higher alkalinity, yield wines often of greater flesh and earlier charm, but still with the classic lime-citrus intensity that the variety should have.

Historically, the Leasingham and Watervale districts of the Clare Valley have produced the great rieslings of Clare, and names associated with these areas were Lindeman's and Stanley. Lindeman's no longer own any vineyards in the Watervale area, though doubtless fruit continues to be purchased from there by its subsidiary Leo Buring (both companies were purchased by Penfold's in early 1990). Stanley, itself sold to Hardy's in 1987, has been since relegated to a cask name, though 'Leasingham' has been maintained by Hardy's as a major wine range of high quality at extremely competitive prices, Rhine Riesling remaining one of the prides of the Leasingham range. The 1989 vintage is a typical example of Leasingham consistency, albeit in a Clare year that cannot be rated one of the best of the decade.

Leasingham Rhine Riesling 1989 (tasted February 1990): pale yellow in hue with a green wash, this riesling showed attractive spicy fragrances on bouquet. Its palate flavours were also quite spicy and forward, making it a pleasing style for present drinking. (15.5 pts) Drink in 1990-91.

Other major riesling forces of high quality in the Clare region today are Petaluma and Tim Knappstein, each with deep reserves of Clare experience—in Petaluma's case since 1977, and in Tim Knappstein's even before that, as he founded his own company in 1976, having previously worked for Stanley Wine Co. when owned by the Knappstein family and afterwards under the Heinz aegis.

Since 1979 Petaluma Rhine Riesling has been sourced from the company's Hanlin Hill vineyard, a poor-looking piece of west-facing hillside 500 metres above sea level 4 kilometres east of Clare, with 20 hectares of riesling, stunted both in appearance and yield. Yet its quality is proven. Famous vintages have included 1980, hardly showing a grey hair ten years on, in early 1990. I noted then a very youthful mid-yellow shade; and though aroma had evolved through lime to a fuller lemon toast fragrance, and palate was becoming lightly honeyed, the wine could safely accept another two to three years in cellar. (18.7 pts) Drink in 1991-93, slowly!

Since 1980, other notable vintages have been 1984, 1985 and 1987. The Petaluma vintage current at time of writing was the 1989. This wine was pale straw-green in shade, with quite intense spicy lime aromas on nose. On palate there was excellent fruit entry and some intensity on mid-palate, but the wine fell away slightly on finish. A very good wine to be drunk now or cellared short-term, two to three years. (16.5 pts) Drink in 1990-93.

Though majority ownership of Tim Knappstein Wines now lies with Wolf Blass International, Tim Knappstein remains very much in day-to-day control. For Tim, rhine riesling is a Clare tradition that should never give way to the inroads of parvenus such as chardonnay; and looking at a line of Tim's top rhine rieslings from the 1980s, which I did in August 1989, there can be no disputing it.

Tim Knappstein Rhine Riesling 1980: this was an appealing medium-yellow in hue with light lemon and honey aromas and similar flavours on a finely balanced palate that will continue to develop well for two to three years yet. (18 pts) Drink in 1991-93.

Tim Knappstein Rhine Riesling 1982: still pale yellow in tone, this wine revealed fragrant citrus and honey aromas in a most elegant bouquet. Its palate showed little development, offering soft but long honey-lemon flavours, and once again excellent balance. This was a veritable Peter Pan of a riesling, which could last another decade. (18.7 pts) Drink in 1994–96.

Tim Knappstein Rhine Riesling 1985: medium-yellow in colour with toast and honey aromas on nose, this one was almost ready to drink, with long toasty flavours nicely accessible to palate. (18 pts) Drink in 1990–92.

Tim Knappstein Rhine Riesling 1988: tasted in October 1989, this wine had an enticing straw-green shade. On a fragrant nose, there were delightful floral aromas, while palate was long and lively, showing intense spicy fruit, a hint of sweetness and a crisp acid finish. (17.5 pts) A riper, more forward style to be drunk in 1991–94.

Tim Knappstein Rhine Riesling 1989: pale yellow-green in hue with quite pungent lime-citrus aromas. Palate flavours were long, citrusy and dry, more steely and less generous than the 1988. (16.5 pts) Though a dry style, this could evolve extremely well for two to three years more. Drink in 1990–92.

Though Tim may not classify 1989 as his best-ever riesling year, the Tim Knappstein Beerenauslese Rhine Riesling 1989 is an undoubted success. When tasted in January 1990, this wine was pale to medium yellow in hue with fine points of gold. Aromas on nose melded apricots and orange peel, but in addition the wine revealed a marvellous freshness and varietal intensity. On palate the flavours were long, concentrated and sweet but the wine retained its wonderful freshness. A simply wonderful botrytised riesling. (19 pts) Drink in 1990–95.

Jane Mitchell is also a vigneron of intense dedication, having made a definite success of rhine riesling over the past decade. In January 1990, I had the good fortune to taste six of the 1980s Mitchell Rhine Rieslings. My notes follow.

1988: pale to medium yellow-green, an outstanding colour, this one offered a lovely lime-citrus nose with just a hint of toast, the first sign of bottle development. Palate was full, ripe and deep, with attractive forward lime-citrus flavours and good balancing acidity. (17.5 pts) Drink in 1991–94.

1987: pale yellow in colour with a reserved nose, revealing light floral–citrus fragrances, this wine showed a slight austerity on palate, drying lime-citrus flavours seeming to lack generosity in the face of firm acidity on finish. But the structure is very good, and the wine should age well. (17.5 pts) Drink in 1992–95.

1986: pale to medium yellow in tone, this wine offered lovely lime-juice and sherbety characters on nose. Palate was ripe with soft, generous, floral–spice flavours suggesting an earlier rather than later maturity. (16.5 pts) Drink in 1990–92.

1985: medium yellow with hints of green still trapped in its colour, this wine revealed very attractive lime-citrus aromas on nose and a deep clean developing palate of good firm structure with lots of fruit and a dry acid finish. (17.5 pts) Drink 1992 onwards.

1984: pale to medium yellow in hue with an agreeable green wash, this one showed slightly developed kerosene aromas on nose. Its palate, however, was still full flavoured with a long citrusy palate and a spicy tangy finish. This was a beautifully balanced rhine in plateau-mode; that is, very pleasantly drinkable and mature but certainly not yet on the downhill path. (18 pts) Drink 1991 onwards.

1982: a bright medium yellow-green in colour, this wine offered a beautifully mature toasty nose. Its palate, however, was the outstanding part, wonderfully balanced and developed with long lime-juice flavours, a most harmonious touch of residual sugar and a long lingering acidity. An elegant wine, mellow and ready to drink. (18.5 pts) Drink in 1990-91.

Virtually every maker in Clare offers rhine riesling, and very little of it is poor. One of the larger makers of riesling in the region is Eaglehawk Estate (formerly Quelltaler, owned since late 1987 by Wolf Blass International). The Eaglehawk Rhine Riesling 1989, tasted October 1989, was a very pale yellow in hue with floral herbaceous aromas on nose. On palate this wine showed long spicy flavours, firm acidity and a dry finish. A seemingly austere riesling that should mature well. (17 pts) Drink 1991 onwards.

Jim Barry Wines is another large regional maker of rhine riesling, now owner of the Florita Vineyard at Watervale, purchased from Lindeman's. The Jim Barry Wines Watervale Rhine Riesling 1989 (tasted December 1989) was pale yellow in hue, showed quite delicate lime characters on nose, with slightly lifted lime-spice flavours on palate, all in good balance either for current consumption or short-term cellaring. (15.5 pts) Drink in 1990-92.

Taylor's, the largest estate in Clare, also makes rhine riesling of good quality.

Vintage 1989 was not without its difficulties in Clare. Intense heat leading up to vintage made conditions uncomfortable, to say the least, and when this heatwave was immediately followed by rain storms and a period of prolonged cool weather, prospects for a favourable vintage were dim. Nevertheless, the riesling harvest was successful, many smaller vignerons making wines of drier style which should cellar very well. Amongst these Skillogalee produced a creditable wine. Tasted in late 1989, Skillogalee Rhine Riesling 1989 was a very youthful pale yellow in hue, its nose showing delicate spice and lime aromas. On palate, long spicy flavours and excellent acid balance were the high points of a wine of great finesse. (17 pts) Drink in 1990-94.

Tim Adams is a former Stanley winemaker, who has now commenced winemaking on his own account at the winery formerly belonging to Rick Robertson. The Tim Adams Rhine Riesling 1989, when tasted in February 1990, held an excellent straw-green colour, while subtle lime-citrus aromas pervaded nose. Palate flavours were full, dry and balanced by good acidity. (16.5 pts) Drink in 1990-94.

Another rhine of note from the Clare vintage of 1989 is that of Dr John Wilson, a modern pioneer of the Polish Hill River region, south-east of Clare. Delicately floral on nose and pale straw in colour, the Wilson Vineyard Rhine Riesling 1989 revealed lime and spice flavours of some intensity and a pleasantly dry finish. (16 pts) Drink in 1990–93. (Tasted January 1990.)

The Polish Hill River region is shared by large and small alike. Not only do Penfold's and Wolf Blass have substantial vineyards there (without wineries), but numbers of smaller vignerons are making wines of great promise. John Wilson has been mentioned, but there is also the Pike Brothers Polish Hill River Estate, makers of good rhine riesling as well as chardonnay, sauvignon blanc and an interesting 'Bordeaux' blend of cabernet sauvignon, merlot and cabernet franc. Pike's Polish Hill River Rhine Riesling 1989 was, in December 1989, pale yellow in hue with spice and lime fragrances on nose, while palate revealed long spicy flavours and balanced acidity. This was a wine quite suitable for current drinking or for short-term cellaring for two to three years. (16 pts)

Other smaller makers of good rhine riesling in the Clare region are Jud's Hill (the vineyard of senior wine judge Brian Barry), Sevenhill, Paulett's, Jeffrey Grosset and Watervale Cellars. Bridgewater Mill, the second label of Petaluma, must also be added; and on the strength of a positively outstanding 1985, chosen in March 1989 by my panel in the Smallmakers Wine Competition of that year as the top Aromatic Dry White, so should Mintaro Cellars.

The Clare and Eden Valleys produce superb rhine riesling with almost boring continuity. Yet these are styles of world quality, deserving not only of proper respect in their birthplace, which they undoubtedly receive, but also of suitable recompense in the market as a whole, which they often do not.

WESTERN AUSTRALIA

A winegrowing area of outstanding potential for the production of quality rhine riesling, as yet only partially realised, is the Mount Barker–Frankland River region of Western Australia. After Eden Valley and Clare, this is most definitely No. 3 in riesling standings in Australia as a whole, and by the end of this century it may well rank equally with the other two. Only a most unjustified neglect by the consumer and a consequent switch to other varieties by the growers will cloud that particular crystal ball.

It is likely, however, that the winegrowers of the Great Southern will persist with rhine riesling, for it is an ancestral and proven variety in a viticultural area less than a generation old, and one should not easily give up one's birthright.

The riesling of Forest Hill is a logical place to start any discussion of this variety, if only because it was with cabernet sauvignon, the first variety planted in the first experimental vineyard in the area, and that vineyard was on the Forest Hill property of the Pearse family, sold in 1989 to a company owned by the late Robert Holmes á Court, which also controls the Margaret River vineyard, Vasse Felix. Future releases of Forest Hill rhine riesling will be as Vasse Felix Forest Hill Riesling.

Though the opportunity to taste the 1989 Forest Hill Riesling had not come my way at the time of writing, the 1988 vintage (tasted in July 1989) was of excellent quality. Bright yellow with hints of green, this wine showed ripe lime-passionfruit aromas on nose. On palate there was intense lime-citrus flavour with the incipient toastiness of slight bottle age. (18 pts) A ripe forward style but beautifully made. Drink in 1991–92.

At the Plantagenet winery which was home to Forest Hill for many years, Plantagenet winemaker John Wade makes not only Plantagenet Rhine Riesling, but also Howard Park Rhine, his right of private practice, so to speak. The two styles are often quite different and certainly were in 1988 vintage, for though both showed good lime-juice aromas, the Plantagenet was riper and more developed on palate in mid-1989 (16.5 pts), in contrast to the Howard Park's leaner and steelier palate (17 pts). Both are excellent rhines, the first to be drunk by 1991, the other with cellaring potential until 1994.

The rhine rieslings of Goundrey and Chatsfield (the latter made under contract at the spanking new Langton Estate winery of Goundrey) have also been a revelation to me in recent journeys to the region. Again 1988 stands out as an annus mirabilis. The Goundrey Windy Hill Rhine Riesling 1988, when tasted in August 1989, held a delightful pale yellow-green hue, while nose and palate, both starting to develop, still showed excellent lime citrus characters. (17.5 pts) Its younger brother, 1989, quite pale in colour, revealed herbaceous aromas with light floral overtones while showing elegant lime-citrus flavours and excellent acidity on palate. A very good rhine for cellaring. (17.5 pts) Drink in 1991–94. (Tasted August 1989.)

By way of contrast to the Goundrey 1988, the Chatsfield Rhine Riesling of the same year (tasted at the same time) was arguably more elegant in its lime-juice aromas and the lighter less-developed fruit on palate and capable of longer life. (18 pts) Drink in 1990–93.

A riesling grower of infinite promise is Castle Rock, whose vineyard is set in spectacular scenery on the northern slopes of the Porongorup Range. Its Rhine Riesling of 1988 vintage was one of the best of the region in that remarkable year, and its successor in 1989 was also very good. When tasted in August 1989, this wine was pale bright yellow in shade, showing attractive floral–lime aromas on nose and long lime–citrus flavours with a crisp acid cut finishing a palate of great promise. (17.5 pts) Drink in 1990–93.

Quality rhines are also made locally at Alkoomi and by the area's largest grower and the state's largest winemaker, Houghton, at its Swan Valley winery.

Arguably (some might say indisputably) the state's most exciting wine area is Margaret River. Not, I am afraid, for rhine riesling. The variety in this region suffers intermittent berry-set problems because of strong sea breezes and, later in the season if the local marri gums are late in flowering, forms what must be a delicious diet for migrating birds. Even if none of these natural disasters affect riesling, the wines produced are generally rather blowsy full-flavoured styles to be drunk up within a couple of years of making. The reason for this is a mystery, though a generally warm climate and a maritime environment may militate against a strongly 'continental' variety such as riesling. In any event it exhibits none of the promise so obviously manifested by the variety in the Mount Barker–Frankland River region.

The remaining grower of notable riesling in Western Australia prefers to blend its own Capel fruit with material purchased from Mount Barker. Capel Vale Western Australian Rhine Riesling 1989, tasted February 1990, held a most attractive pale yellow-green hue, with aromas of passionfruit and spice, while palate showed herbaceous/lime flavours with a clean almost zesty acid finish. (17 pts) Drink in 1991–92.

VICTORIA

Rhine riesling has its place in Victoria also, but one feels it is definitely a second place to that presently more rewarding (both spiritually and financially) variety, chardonnay. Nevertheless rhine riesling of great quality continues to be made in the western and south-western regions of the state (Great Western and Drumborg), in newer higher central areas such as Macedon, and in the alpine regions where in vineyards such as Delatite the end of vintage is sometimes decreed by the seasons rather than the winemaker.

It is appropriate I suppose to begin this survey of Victorian riesling in one of its older-established wine regions, Great Western. There Seppelt has employed not only what might be termed ancestral skill but also modern technique to make high-quality rhine riesling from its local vineyards and those of Drumborg, much closer to Great Western in terms of distance than climate. Basically Great Western is warmer and drier, more 'continental' in the meteorological sense than Drumborg, which is much more variable at critical times of the year such as flowering, when rain, cold and spring gales are often the norm rather than the exception. Yet Drumborg is never a stereotype. Years such as 1989, a little ordinary for rhine riesling at Great Western, saw the variety triumph at Drumborg, producing intense lime-citrus aromas and flavours more Germanic than Australian. Seppelt Drumborg Rhine Riesling 1989, tasted in February 1990, was pale yellow-green in hue, offering persistent lime-citrus aromas. Palate flavours, also lime-citrus in character, are lively and refreshingly zesty on finish. This was a riesling of excellent balance which could be drunk young but had a decade of cellaring potential. (18.5 pts) Drink in 1990 and on during the 1990s.

The Seppelt Drumborg Rhine Riesling 1988 is also a very good wine. Pale yellow in shade, with plenty of lime and the merest touch of lemon on nose, this one was very long on palate, showing riper slightly sweeter lime-juice flavours, spatlese in style but with sufficient acidity to keep the wine in good trim for at least five years. (18 pts) Drink in 1990–96.

Though Drumborg as a riesling vineyard is fickle and capricious, Great Western usually offers more certainty but sometimes less excitement in its riesling wines. The Seppelt Great Western Vineyards Rhine Riesling 1988 was a medium yellow-green in hue with ripe aromas already showing 'kerosene' development. Palate, however, did show pleasant lime-juice character and well-balanced acidity. (17 pts) Drink in 1990–92.

Best's, Donovan, Montara and Mount Langi Ghiran also make riesling of good quality at Great Western. Near Drumborg, the variety is also grown successfully at Crawford River.

East of Great Western is the Avoca Moonambel area (the Victorian Pyrenees), where Taltarni makes the only regional riesling. The Taltarni Rhine Riesling 1989, tasted March 1990, was pale yellow with a green wash, while light floral aromas with hints of lime made an attractive nose. Its palate was light and elegant with a fresh acidity on finish, but there was also a slight toastiness on mid-palate, which foreshadowed good bottle development by 1992. (16 pts) Drink in 1991–92.

Rhine riesling continues its affinity with the Victorian high country by producing eminently satisfactory wines in the Macedon district, though in comparatively small quantity. Riesling growers here are Knight Granite Hills and Rochford.

The Knight Granite Hills Rhine Riesling 1988, tasted in March 1989, was a pale straw green in shade, with lime–floral–spice aromas showing beautifully in a ripe nose. On palate the wine was long-flavoured with lime spice characteristics in the ascendant. Crisp acidity finished off the wine. (18 pts) Drink in 1990–93.

Though Knight is an established name in the area, Rochford is quite a newcomer, making its first vintage in 1988. The Rochford Rhine Riesling 1989 (a year that tested all varieties in the Macedon region to the limit) was a delicate green-yellow in hue, offering elegant lime-citrus fragrances on nose and long lime-spice flavours on palate, beautifully 'cut' by fresh acidity. (17.5 pts) Tasted as a tank sample in February 1990; if successfully transferred into bottle worth 18.5 pts. Drink in 1991–94.

The other grower of rhine riesling in this region whose wine I have not yet tasted is Fearn Hyll.

North of the Macedon massif, the Bendigo area also grows rhine riesling on a very small scale in an area rather more suited to chardonnay and especially to reds.

Riesling country begins again in the Goulburn Valley and in the hills above. In the valley itself, substantial wineries such as Chateau Tahbilk and Mitchelton make wines of quite diverse style.

I cannot confess that I have been greatly excited by Chateau Tahbilk Rhine Riesling over the years. It is usually a soft fuller forward style, very drinkable within that style but lacking the backbone of rieslings of cooler areas. Perhaps its comparatively warm location is its problem.

Realising this, Mitchelton, a few kilometres away across the Goulburn River, has occasionally blended riesling from other areas with its estate-grown fruit, while in more suitable years releasing a Rhine Riesling, totally estate-grown. The second label of Mitchelton is Thomas Mitchell, where also is to be found a Rhine Riesling. Both wines are usually of good quality, the 1989s being no exception.

Mitchelton Rhine Riesling 1989:   pale yellow with points of green, lifted estery lime aromas with high-toned lime–tropical fruit flavours. Good acidity finishes quite a full palate. (16 pts) Drink in 1990–91.

Thomas Mitchell Rhine Riesling 1989:   pale yellow with a green wash with delicate lime–spice aromas, light clean lime flavours and good acidity on finish. A very good rhine slightly lacking intensity. (16.5 pts) Drink in 1990–92. (Tasted January 1990.)

About 20 kilometres to the east of Mitchelton, high in the Strathbogie Ranges lies the Mount Helen Vineyard of Tisdall, from where on the proverbially clear day the witch's hat tower of Mitchelton stands out like some medieval turret. Exposed primarily to the hot and often windy north and west, the Mount Helen Vineyard (about 50 hectares in extent, including 6 hectares of rhine riesling) is necessarily irrigated. The Mount Helen Rhine Riesling 1989, tasted in January 1990, was pale yellow in colour with attractive floral lime aromas. On palate the wine revealed a pleasing balance of lime and spice flavour and crisp acidity with a touch of residual sugar adding a further fullness. (16 pts) To be drunk from 1990 to 1993.

From Mount Helen eastwards the Goulburn River Valley narrows and climbs into the Victorian Alps, where the Delatite vineyard nestles virtually in the shadow of Mount Buller. The Delatite rhine riesling style is usually highly, almost ethereally, aromatic in better years, but alpine viticulture can stretch nature to its extremes with varieties like rhine riesling, and occasionally full ripening cannot be achieved. Fortunately this was not the case in 1989. The Delatite Rhine Riesling of that year, tasted in February 1990, was pale yellow in hue, showing lovely floral lime fragrances. On palate the delicate but persistent lime–spice flavours were cut by a cleansing acidity. A most refreshing white. (17 pts) Drink in 1990–93.

The very antithesis of the Delatite climatic environment are the flat sunscorched plains of the North-East where temperatures often exceed 40°C in January and February. Yet Brown Brothers have grown rhine riesling at Milawa for many years, always treading the path of technical innovation and seeking the freshest style possible in any given vintage. John Charles Brown indeed can be credited with the recognition and exploitation of *Botrytis cinerea* in Australian rhine riesling, discovering the fungus first in 1934, successfully making a sweet botrytis-influenced riesling in 1962 and producing such a wine as regularly as conditions permitted from 1970 onwards. For several years the Browns purchased the Delatite crop and have been largely responsible for the explosive expansion of higher-altitude vineyards in the King Valley, including their own spectacular Whitlands estate, where riesling and many other varieties suited to cool areas are succeeding admirably.

Brown Brothers King Valley Rhine Riesling 1989: pale yellow in hue with complex floral and tropical aromas, lime fruit flavours of fair length, crisp acid on finish. (16 pts) Drink in 1990–92.

Brown Brothers Noble Riesling 1983: burnished gold with a tawny rim, aromas of orange peel and warm raisins on nose, palate showed older bottle-aged characters. In style quite separate from more modern botrytised rieslings. Some lusciousness but more age would be better, fresher. (17 pts) Drink in 1990–92. (Both wines tasted early 1990.)

North of Milawa is the Rutherglen–Wahgunyah region famous for its tokays and muscats, sumptuous fortifieds not forming part of this book but overshadowing the rieslings of the area, which are nonetheless usually of good commercial quality.

Names to look for are All Saints, Buller, Campbell, Chambers, Jolimont and Pfeiffer.

The Sunraysia region of Victoria centred upon Mildura also makes rhine rieslings of good commercial quality. The Mildara Church Hill Rhine Riesling is a typical, quite keenly priced example. Lindeman's vast Karadoc winery also produces a fine Premier Selection Rhine Riesling usually blended from Lindeman's premium fruit from local and other sources. Again value for money is always exceptional.

Of the remaining Victorian areas rhine riesling is most strongly represented in the Yarra Valley, but even here its area is outstripped by chardonnay— wisely so, for in the Yarra's cooler years rhine riesling may remain quite herbaceous on nose, while in other years developing oily 'kerosene' flavours which detract from the mid-palate of the wine.

When these characters are avoided, most agreeable rhines can be made. Alex White at Lillydale Vineyards consistently produces a fine varietal rhine. In February 1990, I tasted Lillydale Vineyards Rhine Riesling 1988.

This was pale to medium yellow-green in colour with ripe floral citrus aromas on nose. Its palate was just starting to develop light honey and toast flavours, though there was sufficient acidity to see good bottle-aging for two to three years more. (16.5 pts) Drink in 1990–93.

Diamond Valley and Seville Estate are other Yarra growers whose rhines are of good quality, Seville occasionally making a botrytised sweet riesling of excellence, 1980 remaining in my mind as a wine of sheer magnificence.

The Mornington Peninsula also offers promise as a vineyard site for rhine riesling, though like the Yarra Valley, much more interest is being shown in more fashionable varieties. However, Elgee Park, one of the older-established wineries in a very small and as-yet young area, produced an excellent 1988 rhine. The variety is also grown by Balnarring and Karina vineyards.

TASMANIA

In Tasmania, location and protection from hostile elements are as critical for riesling as they are for that other later ripener, cabernet sauvignon.

The two majors in the Tasmanian riesling league are Pipers Brook, whose delightful label alone would put most tasters in complete sympathy with its contents, and Moorilla, itself no slouch in the label department.

1989 was a deceptive Tasmanian vintage, promising much until three weeks before vintage, when the heavens opened. Early varieties such as pinot noir and chardonnay escaped the worst, but the riesling harvest had not been completed and as a result some of the fruit left out suffered botrytis infection. When tasted in March 1990 the Pipers Brook Rhine Riesling 1989 was the palest of greens in hue, showing on nose rather herbaceous aromas without the variety's more typical lime-citrus fragrances. On palate the flavours did exhibit some lime-juice characteristics with zesty acidity on finish. (16 pts) Certainly not a classical rhine in the Eden Valley style (though this could not be expected), but extremely interesting nevertheless.

Moorilla, a pioneer of Tasmanian riesling, is located at Berriedale in the Derwent Valley, a few kilometres north-west of Hobart. At this more southerly latitude, the climate is cooler than Pipers Brook, a disadvantage outweighed by the fact that it is much drier than Pipers Brook, so dry in fact that supplementary irrigation is necessary in most years, as it was in 1989 when the infuriating rains that plagued southern Victoria and northern Tasmania mercifully bypassed most of the south of the island state. The Moorilla Rhine Riesling 1989, tasted March 1990, was pale yellow in the glass with attractive tints of green. Its nose was highlighted by intense floral lime aromas, a delightfully fragrant bouquet, while palate offered attractive flavours of lime and spice, amplified by a touch of residual sugar. (17.5 pts) A very successful riesling, its only negative point being that it was a touch short on finish. Drink in 1990–93.

Rhine riesling is also grown at St Matthias, Meadowbank, the Stoney Vineyard and Elsewhere, a quaintly named vineyard in the Huon Valley south of Hobart.

QUEENSLAND

The variety is grown in the Stanthorpe region of Queensland in small quantity. Even less is known of the quality.

NEW SOUTH WALES

In the Hunter Valley the variety is also grown but without much acclaim. Though the wines show little varietal intensity when young, they do occasionally age with some grace, as witness some of the older Rhine Rieslings of Mount Pleasant. Also at Pokolbin, Drayton's grow and market a rhine riesling. In the Upper Hunter, Rosemount usually blend the variety with riesling from other regions.

The major winemaker of the MIA, McWilliam's, is responsible for surprisingly good rhine riesling, considering the warmth of the region, in style much like the better wines of the Riverland and North-West regions of Victoria. Look for Inheritance (750 ml bottle). Lillypilly Estate also makes a very good botrytised sweet riesling.

AUSTRALIAN CAPITAL TERRITORY

Canberra is the last stop on the riesling road. It is an area of some promise for the variety, if the wines of Doonkuna Estate and Lark Hill are a reliable guide; and there is no reason why they should not be, as both produced very good 1988 rieslings (tasted March 1989).

Doonkuna Rhine Riesling 1988: delicately pale yellow in hue, showing attractive floral aromas on nose, this wine offered elegant lime-juice flavours on palate, cut by a crisp acidity that made the wine very refreshing. (16.5 pts) Drink in 1990–92.

Lark Hill Rhine Riesling 1988: pale straw in colour, this riesling revealed delightful lime-juice fragrances and a slight herbaceous aroma. On palate the same lime-juice character reappeared as a most appealing flavour, finishing clean and crisp in the mouth. (16 pts) Drink in 1990–92.

Rhine riesling is deserving of the closest attention in Australia, not only for its value vis-à-vis chardonnay, but also for its unique style. Dry with the merest suspicion of residual sweetness, our riesling styles often show superb fruit that make the wine so different from the dry botrytised often-oversulphured wines of Alsace and worlds apart from the seeringly acid 'trocken' rieslings of Germany.

Traminer

'Every dog has its day', so runs the old proverb. For traminer, or gewürztraminer to give its full name, it has in all probability gone. But let us not be too negative for, despite its enforced association with 'riesling' in seemingly myriads of commercial traminer-rieslings, it does possess on its own account quite positive qualities, which will always assure a well-made traminer of a following, however small. Indeed for any newcomer to wine, traminer is virtually always instantly attractive, if only because of its recognisably musky aroma and spicy palate. Yet that attraction may not always last very long, and I recall how once a new wine-judge, drawn by the seductive muskiness of one of the wine-show entries, took his glass to a senior judge, remarking how fine a wine it was. The response was quite succinct, if not a little condescending. 'That is traminer. Don't worry, my boy! You will soon get over it.'

That has been the problem with Australian traminer. Too many people have got over it.

By repute this highly aromatic variety originated in the former Austrian province, the South Tyrol, where there was a village called Tramin. The area is now part of the Alto Adige region of northern Italy where the variety is still grown, having, during the course of its climb to international fame, prefixed the German word *gewürz* (spicy). That German connection has, in the course of 500 years or so, spread the vine to other countries of Central Europe, formerly parts of the Hapsburg Empire, to Germany itself and to that oft-contested province of France, Alsace. From there it has ventured to the countries of the New Wine World, including Australia, where as at mid-year 1988 it occupied a respectable 650 hectares though, as might be expected, without much enthusiasm (only 18 hectares are still to come into bearing; another 29 hectares are to be grubbed out).

As a grape variety, it is quite precocious, being the first to ripen. Its leaves are medium-sized and downy on the lower surface, being not unlike those of pinot noir in shape, while its bunches, borne in no great profusion, are small and cone-shaped. What does distinguish it is the pinkness of its berries when ripe.

But what of its wines? Undoubtedly it prefers cooler locales or cooler vintages, though paradoxically, when carefully made can perform very well in warmer regions such as the MIA.

South Australia is responsible for more than half the nation's traminer, with substantial plantings in the Coonawarra–Padthaway area (117 ha) and the Barossa (85 ha) as at mid-year 1987. The variety flourishes in the Eden Valley, its Flaxman's Valley vineyard there producing Flaxman's Traminer, a worthy wine highly regarded on the wine-show circuit over many years. Tasted in February 1989, the Orlando Flaxman's Traminer 1988 was pale yellow in hue, showing distinctly musky spicy aromas in a powerful nose. Palate was clean with quite long spice and tropical fruit flavours and a soft finish. (17 pts) Drink in 1990-91.

The Flaxman's Traminer 1989 is also a worthy member of the line. When tasted in May 1990, it held a youthful pale yellow hue with hints of green and showed intense lychee and lime aromas on nose. Palate too offered those same lychee characters adding a dash of spice and excellent balancing acidity which will see the wine age well, if this is required. (18 pts) Drink in 1991-93.

The Flaxman's Traminer style is one of the more elegant in Australia, an elegance most suitable for the more delicate styles of Asian food.

Another traminer of elegance is made by Delatite in central Victoria. Dead Man's Hill Gewurztraminer 1989, tasted February 1990, was youthful in colour, offering a grassy-spicy nose and dry spicy flavours on a well-balanced palate. (16 pts) Drink in 1990-91.

Brown Brothers also produce a similar style from their King Valley fruit, as does the Heathcote Winery south-east of Bendigo.

One of traminer's cooler Australian climes is Tasmania, where Andrew Pirie at Pipers Brook makes another very elegant style. The 1989 Pipers Brook Traminer was pale green in hue, with spicy-lychee aromas and hints of grass. Palate was bone-dry showing quite long spicy flavours and good acidity. Suitable for simple seafood entrees. (16 pts) Drink in 1990-92. (Tasted February 1990.)

Like sauvignon blanc, traminer needs extreme care in making. Otherwise it may 'go over the top', exuding an overly aromatic 'hair-oil' nose and a palate that recalls stewed lychees, though certainly the fuller style when carefully made is a valid expression of its varietal identity; and like an auslese rhine riesling it is suitable as an aperitif or with bigger richer Asian foods.

Robert Fiumara at Lillypilly Estate at Leeton in the MIA makes a bigger yet clean style, avoiding the unpleasant oily characters on nose and palate that ill-made traminer all too freely offers. Lillypilly Traminer 1988 is a typical case in point. Tasted in October 1989, the wine was pale to medium yellow in tone, offering on nose quite full spice and rose-petal aromas. In flavour, spice and lychee were dominant, while a touch of residual sugar filled out middle palate very well. (17 pts) Drink in 1990-91.

Another maker of a pleasant full style is Tolley's Pedare at Hope Valley north-east of Adelaide.

Other aromatic varieties

There are many other aromatic varieties planted in microscopic numbers throughout Australia. Some such as sylvaner may already have proved that they are unsuitable to most Australian vineyard regions. Others such as müller-thurgau and some of the more modern German hybrids exist in small quantities in cool-area vineyards and nurseries, awaiting the day when Australian consumers return in overwhelming numbers to aromatics. They may have to wait a very long time.

The most typical of all aromatics are the variants of muscat grown in most of our warmer areas, wines like white frontignac. There is little to be said of such wines except that, if cleanly made and lacking 'oiliness' on nose and palate, they should be enjoyed while they are in their first flush of youth, for they age with little grace.

THE REDS

LIGHT AND MEDIUM-BODIED, SOFT FINISH

PINOT NOIR

What can one say about pinot noir? Fickle, capricious, irresponsible are all suitable epithets if one was minded to attribute human frailties to mere vines. If pinot noir were a mere vine we could perhaps stop there. However, as it is one of the great varieties of Burgundy, whose red wines are hallowed throughout the wine-drinking world, let us just call it 'variable'.

The vine scientists and viticulturists have shown that though pinot noir is very old it is not yet civilised enough to conform to their accepted rules of plant genetic behaviour, in that it undergoes mutations and produces genetic characteristics that are unstable. Thus it has been found with white grapes and grey grapes as well as the more familiar black. Its juice also has occasionally been seen to be coloured. Its 'cousin' (or is it its 'grandfather'?), pinot gris, sometimes upon propagation produces white and black descendants. Its other relative, meunier, often changes the downy appearance of its foliage so as to become almost indistinguishable from pinot noir.

Anthony Hanson in his book *Burgundy* (Faber & Faber, 1982) mentions the existence of more than a thousand different clones of pinot in that region. The late Allan Antcliff (*Some Grape Varieties for Australia*, CSIRO, 1976) notes 'about a dozen different recognized clones' in Australia at that time. There have been more since, for these days throughout the world clones are being constantly evaluated. While clonal selection has produced pinot noir with loose bunches, bred to be free of disease on Swiss hillsides as well as pinot, designed to grow conveniently upright for ease of cultivation in Burgundian vinerows, its goals these days are not only crops of reasonable size with vines free of viral infection in whatever locale they are planted but also the production of fruit of the best quality that can be achieved in any given vineyard area. With this in mind the end products of such selection are now being vinified and tasted in both Burgundy and Australia.

Physiologically the vine is not vigorous, taking rather more years than normal to grow to a mature size. Its leaves are small to medium, usually entire and rarely lobed. Its bunches are, as its name suggests, small with a shape not unlike a pine cone, and slightly oval berries densely packed.

In France there are 18 000 hectares planted to pinot noir, equally distributed between Burgundy and Champagne, not to mention other outposts of the vine such as Alsace, Sancerre, Savoie and the Jura, all northerly or comparatively high in altitude, sharing predominantly cool ripening conditions. Elsewhere in Europe, the vine is found in similar climes, in Germany as Spätburgunder, in Northern Italy as pinot nero, and in Switzerland as klevner. It is very much in vogue also in Oregon, the cooler areas of California and New Zealand, as winemakers go in search of the perfect pinot much as medieval heroes sought the Holy Grail. As a rule it ripens early in season; only in Germany does it seem at all prone to differ—its name *Spätburgunder* (late burgundy) indicating a later development.

Its area in Australia as at 30 June 1988 was 785 hectares (525 ha bearing; 260 ha non-bearing). Its yield was 3967 tonnes, an average, paltry as it seems, of 7.5 tonnes per hectare. The variety was seemingly introduced to Australia quite early, even before the Busby Collection, probably being grown at Ryde by the explorer Gregory Blaxland. Certainly it was reintroduced with that collection in 1832. It was cultivated at Geelong by Swiss and German growers in the mid-nineteenth century, at Great Western slightly later, and more or less continuously though on a minor scale since the inception of winegrowing in the Hunter Valley. Elsewhere in Australia its history is quite obscure, though John Reynell found that it did not succeed at Reynella. It seems but rarely to have been used as a straight varietal red wine, except very occasionally in the Hunter Valley, winemakers there preferring to blend it with greater amounts of shiraz to make a pleasant soft 'burgundy' style red.

Since 1973, however, Tyrrell's have produced a Hunter Valley Pinot Noir each year, following conventional crushing and fermenting techniques until 1978 when the Burgundian practice of partial carbonic fermentation was adopted for the first time. This procedure has been continued ever since, in some years, such as 1980, capturing true Burgundian style.

The Rothbury Estate, that other pinot experimenter of the Hunter Valley, has made trial batches of pinot noir from 1976 onwards, itself opting for the partial carbonic system in 1982. It too has had its successes, notably 1986.

Since the mid-1970s as the propagation of the variety spread throughout Australia, it has become increasingly popular in both newer and older wine areas and in both cool climes and warm. In South Australia half the area of pinot noir in bearing (249 hectares) as at 30 June 1988 was in the Padthaway and Coonawarra districts (129 hectares), while in the Barossa Valley there were 45 hectares, and in the Central District (Adelaide, McLaren Vale and the Adelaide Hills) 35 hectares, the total production for the whole state for that year being 1953 tonnes, a little over half of 1 per cent of the state's total grape crush.

Its area in New South Wales as at the same date stood at 99 hectares in bearing, its production being 746 tonnes (0.44 per cent of the state's total production). Its traditional home, the Hunter Valley, with 308 tonnes, supplied the major share, while the Murrumbidgee Irrigation Area yielded 211 tonnes. Elsewhere in New South Wales a further 228 tonnes were produced in places as far apart as Tumbarumba and Port Macquarie—such is the interest in this variety.

In Victoria, interest in the variety is growing even more rapidly than in New South Wales if areas not yet in bearing are taken into account. Though Victoria trailed New South Wales by a few bearing hectares, the southern state had nearly twice as many hectares of pinot awaiting their first crop. The Yarra Valley, Geelong, Mornington and the Mount Macedon regions all show tremendous pinot promise, though none of these areas are as yet consistently good enough in quality for ultimate honours to be bestowed.

Attention is also focused on the variety in Western Australia, particularly in Margaret River and the Great Southern region. Though production is extremely small (only 18 hectares planted and 88 tonnes produced as at 30 June 1987), the Moss Wood Vineyard and to a lesser extent the Leeuwin Estate have been successful enough in their pinot reds, though as in all other Australian areas, consistency is lacking.

Pinot noir may become the specialised red variety of Tasmania, though whether for red or for sparkling-wine 'base' it is as yet difficult to say. Perhaps even for both. As at 30 June 1987 there were 24 planted hectares, making it the most popular wine variety with chardonnay and cabernet sauvignon in that state.

Pinot noir as 'base wine'

Pinor noir is a dual-purpose variety in all states. In the Hunter Valley, Tyrrell's pick pinot noir as sparkling-wine base every year. If the wine is slightly pink in colour, then so be it; it is often on the top rung of Australian sparkling wines. Rosemount too use Hunter pinot noir for this purpose, producing a style that has readily gained public acceptance. In the new winegrowing areas of Tooma and Tumbarumba, high in the Snowy Mountains, pinot noir is also used as 'base' wine.

It is south of the Murray River, indeed south of the Great Dividing Range, in those cooler parts of Victoria, that pinot is much sought after for its contribution to 'base' wine. Thus near Ballarat, Yellowglen uses all its 10 hectares of pinot as 'base' wine for its Cuvée Victoria. The Yarra and Mount Macedon have both shown extreme promise as areas of great quality for this purpose. Indeed Domaine Chandon Australia Pty Ltd after exhaustive trials has chosen the Coldstream area of the Yarra Valley as its chief vineyard and headquarters, though it is also extremely interested in Tasmania. At Great Western, the home of Australian sparkling wine tradition, Seppelt also vinifies the whole of its local pinot noir as 'base' wine, supplementing it as necessary with fruit from Padthaway in South Australia and other areas.

Though Coonawarra is justifiably famous as a red wine area, and Padthaway bids fair to emulate the Coonawarra reputation in white wine, pinot noir from each district is made as 'base' wine. In Coonawarra Wynn's have the lion's share of pinot, making about 25 per cent of it as red and the rest as 'base'. Lindeman's, on the other hand, process very little as 'base' (only about 5000 litres in 1988), preferring instead to continue to master the intricacies of pinot as a red variety. At Padthaway Hardy's also utilise about half their pinot noir in their Classic Cuvée sparkling range.

The most exciting wine area that has adopted pinot noir as an integral part of its raison d'être is undoubtedly the Piccadilly Valley, pressed into a fold of the Mount Lofty Ranges about 20 kilometres south-east of Adelaide and planned as a region for quality sparkling and table wines by Brian Croser as long ago as 1969. Selected for its extremely cool and slow ripening conditions to maximise flavour complexity, the site has brought with it high rainfall and humidity, two factors that Australian winemaking tradition holds inimical to fine wine. Nonetheless there are now 28 hectares of pinot noir marching in orderly rows up and down the cool slopes of this 500-metre-high valley, which, with its scattered stands of pine, could easily be mistaken for a French *climat* of impeccable reputation. Croser's dream for the region is beginning to be realised by the exciting quality of the 1985 and 1986 'Croser' sparkling wines, which, though predominantly chardonnay in content, augur well for the success of future wines which will see the pinot noir content increase to 50 per cent.

As for technique, pinot noir 'base' is treated very similarly to any white wine. The fruit is crushed and drained in any of the customary crusher-destemmers; the free-run juice is chilled down to 5–8°C and then settled over some weeks after the addition of pectolytic enzymes. Freed of its lees, the juice is then raised slightly in temperature, a yeast culture is added and the ensuing fermentation is completed in about two weeks. After the 'base' is racked, it is then ready for taste assessment.

So, what do Australian winemakers seek as the quintessential characteristics of pinot noir in 'base' wine? Brian Croser himself seeks 'apples', preferring to avoid 'strawberry' aromas on the nose. Warren Randall, architect of the exciting Seppelt styles of méthode champenoise, strives for perfumed fruit, permitting a suspicion of 'strawberry'. On palate, Croser feels that pinot base should be austere, whereas Randall allows a little 'Marmite' character. Both agree that pinot should add length and firmness to a sparkling wine palate.

The future is indeed bright for Australian méthode champenoise wines, of which pinot noir in greater or lesser proportion should always be an integral part. In the comparatively short time since small quantities of pinot noir have been available for such winemaking purposes—and no-one will deny that the quantities are still far too small—the quality of Australian sparkling wine has soared, but the challenge yet remaining to be answered is that of serious red.

Pinot noir as red wine

There is little doubt that the most successful Australian pinot noir styles, made so far as serious 'dry red', have been achieved by means of the semi-carbonic maceration method, widely practised in Burgundy, as adapted to Australian winemaking usages and law.

Alternative techniques are true carbonic maceration, seemingly quite uneconomic unless the supply of pinot is plentiful (an unlikely situation) and cheap (even more unlikely), given that Australians seem unwilling to pay more than mid-market prices for soft fruity carbonic styles that are meant to be drunk within a year of vintage; and the traditional method of dry red crushing, which often produces light red wines of unbalanced tannic structure, harsh and without any of that archetypal softness on palate that lovers of the wines of the Côte d'Or expect in the variety.

When employing the semi-carbonic technique the winemaker must first make critical decisions. How much whole fruit should be included? What quantity of stalks (if any) should remain in the must? Too much whole fruit may result in a wine that is overly soft and lacking in staying power. Too many stalks may mean a green and hard wine.

Having decided, the winemaker crushes the remaining fruit, adding the whole fruit when fermentation is under way. The alternative here is of course to ferment each proportion separately, combining the musts later for pressing, the winemaker hoping that the colour extraction is satisfactory and again that the separately treated carbonic material does not dominate the final blend by excessive early-drinking character.

Some sulphur dioxide is usually added at this stage (about 20 ppm) but not enough to hinder malolactic fermentation, whether such is to be allowed to occur naturally or to be induced by the addition of an MLF culture. At this time also the pH (acid level) of the must may need to be adjusted by tartaric acid, and a yeast starter is added to ensure a rapid start to fermentation. The temperature of the must is also important. Lower temperatures (15–25°C) produce a fruitier one-dimensional wine; higher (25–32°C), a wine with more complexity, tannin and colour but sometimes less fruit character.

During fermentation, the must may be (a) pumped over the cap of skins using an ultracooler if necessary to reduce temperature, (b) headed down by using traditional header boards, or (c) plunged manually at least twice a day or even foot-trodden (*pigeage*), if the maker is wedded to true Burgundian methods. Such techniques aid colour extraction and help to remove 'hot spots' (areas of ferment hotter than others).

Before the completion of fermentation, the wine may be run off into new wood as a further measure of complexity.

Thus the wine completes its primary fermentation and is pressed. All but the heaviest pressings are returned to give more 'body' to what is usually a light-bodied wine. After malolactic fermentation the sulphur content is checked, being adjusted if necessary to no more than 50 ppm. Then it is time for maturation in new or one-year-old small oak, mostly of 225 litre capacity, though occasionally larger barrels are used. Popular French oaks used nowadays by our winemakers are Nevers, Tronçais, Allier and Vosges. Even the cheaper American oak is put into service. Only in Limousin oak does pinot noir seem ill at ease, being overwhelmed by its overt tarry–spicy flavours. Length of such maturation should also be carefully watched, as light-bodied pinot (like chardonnay) can easily be overwooded. Thus Australian pinot rarely spends more than a year in wood and often very much less, sometimes little more than three or four months, if the wine is light.

After an appropriate number of rackings, depending on its time in wood, the wine is fined usually by the addition of egg-white, sometimes pad- or membrane-filtered (though often not), and bottled. Thus our pinot noirs may find their way on to the market even in their year of vintage, though the methods of vinification differ little from those used in Burgundy except in the absolute exclusion of sugar from any part of the process.

Whether these pinots merit much further consideration depends very much on whether the maker has overcome the problems outlined above. Is the colour satisfactory? Is the bouquet complex and interesting? Does the palate have enough weight or is it little more than rosé? What is the palate structure? Are the flavours recognisably pinot noir?

THE COLOUR OF PINOT NOIR

It is of course a truism to say that pinot noir is light in colour. Its colour range in Australia varies from an anaemic pink to a serious ruby red, rarely more intense. This was, in the early years of our pinot experience, considered a gross defect, but time cures most things, including winemaking attitudes in respect of pinot colour. These days a spectrum from vibrant cherry to ruby red is considered quite acceptable and even respectable. We need not worry too much about this as colour variation seems endemic in pinot and occurs just as frequently in Burgundy. The reason appears to be that pinot noir is deficient in phenolic compounds—anthocyans and tannins, both important to the colour and flavour components of wine. One of our leading oenologists, Dr Tony Jordan, puts it this way: 'Compared to other classic red varieties, pinot noir on average appears to have less phenolic weight, less flavour and less complexity of flavour. Thus, what would be a relatively small change in colour and tannin or flavour level in another variety such as cabernet, due to, for instance a difference in climate or change in viticultural practice, may appear as a dramatic change in pinot noir because of its lower overall phenolic and flavour level.' (*Proceedings of the Australian Society of Viticulture and Oenology*, November 1987.) He further states that satisfactory colour can be obtained by correct viticultural practice, such as crop level, leaf/fruit ratios, canopy management and sunlight exposure. Though to scientists this unpredictability of colour is a matter for viticulture, it is important that the retail purchaser of pinot noir be aware of such colour variations, so that the variety is not regarded as an expensive, current-drinking rosé style (unless that was the winemaker's intention). What the winemaker should not attempt is the amelioration of colour by the use (quite legal, unfortunately) of the 80% varietal rule, which in the case of a pallid pinot would allow the addition of 20% of another bigger-coloured variety—for after all, colour is only one component of the total enjoyment of pinot. More important are the aromas of young wines and the bouquets of older ones, those complex factors simply summed up as 'nose'.

THE 'NOSE' OF PINOT NOIR

What an imposing and sometimes startling array of aromatising adjectives pinot noir has inspired! These evocative epithets usually include fruit fragrances such as 'cherry', 'strawberry' and 'plums', vegetative smells such as 'sappiness', and kitchen odours such as 'stewed rhubarb', 'cooked beetroot', or 'macerated fruit'. Most unfashionably, 'tobacco' is sometimes noticed, as are the outdoor scents of 'undergrowth', 'bracken' and 'compost', not to mention those great companions of noble Burgundy, 'truffles' and 'game'. The Burgundians, fundamentalists that they are, even use *merde*.

The aromas, however, depend on the age of the wine in the bottle, its area of production and indeed the techniques used in its making. In this respect, our benchmark must be the Côte d'Or, for what other starting point can there be! Of course, to a Burgundian, this too begs the question, for the nose of pinot noir will vary according to the *climat*. Gaston Roupnel, a Dijonnais academic and author of much purple prose on Burgundy half a century ago, once described le Chambertin as having the aroma of reseda (mignonette) and le Musigny as being redolent of 'roses and violets beneath a morning dew'. While I do not command such expertise either in purple prose or aromatic assessment, in young Burgundy I often do sniff 'strawberries' (an aroma typical of wines made by the semi-carbonic maceration technique). It is a nose I prefer, and I carry that aromatic heart on my sleeve when assessing our own young pinot noir; and if the 'strawberries' have the added dimension of some 'sappiness' and the 'vanilla' of some excellent wood, the resultant combination makes for a fascinating nose. True, there are other fruit aromas: 'cherry', quite light but elegant, and 'plum', a deeper nose more cognate with merlot. 'Stewed fruit', 'rhubarb' and 'beetroot' I usually associate with overripeness and often a heavy palate.

With bottle age the simple strawberry aromas may change to 'undergrowth', 'compost', 'tobacco', 'game' and 'truffles' (an expensive nose, indeed), but never quite in my nose to basic human byproducts.

Again, the nose of pinot is sometimes different in that it is described as 'spirity', a lifted character that I do not always associate with the typical volatility of a faulty wine. True, pinot noir when badly made can be wildly volatile, but that 'spiritiness' is just another fascinating feature of the natural aromaticity of pinot.

Thus the nose of good pinot will always tend to lightness, rarely matching the opulence of richer shiraz or cabernet sauvignon, but the ideal pinot noir should be just as multifaceted and complex as any other red variety.

THE PALATE OF PINOT NOIR

It seems to be generally agreed what the palate structure of pinot noir should be. Soft entry, a soft and moderately full middle palate and a soft but persistent finish. 'Velvety' is a term most appropriate for some Burgundian pinot noirs. Softly, softly. The palate should possess enough body to be a serious red, with soft tannins and sufficient acidity not only to keep the wine alive in the mouth but also to ensure improvement in bottle over the medium term (three to four years). There should certainly be no jarring factors such as excessive tannic bitterness on the finish of the wine. Such are the conventional specifications.

But what are the flavours and how are these flavour components created? When discussing colour I mentioned the phenolic inferiority of pinot noir compared to other varieties. Such an 'inferiority' also impinges on flavour and complexity of flavour. Many have pointed out that pinot as a grape variety is a poor traveller. Some point to warmer climates as a reason for its phenolic deficiency, and there seems little doubt that pinot likes to keep its 'cool'. Even in warm areas such as the Hunter Valley, pinot noir does best in cooler years. I particularly recall a Tyrrell 1980, tasted in 1988, having a soft full palate structure with 'gamey' overtones almost like a Côte de Beaune wine of a ripe year. 1980 was a mild, slightly slow vintage by Hunter standards, which had obviously allowed pinot noir to develop greater intensity and complexity of palate flavours. So pinot noir should be permitted to ripen fully but slowly, if climatic conditions are favourable.

Though little research has been carried out, another reason for pinot flavour may be soil. The Burgundians certainly agree, as limestone content is a common factor in the best *climats* of Burgundy. So too is this factor evident in some of Australia's better areas, the Hunter Valley (in parts), Coonawarra (generally) and Geelong (in parts). In fact this would be a superb theory if the Yarra Valley shared this limestone factor, but alas it does not. Perhaps what is critical in the Yarra is, as Dr John Middleton (himself a veteran of 22 vintages of pinot) believes, the ability of the soil to hold moisture in times of heat stress. Who knows what the solution for successful pinot noir really is? In Australia the natural home for pinot noir may even yet await discovery. When that discovery is made, I am confident that no one factor will provide the ultimate answer; it will surely be a synthesis of clonal selection, soil, aspect, climate and technical expertise, all based on a devotion to Burgundian style!

NEW SOUTH WALES

In the Hunter Valley there is one totally committed devotee of pinot noir and the Burgundian style, Murray Tyrrell. It is Tyrrell and his band of winemakers who have come closest to mastering pinot in its Hunter environment. In one of the many retrospective tastings carried out for this book, I evaluated all the Tyrrell pinots with four exceptions from 1976 to 1987.

1987 was the last of a trio of outstanding Hunter years. The Tyrrell Pinot Noir is dark ruby in colour, with a lifted, 'stewed fruit' nose. Its palate is full-bodied and complex, with sweet fruit and 'tobacco' flavours and a lifted character that makes me reserve judgment about its future prospects until 1991. (17 pts)

The most notable 'red' year in recent memory, however, was 1986 and the Tyrrell Pinot certainly confirmed it. Light to medium ruby in colour, with a 'cherry' nose and a palate that was all 'crushed strawberries', the wine promises well for the future. (17.5 pts)

Though 1985 was the first of that trio, the Tyrrell Pinot 1985 was lighter in colour than the 1987, as would be expected, yet paradoxically darker than the 1986. Its nose is intriguing, showing 'undergrowth' against a vanillan wood background. The palate was soft and straightforward with a slight woody finish which was a mirror-image of the nose. (16.5 pts) The wine was probably entering a cocoon phase, perhaps to emerge as gracefully as the 1983, itself the product of a warm year but no whit inferior for that. Its colour is still full and bright even with a degree of density, the nose having the 'undergrowth' cast that typifies pinot noir in middle age. It was the palate with a fruit character I can only describe as 'explosive' that was the highlight of the wine. Certainly there was no volatility, just complex strawberry flavours, which were delightful to taste in a wine then five years old. (18 pts)

Warmer vintages do have their problems, however, and this was exemplified by the 1981, the product of a Hunter drought, now rather brown in colour with 'mushrooms' and 'compost' on nose and a soft fading palate. (14.5 pts)

Much more satisfying, however, was the 1980 vintage, a revelation of how Hunter pinot can develop. The wine was browning of course, but had evolved a strawberry-gamey bouquet that was authentically Burgundian, while the strawberry palate was full and soft. It was a wine that could have easily originated from any warm vintage in the Côte de Beaune. In mid-1988 it was a very definite success. (18 pts)

The years before 1980 were not so remarkable. The 1979 Pinot was distinctly red-brown in colour, and though the nose showed nuances of 'undergrowth' and strawberries, the palate, soft and quite long, was manifestly of the Hunter rather than Burgundian. (16 pts)

What of the famous 1976, the wine that captured the Pinot Noir class at the 1979 Gault-Millau Wine Olympics and humbled the might of Burgundy? Twelve years on it was rather brown, with an aged nose, revealing a slightly burnt character. Its palate, quite mature, was exhibiting all the flavour traits of an old Hunter red. At that stage of its development, there were no particularly Burgundian attributes. (15 pts) (Tasted July 1988.)

The learning curve at Rothbury in respect of pinot noir rose rapidly during the 1980s. After using complete carbonic maceration in the early years of the decade, Rothbury employed 'sandwich' fermentation for the first time during 1985 vintage. As the base of the sandwich, a layer of whole bunches is placed in the bottom of a vat; on top is an almost equal quantity of grapes crushed in the normal way (the 'meat'); and then to complete the sandwich a further layer of whole bunches equal in quantity to the first is spread over the crushed fruit. To this sandwich is added a yeast culture, dry ice (to ensure an anti-oxidative supply of carbon dioxide) and tartaric acid to reduce pH. The vat is then sealed to allow fermentation to commence. Twice a day the vat is opened, and the 'cap' (the skins and whole bunches on top of the must) is 'walked'—that is, the winemaker (or more usually, one of his staff) wades into the must crushing the whole bunches beneath the feet. The Burgundians call this procedure *pigeage*. Except for the 'walking', which evens out the temperature of the must to a small degree, temperature is not controlled, the ferment being allowed to run hot. After about a week the free-run wine is pumped off, and the remaining bunches and skins are pressed. The light pressings join the free run in small two-year-old barrels, where the final flicker of primary fermentation continues. On completion of primary fermentation the wine almost always begins its malolactic fermentation within a few days and then remains on lees for a month, when it is racked and stored in old barrels or stainless steel for further appraisal.

One important result of this technique has been wine of greater complexity on both nose and palate, since wines made by pure carbonic maceration, after an initial burst of fruit intensity on nose and palate lasting about a year, generally slump into a pit of one-dimensional flavour from which they rarely if ever emerge.

Such has been the technical approach to recent Rothbury pinots, yet like the apocryphal pudding, the proof of all pinot techniques is in the tasting. Rothbury generally release two levels of pinot quality: Black Label as the higher standard, and White Label as an earlier-drinking forward style. In June 1988, I retasted for the purposes of this book all the Black Label Pinots made from 1982 to 1987.

1987: medium ruby in colour with a 'cherry' nose and a hint of tobacco and beetroot. There was a soft entry to palate, which grew to a velvety fullness on middle palate, all of this being balanced by a fresh but not too obtrusive acidity. It is a wine that should develop well over three to four years. (16.5 pts)

1986: the warm yet slow summer, with cooler dry intervening periods, made this vintage a joy. For Rothbury its 1986 Black Label Pinot Noir is a delight. With a nose of ripe strawberries the wine has a soft entry yet very full flavours of crushed strawberries on mid-palate with quite a long soft finish. It is a most harmonious pinot noir with great development potential. (18 pts)

1985: a nose of 'cherries' preceded soft straightforward 'strawberry' maceration flavours with a slightly 'furry' tannin finish. Though quite well balanced, it is not to be compared with the previous two wines. (15 pts)

1984: a wet year in the Hunter Valley, producing a Black Label Pinot Noir with 'stalky' vegetative characters on nose and now-fading 'strawberries' on palate. Drink up. (15 pts)

1983: Directors' Reserve Pinot Noir: with a lifted 'strawberry' nose and a degree of volatility, the palate shows strong flavours but the volatility component can certainly be tasted and will only become more obvious. Drink up. (14 pts)

1982: medium red with brown tints, this wine has evolved a complex nose of 'undergrowth'. The palate too is quite complex in a framework of soft round flavours. It is now at its peak. (17 pts)

There are of course other Hunter growers of pinot noir, their wines to my palate being too heavy in tannin. And though they do age, having the wrong structure in the first place, they age as ordinary tannin-dominated reds.

VICTORIA

Victoria, so its winemakers often pronounce, is the natural Australian home for pinot noir. Self-proclaimed though it may be, there is no doubting Victorian progress in the fulfilment of this prophecy. The Yarra Valley in particular has at least six makers, some of them brand new (even by born-again Yarra standards), who in any given year might make a marvellous pinot. The question as always is whether it is done consistently.

David Fyffe of Yarra Burn has been as consistent as any. His first pinot was made in 1981, and though that wine is now past its peak, its successors are very much alive and track a steady progress towards a recognisably Burgundian style of consistent quality.

Yarra Burn Pinot Noir 1987: this product of a very cool year is a light pink-red in colour, with a charming 'cherry' bouquet and a palate of similar fruit quality with a slight lift. It is a good wine but rather light. (16 pts)

Yarra Burn Pinot Noir 1986: a fuller colour than others, this wine has a cherry–strawberry nose and an excellently structured, strawberry palate that needs a little time to develop further. (17.5 pts)

Yarra Burn Pinot Noir 1985: another pinot noir of light to medium red with a 'cherry' nose and quite a firm palate with some 'sappiness', just a little lacking in generosity. (15.5 pts)

Yarra Burn Pinot Noir 1984: I saw this wine first soon after its release. It was outstanding then. It still is. Comparatively pale in colour with an excellent 'strawberry' nose, full soft fruit in a generous middle palate with 'sappy' overtones, it is quite 'Burgundian' and a benchmark for the variety in the Yarra. (18.5 pts)

Yarra Burn Pinot Noir 1982: though browning at the edges, this wine is similar in nose and palate structure, though the palate flavours are rather too 'sappy' and a little out of balance. (15 pts) (All the above wines were tasted in August 1988.)

Diamond Valley is an offshoot of the Yarra to the north-west of the generally accepted viticultural area. There at Diamond Valley Vineyards, David and Cathy Lance, like David Fyffe, are also experiencing a learning curve with pinot noir. Since 1982, Diamond Valley pinot noir has won many trophies and gold medals including the Peaches Trophy at the National Wine Show twice. At a tasting in August 1988, I tasted the Diamond Valley pinots from 1981 to 1986.

The 1981 vintage had during that time aged extremely well, showing that 'spirity' (not volatile) nose peculiar to the variety. The palate was definitely mature with 'gamey' flavours and a soft lingering finish. Though the wine is now beginning to fade, David Lance had certainly captured true Burgundian style. (17 pts)

Despite its Peaches award at the 1985 National Show, I found the 1982 Diamond Valley Pinot slightly closed on nose. True there were 'tobacco' aromas and there was a clean, correctly structured palate, but the wine as a whole was just a little dull. (16.5 pts)

In that year of adversity, 1983, Diamond Valley Pinot Noir excelled. With its 'cherry' nose and 'sappy' delicate palate, the wine though light is still lively and elegant. (17.5 pts)

The extremely cool vintage of 1984 continued the light 'cherry' style of Diamond Valley Pinot (16 pts), while the ripe 1985 showed more complex 'berry' and 'tobacco' aromas and a fuller fruitier palate. (17 pts)

My pick of the group, however, already with four trophies by late 1988, was the 1986. With intricate cherry/oak aromas on nose and an elegant classically structured palate the wine was marvellously full-flavoured and worth every one of four trophies. (18.5 pts)

So it is fair comment that the pinot noir future for Diamond Valley seems bright. David and Cathy Lance have evolved an elegant wine with 'cherry' aromas aging into 'tobacco'. The palates are usually long and soft, aging well for four to five years.

Dr John Middleton is one of the modern pioneers of Yarra Valley pinot, which has always been close to his heart. During the past decade some marvellous pinots have been made; 1978 and 1980 are just two. Of more recent vintages the 1984 had the typical complex 'spirity' nose of Burgundian pinot (not volatility, in the wine-fault sense). On palate there was a soft strawberry fullness which dominated an excellent wine. (17 pts) Fuller still was the 1985, with a more straightforward strawberry nose but seductively velvety on palate. (18 pts) Both wines were beautifully balanced. (Tasted March 1989.)

Yarra Yering (Dr Bailey Carrodus) has a splendid reputation for pinot, 1984 and 1986 being particularly good (both pointed at 18 in late 1988). St Hubert's too have had success with pinot, the 1986 being especially good, with a slight 'beetroot' nose and a full soft well-balanced palate. (18 pts) (Tasted February 1989.)

Of the new guard of Yarra makers, Coldstream Hills, the winechild of James Halliday, has in its initial vintages produced most promising pinot. Like Garry Farr at Bannockburn in Geelong, Halliday has spent a vintage with Domaine Dujac at Morey-St-Denis, no doubt picking up a Burgundian secret or two. Of the wines released to date, the 1987 Miller Pinot Noir is top quality, while the 1987 New Pinot (a style admittedly made to be drunk young) was decidedly light. 1988, covered in Show glory, is undoubtedly the best yet.

Coldstream Hills Pinot Noir (Rising Vineyard) 1988 (tasted several times during 1989 and early 1990): another pinot of excellent medium to dark red hue, showing aromas of ripe strawberries and smoky spicy oak. On palate there was just the right arrangement of medium to full berry softness, skilfully handled spicy oak and balanced tannin to allow this wine to age extremely well. (18.5 pts) Prophecies often return to haunt, but this pinot has more than enough substance to justify cellaring patience until 1993 at least.

Coldstream Hills Pinot Noir 1989 (tasted March 1990): medium to full red in hue with hints of purple, revealing a delicious nose of cherry–plum and tobacco, this wine offered ripe berry fruit and spicy oak on initial entry to palate, then fell away ever so slightly into a leafy finish, lacking a little length. Very elegant, nonetheless. (17 pts) Drink in 1991–93.

Yarra Ridge is also a rising star in the pinot constellation. Its 1989 Pinot Noir, tasted in April 1990, was one of the great successes of that uncertain Yarra vintage. Medium to full red in colour, this wine offered lively sappy, cherry aromas on nose and quite intense cherry–plum flavours on entry to palate. Mid-palate showed softly sweet carbonic maceration characters, while finish revealed light well-integrated tannin. (18 pts) Drink in 1991–93.

So the Yarra is building an excellent reputation for pinot noir and may indeed prove to be the ultimate Australian home for the variety. In virtually every year, one vineyard or another will make a delightful pinot. It is all a question of consistency of performance. That is the one virtue lacking in the Yarra at the present time. As winemaking experience with the variety increases, doubtless the consistency will arrive.

Geelong is the ancestral home of pinot in Australia and the chief rival to the Yarra Valley for pinot predominance in Victoria. There winemaker Gary Farr at Bannockburn has at least as much hands-on experience with the variety as anybody in the state except Dr John Middleton at Mount Mary, Dr Peter McMahon at Seville Estate and Dr Bailey Carrodus at Yarra Yering. I tasted the five Bannockburn vintages from 1982 to 1986 in late 1988.

Remember the hyperbole (described earlier) inspired by pinot in Burgundian prose? I realise that Australian wine of any description rarely qualifies for such epigrammatic enthusiasm, but the 1986 Bannockburn Pinot Noir proved a marvellous exception. Violets! That wine removed the filter of pragmatic realism from my nose, and I smelt violets, real violets in an Australian pinot. On palate there were delicate strawberry flavours—not the crushed carbonic characters of some warmer-area wines, but 'strawberry' with finesse. The palate structure was also classic: soft entry, a full, even sumptuous middle palate and a long finish, yet withall sufficient acidity to guarantee a long and harmonious cellar life. It is surely another of the benchmarks for Victorian pinot noir. (18.5 pts)

The 1985 vintage was a little more austere on nose, showing slight strawberry with some stalkiness. Nonetheless the palate was big enough though not quite as full as the 1986, to ensure that the wine would age well. (16.5 pts)

Like 1986 and 1985, the Bannockburn 1984 had an excellent deep ruby colour. On nose there was strawberry again with a hint of vanillan oak, while on palate cherry and strawberry flavours with a touch of sappiness preceded a long finish. A complex wine which will continue to mature well. (17 pts)

The wine of 1983 was possibly the least of them, not that there was anything actively wrong with it. Paler than the others, though without browning, the wine showed slighter fruit characters on nose and palate. Nor was it as full on middle palate as the later wines. However respectable it would have seemed in any other range of pinots, amongst its brothers it seemed to be a product of its difficult birth year, slightly stressed perhaps by the extremely hot and dry conditions of 1983. (15.5 pts)

The oldest wine was the 1982, still a very good light ruby red without browning. On opening, the nose suggested cherries but after a few minutes, nuances of aged wine began to appear—'undergrowth' and a slightly 'gamey' bouquet. On palate there were developed 'sweet' fruit flavours, quite full but soft but definitely 'Burgundian'. (17 pts)

This range was the most consistently 'Burgundian' of all the pinot ranges tasted for this book and certainly promises very well for the future, the wines being remarkable for their fullness of fruit and elegance, qualities not often found together, the palates treading a fine line between the bluff coarseness of some pinots and the tissue-thin spindliness of others.

Though it might have seemed an impossible feat when I tasted the

1986 (after all, how does one surpass perfection?), the Bannockburn Pinot Noir 1988 is also a marvellous wine. When tasted in January 1990, I noticed a medium to full red hue with tinges of purple, concentrated aromas of black cherries and tobacco, and an intensely concentrated and rich palate of strawberries and tobacco with soft beautifully integrated tannins on finish. A gorgeous wine. (18.5 pts) Drink in 1992–95.

Bannockburn, however, is not the only Geelong vineyard producing pinot noir. The only local pinot to rival Bannockburn in 1988 was Hickinbotham Geelong Pinot Noir 1988. This wine, tasted several times during 1989, was medium to full red in tone, revealing dark cherry and tobacco/undergrowth fragrances in a very complex nose. On a very deep palate, this wine unfolded an intricate array of flavours, ripe cherry, sweet strawberry, truffle and tobacco being but a few of the sweet and savoury tastes that multiplied in the mouth. This was a wine of excellent balance and a pinot that could be cellared with absolute confidence. (18.5 pts) Drink 1993–95.

The Prince Albert vineyard, 2 hectares in area and planted wholly to pinot, is another Geelong estate in renaissance, having been planted by the Geelong pioneer Pettavell 120 years earlier. After initial success and then some uneven wines during the early 1980s Prince Albert seemed to be returning to form with 1986 and 1988 vintages.

In Victoria, however, the Yarra Valley and Geelong have their rivals. The most promising of the newer regions, some say, is the Mornington Peninsula. There it is only fair to state that pinot is still in its infancy, and again consistency of quality will be the essential virtue demanded by the public, though wines such as Stoniers Merricks Pinot Noir 1987 would be outstanding in any company, especially in such a young area.

In the few years of its existence, Dromana Estate has added considerable lustre to the reputation of the Mornington Peninsula. It too made marvellous pinot noir in 1989. Tasted in March 1990, Dromana Estate Pinot Noir 1989 was medium-red in hue with deliciously fresh strawberry–cherry fragrances on nose. Palate was quite complex offering not only a delicious transference of those sweet fruit aromas into ripe generous cherry flavours but also a spicy oak underpinning that promised well for the future cellaring life of the wine. Its structure was quite classical, soft entry, full velvety middle and soft finish with persistent soft well-integrated tannins. (18.5 pts) Drink in 1990–94.

Yet another district virtually undeveloped as a pinot clime is Macedon. There Cope-Williams made a 1986 Pinot Noir with an entrancing nose, the wine disappointing only because of a slightly unbalanced palate.

Elsewhere in those cool southern parts, Reg Egan at Wantirna South, a south-eastern suburb of Melbourne, has produced pinot in small quantities for more than a decade.

And in the mountain fastnesses of the Victorian Alps, the Ritchie family at Delatite make a light elegant version, which to me does not yet have classic structure.

There remains, however, one region that does offer serious competition to the Yarra and Geelong and those postage-stamp vineyards in Mornington: Bendigo, where Stuart Anderson at Balgownie has made some fascinating pinots during the past decade. On the whole they are a little more weighty and less ephemeral than those of the cool south, but they nonetheless are wines of classic structure, grace and, importantly, staying power, being able to withstand that most exacting of all tests for a red wine, bottle age. Of older vintages, I recall vividly the excellence of 1982. Of more recent, in October 1988 I tasted four Balgownie Pinot Noir from 1984 to 1987. Only 1984, light in structure because of that extremely cool vintage (shared by the rest of southern Australia), is yet ready for consumption. Pale coloured and now showing traces of brown, the wine has a sappy 'spiritiness' on nose, quite typical of the variety. The palate is light-bodied with cherry and green-stalk flavours, finishing with soft spice. As there is an oxidative element in the wine, palate flavours are broadening and the wine should be drunk.

The common thread in all three of the younger wines is, as Stuart Anderson puts it, some 'skeleton and flesh with a capability to age a bit'. The wines all show excellent fruit of cherry/strawberry flavours, well integrated with fine Allier oak barriques, themselves ranging in age from new to three years old. Despite this greater weight of palate, the wines are not heavy or clumsy. The palate structure is quite classic, the 1987 in particular showing much promise.

Undoubtedly, the hectares of pinot noir grown in Victoria will increase impressively in coming years, and the supporters of the Yarra Geelong and Mornington will grow in numbers, but Bendigo, even in the face of such competition, will always be, in those Michelin words, 'worth a special trip'.

SOUTH AUSTRALIA

In South Australia, pinot noir is not as advanced as it is in Victoria. Perhaps until very recently too little attention has been paid to correct vineyard location or winemaking technique. Though plantings are now proceeding apace in the Adelaide Hills, these are intended for sparkling wine, only a few drops of red having yet been made. In quantity terms the leading area of production is Coonawarra–Padthaway, followed at a very respectable distance by the Barossa Valley and Southern Vales.

So how has pinot fared in what is undoubtedly Australia's best red wine area? Regrettably it must be conceded that the majority of Coonawarra winemakers have not treated the variety with extraordinary care. Mostly it has been vinified just like the other reds, though certainly experience with the variety is not lacking.

Lindeman's Padthaway Vineyard has produced pinot noir since 1979, and the Rouge Homme wines from Coonawarra have appeared since 1983. Lindeman's vinification has been mostly traditional, though in recent vintages whole bunches have been added to the traditional fermentation, as well as about 15 per cent carbonically macerated wine being included in the final wine, which is matured in Nevers oak. Such techniques must contribute complexity to the final wine.

Of the Padthaway range tasted early in 1989, the 1980 vintage was most impressive, with cherry/tobacco aromas and bottle age combining to show some complexity and a full middle palate and soft finish that makes for a very satisfying table wine. (17 pts) Another vintage of similar though slightly lighter mould was the 1982. (16.5 pts) The older wines (1979 and 1981) had faded, and the younger (1983 to 1986) were curiously one-dimensional, as if made in lighter style for almost immediate drinking.

The Rouge Homme wines (1983 and 1985) were also of the same light mono-dimension. Only the 1984 showed slight 'undergrowth' characters on nose, and good fruit and weight on the middle palate. (16.5 pts)

Other Coonawarra pinots from Hollick and Brand have been very much in the same style: light- to medium-bodied reds of one-dimensional fruit flavour, pleasant drinking but by no means exciting to the pinot enthusiast. Indeed much the same can be said of the Hardy pinots from Padthaway.

Far more exciting in prospect for pinot, if the 1986 vintage is a true foretaste, will be Wynn's Coonawarra Estate. A late arrival on the scene, but understandable as Wynn's had previously employed all their pinot in the making of sparkling wine, the 1986 (tasted in August 1988) was dark ruby red, highlighted by tints of purple, with cherries, strawberries and a hint of 'undergrowth' highlighting the nose. In a beautifully made palate, elegant strawberry flavours balanced by well-handled wood completed the harmony of the wine. (18 pts)

The marvellously ripe Coonawarra vintage of 1988 also continued Wynn's mastery of pinot noir. Tasted in March 1990, Wynn's Pinot Noir 1988 presented quite positive ripe cherry and spicy oak aromas on a delightful nose, while offering on palate soft ripe berry and tobacco flavours with a touch of cloves. A complex and Burgundian palate that should develop well in bottle for three to four years, and a worthy successor to the 1986. (18 pts) Drink in 1993–94.

In the Barossa, pinots made so far have been of bigger, more 'earthy' character, with generosity rather than elegance the keynote of palate. At High Eden, in the Barossa Ranges, Adam Wynn has now experienced several pinot vintages. Though his pinots reflect his tremendous skill, they are elegant soft reds with beautiful spicy wood/fruit integration on middle palate, not owing much to Burgundian style. Even more straightforward are the Tollana pinots and those of Pedare.

Pinot is also grown in a minor way in the Riverland areas, and there makes simple red wines of one-dimensional fruit, sometimes with light strawberry flavours.

The South Australians, however, will not despair. Further experience with the variety and increased plantings in cooler or higher regions may yet see a 'Burgundian' pinot, capable of competing with the best from other states.

TASMANIA

In Tasmania, pinot certainly has found a home, if only for sparkling-wine purposes. In the north, Andrew Pirie at Pipers Brook has had his successes. At Berriedale near Hobart, Julian Alcorso is staking Moorilla's reputation on pinot noir. On the faith of his 1986, a lovely wine of strawberry and 'undergrowth' nuances in bouquet and a soft full middle palate of strawberry and 'tobacco', he is on very firm ground. (18 pts)

WESTERN AUSTRALIA

In Western Australia, pinot noir prospers in the Margaret River region, where Moss Wood has made some outstanding wines. The 1981 was of great style and received great critical acclaim. The 1986 may be even better. Here is a pinot of a lovely deep ruby hue with a nose of strawberry and light 'undergrowth' characters. In the mouth there is a soft, yet voluptuous middle palate, quite velvety and a discreet tannin-integrated finish. In flavour, intense but elegant strawberry, 'tobacco' qualities predominate. Moss Wood 1986 is a pinot noir of power and presence, a tremendous success. (17.5 pts)

In the same area Leeuwin Estate has also built a good reputation for pinot noir, its 1983 being particularly fine, while Cullen's and Pierro are also wineries to watch.

The Mount Barker region also augurs well. There the Plantagenet Pinot Noir 1987 was of excellent palate structure and flavours, the first of, hopefully, a famous line. Close to Albany, Wignall is a pinot name to be reckoned with.

There is no doubt that the search for the perfect Australian pinot will go on. Even as I write, Coldstream Hills has become the high-flyer of Australian pinot, winning acclaim not only at our wine shows, but in wine events of international importance, such as the Qantas Cup. Pinot enthusiasts will continue to seek out such wines, but for most consumers Australian pinot is a confusing rag-bag of styles that certainly do not justify high price tags. In the search for perfection, consistency must have its part to play.

MEDIUM-BODIED, FIRM FINISH

SHIRAZ

'Familiarity breeds contempt.' A weathered old chestnut, certainly, but true indeed when applied to shiraz in the 1970s and early 1980s. Yet perhaps no longer, as a new respect grows for shiraz in its more-favoured Australian sites.

Regarded almost with scorn as the white wine boom of the mid-1970s undid all the predictions of the 1960s, shiraz vines were grubbed out by the wagonload or topgrafted to white varieties as winemakers tried frantically to cope with the fickleness of public taste. Whatever red excitement was left in the consumer (and there was not much) was centred almost entirely upon cabernet sauvignon. By the early 1990s shiraz was fortunately regaining its public favour.

In the world at large, its bigger producers are France which has, with 13 000 hectares, nearly three times the Australian area of 4904 hectares (as at June 1988), a tremendous decline from its heyday in the late 1970s of more than 10 000 hectares. Third is Argentina (2000 hectares), South Africa and California having much smaller areas. Elsewhere shiraz has made very little impression, lacking perhaps the varietal distinction or more probably the sales excitement of those well-known international travellers, cabernet sauvignon and chardonnay.

Its ancient origins are shrouded in myth. Did it originate in its namesake city in Iran and then proceed via the Middle East to Syracuse in Sicily, Marseille and on to the Northern Rhône? Who was responsible for its tortuous journey: Phoenician or Greek traders, Roman legions or hermit knights returning from crusades? Why not add Arab caravans or throw in a magic carpet or two? The truth is that only the immediate origins of shiraz are known and that the Northern Rhône is most probably its ancestral home as well.

In Australia its origins are more certain. It came virtually with a passport—'Hermitage' (Vine 9) and 'Ciras (Scyras)' (Vine 45) in the Busby Collection of 1832—and was immediately planted in Sydney's Botanical Gardens, its authentication being Busby's own words: 'this variety alone is used in making the best red wine of Hermitage.' Within the same decade it found its way to the Hunter Valley and perhaps even to South Australia.

By the late nineteenth century it was established in every winegrowing area in Australia. Its present distribution shows South Australia with 2840 hectares, New South Wales with 1459 hectares, and smaller areas in Victoria, Western Australia and Queensland. Only Tasmania does not grow shiraz.

As a cultivar it is vigorous, has a spreading growth habit and produces five-lobed leaves of a bright green with white-green growing tips. Its bunches are long and rather loose, cylindrical in shape. Its berries are oval, dark purple-black in colour, fleshy and thinner-skinned than cabernet sauvignon, a propensity that makes the variety more susceptible to damage and disease. Shiraz ripens mid-season, and whether cane- or spur-pruned it crops moderately well, as witness its Australian average in 1986 vintage of nearly 10 tonnes to the hectare.

Shiraz is, it is often said, a workhorse, worthwhile but lacking the glamour of cabernet sauvignon. It is found at all price levels from the cheapest to the most expensive and in all red wine styles from rosé and sparkling 'burgundy' to vintage 'port'. Decolorised, it has even found its way into bulk white wine and cheap sparkling white.

Clonal selection work has continued since the 1960s in the various states, and most states now have their favourite clone, though in some regions the shiraz vines are old enough to antedate clonal selection.

NEW SOUTH WALES

Historically it has always been the most important red variety in the Hunter Valley. Even in the 1950s when the fortunes of the region were at a low ebb, famous wines from 'hermitage' (as the area insists on calling it) were made by Lindeman, McWilliam and Tulloch, 1954 and 1959 being years of renown. Right through the 1960s, 1970s and 1980s the distinctive Hunter hermitage style continued, and though to some critics outside the region used to more fruity and uncomplicated flavours it is something of an acquired taste, the traditional 'leathery' nose and the earthy, smoky palate are still to be found, Tyrrell for one maintaining the customary style.

Whether this style will continue beyond the present generation of winemakers depends on market acceptance and the impact that new winemakers and criticism will have on it. If the style is merely a function of Hunter heat, lack of proper equipment and 'tradition', which may be translated as a reluctance to improve it, then perhaps it may be allowed to fade into history, for after all the white wine making customs of the past have been completely changed during the past 30 years. Why not the red? Yet I would be sad to see such a distinct regional style disappear completely.

Nevertheless with better cooling and cleaner fermentation and skilful use of American oak, a newer, fruitier style of Hunter shiraz is already evolving, free of the earthy 'tarry' flavours of earlier years. However the traditional Hunter style was caused—and it is most probably by sulphide generated during a hot fermentation—the new, cleaner style is receiving great public acceptance. Whether such wines will age with as much complexity as the older style is another question, but does the present-day consumer want to wait so long anyway?

It is no secret that the best hermitage reds have come from the best soils, which in the Lower Hunter are the distinctive red loams, found mostly on hillsides but all too sporadic in occurrence. Such soils are well drained, often with some subsoil limestone, factors shared by Rose Hill (McWilliam, Lake and Drayton), parts of Ashman's (Tyrrell), the slopes around the Lindeman Hunter River Winery, the McWilliam Mount Pleasant Winery and the hills behind, and also the Howard and Stephen family vineyards along the undulating Marrowbone Road. The winemaking relevance of such soils is not that they impart any particular characteristic to the wine, but that they provide a favourable environmental factor (one of several necessary) for the growth of a vine. Both moisture retention in periods of drought and good drainage in times of heavy summer rainfall (the Hunter may experience both during the one season) are necessary for the vine to produce optimum quality and quantity during any given season. Vine stress must be avoided; healthy vines yield healthy wines.

Shiraz originating from the lighter clay-based red podsols is usually stressed to some degree, and though quality may be satisfactory, quantity, another important factor for the producer, often suffers. That other common Hunter soil (the deep silty river sand) is most often used for whites, rarely for red.

Of all the longer-established Hunter winemakers, Tyrrell still makes the most traditional style of hermitage, for that synonym for shiraz is also a tradition in the area. In warmer years the Tyrrell style is dense red-purple in colour when young, with aromas of smoke and earth and hugely structured palates of great extract and tannin, certainly amongst the firmest in the Hunter. The Tyrrell aficionadoes are prepared to wait a decade for such wines (they often need it), but with time the smoke and earth aromas (less-charitable critics use terms such as sulphide and mercaptan) meld into the bouquet heightening its damp leather complexity, the firm tannins soften, and the whole wine assumes a mature garb; it is a firm harmony in most cases, for Tyrrell Hermitage can rarely be accused of being overly soft or namby-pamby. Vat 5 is usually the most typical and the best of the range. That wine in 1983 vintage, a warm Hunter year if ever there was one, was in February 1989 still quite dense and purple tinted in colour, earthy in aroma, but firm and slightly closed on palate. The wine, made for a 12- to 15-year life span at least, was only then emerging from a rather shy youth and should not be drunk before 1996. (16 pts)

Though the Tyrrell shiraz styles are classically loyal to Valley tradition, another Hunter maker whose style has altered considerably in the 1980s is McWilliam's at Mount Pleasant. Gone is the excessive 'tarriness' of the 1960s and 1970s, and though traces do remain in warmer years, they are factors for complexity rather than a sum total of fault. The finest and longest lived of all the Mount Pleasant Hermitage reds are from Rosehill. The 1986 Rosehill Hermitage, tasted in March 1989, showed all the wealth of character of that generous year. Deep red in colour with a bouquet of ripe berries and black pepper and a sumptuously rich palate, here was a top Hunter hermitage, ranking with the best of the breed in Australia in that year. (18.5 pts) Under winemaker Philip Ryan's stewardship, the Mount Pleasant Hunter reds go from strength to strength.

Lindeman's these days use much more Broke shiraz in their Hermitage and 'Burgundy' wines than formerly. The soils at Broke are deep friable loams, which produce reasonable shiraz crops of 'berry/pepper' flavours rather than the 'smoky' tastes often seen in Pokolbin fruit. The fruit character seems to be changing in the 1980s, and it is surely not because of winemaking changes, for there certainly has been continuity, with Karl Stockhausen in the position from the late 1950s until 1986 except for a Barossa stint in 1980–81, and Gerry Sissingh from 1986 to 1990. I do not lament the change, if change it proves to be, for I was most impressed with the 1986 Steven Hermitage Bin 7210 tasted in March 1989. Deep red-purple in hue with a nose that epitomised black peppercorns, this wine unfolded a rich harmonious palate, showing an elegant pepperiness integrated most acceptably with soft tannins. A lovely style, which will drink well into the 1990s. (18.5 pts)

Drayton's, whose hermitage style in warm years sometimes shows the traditional Valley leatheriness, made very good shiraz in the cool 1987 vintage and also in the more difficult and drizzly 1988 year, Bin 5555 Hermitage of 1987 having a fine strawberry fruit nose and big palate with black-pepper flavours, balanced tannins and good potential for development. (17 pts) (Tasted October 1988.) Its successor, Bin 5555 of 1988, tasted in October 1989, was understandably lighter in weight but by no means thin. Very clean on nose, it too showed excellent fruit on palate, being ready for drinking in 1991. (17 pts)

Hungerford Hill also enjoyed success with shiraz in 1987. Its 'merchant range' Shiraz 1987 was full bodied, showing a lovely berry and American oak nose with excellent integration of wood and fruit on palate. (17.5 pts) (Tasted October 1988.) The Pokolbin Collection Shiraz 1988 was also a worthy wine. Lighter in body than the 1987 wine but of medium weight with a cellaring potential of three years. (17 pts) (Tasted October 1989.)

With the advent of the red wine boom in the mid-1960s, one of the most sought-after shiraz reds at that time was that of Tulloch, then a family-owned concern, which closed promptly at one o'clock on Saturday afternoons so that winemaker Keith Tulloch could go off to bowls. So on a Saturday morning trip from Sydney, I usually made Tulloch the first port of call to taste the latest release of the Private Bin Pokolbin Dry Red. Three memorable vintages, 1965, 1966 and 1967, spring to mind. Soon after, in 1969, the Tulloch family sold the vineyards and winery to Reed International, in one of the first of several multinational takeovers of the Australian wine scene. In 1974 Tulloch was sold to Gilbey's, which in turn sold off vineyards before disposing of the company once more to Allied Vintners, itself absorbed in the 1980s by the Penfold's group. This rollercoaster ride of ownership and the white wine boom of the mid-1970s may have been the cause of the downturn in red wine quality that occurred during the 1970s. On the positive side, however, there have been continuing threads: in local management, where Jay Tulloch has held the reins for some years, and in winemaking, where Patrick Auld has been in control since 1980.

Tulloch shiraz these days is selected from all over the Lower Hunter and Fordwich (the area adjacent to Broke and with similar soils and climate). In 1990, a flagship Tulloch Hermitage, 'Hector', named after the late Hector Tulloch, was launched from 1986 vintage. The 1991 release is the 1987 vintage, and thereafter the wine will be released from year to year, quality permitting.

The 1986 'Hector', tasted December 1989, was a limpid medium to full red in colour. Its bouquet was most pleasing, revealing scents of chocolate and earth with hints of sweet vanilla oak. Its palate was similarly generous in flavour: sweet tastes of chocolate and charred oak dominant against a canvas of soft tannin and acid. It was a pleasantly accessible wine to be drunk in 1990–94. (17 pts)

In contrast, its younger 1987 brother was tighter knit. Still full red in hue and purple-tinted, this youthful wine showed berry and black-pepper fragrances on nose with the more subtle influence of French oak. Its elegant palate offered black-pepper flavours and firmer tannins on finish. A wine of excellent structure, it should age well. (17.5 pts) Drink in 1993–96.

With shiraz wines such as these and the technical expertise and backing of the Penfold's group, Tulloch is now well placed to regain its reputation as one of the leading makers of fine Hunter Hermitage.

Of all Hunter makers, Wyndham makes the least recognisably regional style of shiraz, most probably because it is the Hunter Valley's largest producer by far (Wyndham crushes about 70 per cent of all Hunter fruit) and therefore has access to shiraz from many sources and different soils. The Wyndham shiraz style is like the menu of an international hotel, perfectly adequate but rarely exciting or even controversial when it comes to typical regional characteristics. In August 1989, I tasted the appropriately-enough named Wyndham International Hermitage 1988: medium to full red in colour with a clean berry nose, this wine showed a medium-bodied palate of forward-drinking style which would be quite ready by 1991. (16.5 pts)

With the almost Australia-wide acceptance of American oak as the most appropriate maturant for shiraz, the Hunter Valley too has joined the fray. Brokenwood has matured its Graveyard Hermitage in American oak each year since the glorious 1986 vintage. The intervening years, 1987 and 1988, have been equally successful though in different styles: 1987 long palated and elegant, to be kept until 1994; and 1988 softer and more accessible and ready about the same time. (1987: 17.5 pts) (1988: 18 pts)

Almost all the smaller makers of the Hunter Valley offer a shiraz (or hermitage) on their lists. Quality is usually good, but the consumer should always taste if possible before purchasing as a trace of sulphide sometimes intrudes. Reliable makers of often-superb wines include Marsh Estate, Allandale, David Paterson at his amusingly named Chateau Pato, Oakvale, Peterson's, Sutherland, Tamburlaine, Thalgara and Terrace Vale. Other vignerons with excellent reputations for other varieties whose shiraz I have not tasted are Fraser, Allanmere, Briar Ridge and Little's, nor have I seen any Murray Robson wines since his departure from the Robson Vineyard (now Briar Ridge).

All of which leaves one remaining Pokolbin maker of shiraz, the Rothbury Estate, very much the child of fickle fortune in its early days as it struggled to establish a reputation for reds in a market that was rapidly attuning itself to white. Since 1982 there have been some great years of Rothbury Hermitage: 1983 ripe and robust; 1986 big, soft and flavoursome; 1987 quite elegant. And 1989? A year saved by a fortnight of fine February weather amid an ocean of rain. Huge coloured wines of deep peppery flavours, very true to variety and almost Rhône-like in their intensity, though lacking the softer more voluptuous characters of years such as 1986. At the time of writing, I had seen the 1989 Rothbury reds only once as barrel samples, but they hold tremendous promise. The wines of 1986 and 1987 are of course in bottle. My notes from late 1989 follow:

Rothbury Reserve Shiraz 1986: deep red in colour with a very slight touch of maturing 'brick', this wine revealed distinct chocolate and vanilla aromas on nose, its palate being soft ripe and full with well-integrated peppery wood tannins on finish. It was quite harmonious and almost ready to drink in late 1989. (17 pts) Drink in 1990–93.

Rothbury Reserve Shiraz 1987: slightly paler than the 1986, but with a more vibrant purple-tinted red, this wine offered a most pleasing bouquet of fine fruit and sweet oak, ripe without being overpowering. In the mouth, flavours were lighter and fruitier than the 1986, but at the same time were long and well balanced. This was a very elegant shiraz style to be drunk in 1992–95. (17.5 pts)

These are both excellent examples of modern Hunter shiraz from a maker more widely known these days for its chardonnays.

To the west of Pokolbin is the Fordwich–Broke area, always recognised as separate, but often used as blending material for lighter Pokolbin reds. From its richer red loams, quite powerful shiraz wines are produced, often lacking the finesse of those from the Pokolbin area.

The two names of importance from the Broke region, whose shiraz wines are usually made from fruit grown locally, are Saxonvale and Simon Whitlam. Saxonvale, owned by Wyndham since 1987, makes a solid Hunter shiraz, rarely subject to the sulphide idiosyncracies occasionally shown by other wines of the Lower Hunter. Its 1986 vintage, however, produced a Hermitage of exceptional quality, showing a delightful black-pepper and vanilla nose and soft voluminous fruit on palate. A most harmonious wine. (17.5 pts) Since the departure of Alasdair Sutherland as winemaker in May 1989, Saxonvale seems to have adopted a lower profile, and opportunities to taste later vintages have not yet come my way.

Simon Whitlam wines have been made in recent years at the Arrowfield winery by Simon Gilbert. The Simon Whitlam wines remain separate, having their origin in the company's Wollombi Brook vineyards at Broke. The Simon Whitlam Hermitage 1987 tasted in late 1989 was full red-purple in colour showing attractive dark chocolate aromas on a full nose. Flavours on palate were rich, ripe and long, being highlighted by excellent smoky oak. (17.5 pts) Drink in 1992–93.

McWilliam's also are going for Broke, having purchased a substantial area of land there in 1989. No doubt a Broke Hermitage will be available before the end of the 1990s as an interesting comparison to its Pokolbin styles.

In the Upper Hunter, shiraz has never earned as much winemaking attention as in the Lower Hunter Valley. The largest denizen of the district, Rosemount, prefers to blend its local shiraz with wine from other areas to produce a multi-blend Diamond label Shiraz of excellent quality. Shiraz was a positive embarrassment to Arrowfield in its early days. There was simply too much for a market swamped with ordinary red. The Arrowfield red experiment was an admitted failure. Many hectares of shiraz vines were either grubbed out or grafted over to more popular white varieties. Since that time, under winemakers Gary Baldwin and then Simon Gilbert, Arrowfield has become more renowned for its quality whites, particularly chardonnay.

Other changes were forthcoming in the Upper Hunter. In 1989, Dr Bob Smith sold his Hordern's Wybong Estate to Wyndham winemaker Jon Reynolds, who has renamed it 'Reynolds Yarraman'. Doubtless under its energetic and enthusiastic new winemaker-proprietor, it will continue to show the shiraz promise revealed in 1986 and 1987 vintages by his predecessor.

Regrettably the Upper Hunter seems unsuited to excellence in shiraz. Perhaps the deep rich loams, ready access to irrigation and the uncommonly hot midsummers provide too encouraging an environment for a variety often not so favoured in the Pokolbin area.

That is shiraz in the Hunter Valley late in 1989. Certainly it is the Hunter's best and most important red variety and likely to remain so, unless in the decade of the 1990s merlot assumes a more dominant role—as well it might, by confirming and continuing the pleasing plumminess of nose and softness of palate shown by several Hunter cabernet–merlot

ABOVE: *Rhine riesling grapes, Petaluma Vineyard, South Australia.*
BELOW: *Semillon grapes on the vine, Delamere, Tasmania.*

Chardonnay grapes on the vine, Camden Estate, New South Wales.

and merlot–cabernet blends from the 1986 and 1987 vintages. If such attractive wines continue, shiraz either as a single varietal or as a blender with cabernet may well find a true rival in merlot. There is, however, a great deal of room for co-existence.

Shiraz holds sway in Mudgee also, producing earthy robust wines, not dissimilar to those of the Broke–Fordwich area of the Hunter Valley. Bob Roberts, owner-winemaker of Huntington Estate with 20 years' experience of shiraz in the region, does not quite agree. He sees 'crushed pepper' character in the Mudgee shiraz of good years and 'tar' in bad. Whether the 'tar' is a function of stress and the black pepper one of equilibrium might well merit some local research.

During the 1980s, 1984 and 1985 were among the best of the Huntington vintages. In late 1989, Huntington Shiraz Bin FB21 1984 (FB in Bob's terminology means 'full-bodied') was only just starting to show signs of maturity in colour, still being of a bright medium red hue. On nose the wine shows complex black-pepper and camphory oak aromas, while its open palate was highlighted by intense black-pepper flavours and moderate tannins. The wine was a great success and should continue to age extremely well. (18 pts) Drink 1991 onwards.

Tasted at the same time, Bin FB5 Shiraz 1985 is typical of Mudgee. An undeniably big wine, it still held a youthful and quite dense red colour. Its bouquet was muted, revealing little besides subdued vanillan oak and hints of berries and black pepper. Its palate was full-bodied, but was tannic, tightly structured and rather closed. Though well balanced, it needed to open out and required at least three years to do so. (16.5 pts) Drink 1993 onwards.

Mudgee's largest winery, Montrose, now owned by the Wyndham group, also makes typical regional shiraz. Good years of the 1980s have included 1982, 1984 and 1987. The 1988 Montrose Shiraz recalled the lighter nature of that vintage in Mudgee, the Hunter Valley and other parts of northern New South Wales. Medium to deep red with some purple tints and lacking density, this wine showed spice, vanilla and 'fruit pastille' aromas on nose. Its palate was light to medium weight revealing well-balanced fruit and acid on mid-palate and slightly furry tannin on finish. (16.5 pts) This was a pleasant red of forward development. Drink in 1990–92.

Through its ownership of Montrose, Wyndham is also proprietor of Craigmoor and Amberton, each of which have produced good shiraz from time to time, though both these wines have been made at Montrose in recent vintages.

Other producers of good shiraz in the district are Miramar, Botobolar Burnbrae and Erudgere.

The largest shiraz-growing region in New South Wales is the Murrumbidgee

Irrigation Area (MIA), centred on Griffith. There, lacking depth of palate, most of it finds its way into the bag-in-box reds, which provide Australia's current drinking, while the better examples are often blended with local cabernet and are sold at cellar door.

Another region of New South Wales which should provide excellent shiraz is the Hilltops region near Young. Here McWilliam's purchased the Barwang Estate in 1989 and were, at time of writing, rapidly expanding its vineyard area. Future vintages are awaited with interest.

Only one more winery need be mentioned in connection with New South Wales shiraz, and that is the Port Macquarie establishment of Cassegrain, which sources most of its shiraz from its Hillside vineyard at Pokolbin in the Lower Hunter. The wines are usually extremely well made, exhibiting the normal characteristics of the region. Very good Cassegrain years in the eighties have been 1985, 1987 and 1989. The first crop from young shiraz vineyards at Port Macquarie is to be the 1991 vintage.

VICTORIA

Though some winemakers in the Mount Barker–Frankland River region of Western Australia may disagree, the most exciting recent developments in Australian shiraz have taken place in Victoria. There it is not the more fashionable southern regions of the Yarra Valley, Geelong and Mornington that are making the pace, though good shiraz is certainly grown in the Yarra and Geelong; it is the Central Highlands, Bendigo, Avoca–Moonambel and Great Western regions that are certainly achieving great quality. Rutherglen (the North-East) continues to make wines which, though bigger than most other Victorians, are these days almost puny compared to the heroic Rutherglen shiraz wines of a generation and more ago.

I have mentioned elsewhere that Stuart Anderson rediscovered just how well suited the Bendigo region was for most red wine varieties. Shiraz is no exception. Balgownie Hermitage 1988 (Stuart also prefers that term to the synonymous shiraz), tasted December 1989, was intense in colour, a dense purple with a ripe bouquet redolent of crushed black peppercorns. Its palate was also intense but soft and balanced with a lingering licorice flavour and subtle well-integrated tannins. This was a most promising wine that needed at least three more years in bottle and then would keep for many more. (17.5 pts) Drink sparingly from 1993 onwards.

Eucalypt is said to be a distinctive feature of shiraz nose and palate in the Victorian Central Highlands. Though Balgownie wines rarely show it, the 1986 and 1987 Chateau Le Amon Shiraz do. The 1986 was dark red in hue, still with some density, showing distinct aromas of mint and eucalypt. On palate the flavours were quite generous and long, offering an interesting combination of mint and spicy oak. (16 pts) (Tasted April 1988.)

The 1987 Le Amon Big Hill Shiraz, on the other hand, lacked mint on nose but made up for that with generous aromas of pepper and eucalypt. Its palate was leaner and more tannic than the 1986, but it had sufficient fruit to ensure harmonious development. (16 pts) Drink in 1992.

Though Jasper Hill was devastated by a bushfire a few weeks before vintage in 1987, its 1987 Friends Shiraz showed no sign of it in April 1989. A huge purple red in shade with a typical peppery nose, this wine recalled the excellent shiraz wines of the Northern Rhône in the intensity of its pepper and spice palate. (17.5 pts) Drink 1994 onwards.

Jasper Hill is located to the east of Bendigo and importantly just to the north of Heathcote, which is the centre of what is arguably the most outstanding area of the Central Highlands, a region which, if ever Australian law insisted on such things, would most definitely be an appellation area for shiraz. Growers of quality for shiraz are Mount Ida and Heathcote. Other growers of good repute whose shiraz wines I have not recently tasted are Zuber Estate (close to Heathcote) and Harcourt Valley (near Castlemaine).

To the south-west of Heathcote lies the Mount Macedon region, the isolated massif between Melbourne and Bendigo. The winemaker of longest standing in the region is Lew Knight, whose Granite Hills vineyard pioneered viticulture there from 1970 onwards. The Knight Heathcote Shiraz of 1985, tasted in October 1989, was full red in hue, showing subdued black-pepper and smoky oak aromas on nose. Supple palate flavours again showed typical black pepper, and the wine, though beginning to mature, was well balanced and able to age well for three to four years more. (17.5 pts) Drink in 1990–94.

John Ellis also is a winemaker of vast experience though relatively new to this region. His Hanging Rock Heathcote Shiraz 1987, tasted at the same time as the Knight, was a marvellous wine of a fulsome red-purple colour with a deep pepper and spice nose and a palate showing most attractive plummy flavours and soft integrated tannins. This is a classic cool-area-fruit style of shiraz, showing no eucalypt whatsoever. (18.5 pts) Drink 1992 onwards.

The Hanging Rock Heathcote Shiraz 1988 is a bigger riper wine but just as impressive. A very dense red-purple in hue, this wine offered a very open yet complex nose of berry, leaf and vanillan oak. Deep ripe berry flavours and quite full tannins left a most favourable imprint on palate. Beautifully balanced and should be at its best towards the end of the 1990s. (18.5 pts) (Both wines tasted October 1989.)

Craiglee, one of the famous names of nineteenth-century Victorian viticulture, is located at Sunbury, virtually an outer suburb of Melbourne these days and well south of the Macedon massif. Its 1986 Shiraz offers typical black-pepper aromas of the area, with its long and balanced palate showing excellent pepper and spice flavours. (17.5 pts) Drink in 1991–94.

The ensuing vintage, 1987, was also a great success for Craiglee Shiraz.

This wine was chosen among the top 100 Smallmaker wines during the 1989 Sydney International Smallmaker Competition, which I was fortunate enough to chair. Tasted in April 1989, the wine remained very youthful in its red-purple hue, showing delightful aromas of black pepper and vanillan oak, while its elegant palate showed excellent fruit depth and soft, powdery tannins on a clean dry finish. (17 pts) Drink 1991 onwards.

Westwards about 120 kilometres from Macedon lies the Avoca–Moonambel region in the shadow of the Victorian Pyrenees, mere foothills when compared to their French counterparts but useful enough as gatherers of rain clouds in a district which would otherwise be very dry.

At Moonambel, Dominique Portet made his first shiraz (or French Syrah, which his labels prefer) in 1977, a wine that I tasted in April 1989, very much alive but still closed and tannic, in a vertical tasting of the first decade of Taltarni reds. The notable shiraz of that tasting were 1978, 1979, 1981, 1984 and 1986. When tasted again in August 1989, my initially favourable impressions of the 1986 Taltarni French Syrah were confirmed. A rich purple-red in hue, it revealed full black-pepper aromas in a nose which also showed just a suspicion of eucalypt. Its palate was ripe, supple and well balanced. A wine with the capacity to age well for five years. (17 pts) Drink in 1995, but be in no hurry.

Dominique Portet is an empirical winemaker, and it was noticeable during that tasting how his shiraz style had lightened over the decade. That said, Taltarni French Syrah is most definitely a wine in need of bottle age, five years in cellar at least being required, but it has ceased to be herculean.

That intriguing eucalypt character, sometimes seen in Taltarni shiraz, also occurs in other shiraz wines of the district. Nonetheless, provided it does not overpower the typical black-pepper characters of the variety, the shiraz wines of other makers of this region can be extremely attractive. Labels to look for are Dalwhinnie, Mount Avoca, Redbank and Warrenmang.

A mere 60 kilometres to the south-west is Great Western, for many years a surviving but isolated outpost of the vine in the rolling pastoral vastness that is western Victoria. Here too shiraz has been a sturdy veteran, providing many a famous red from the hands of the almost legendary Colin Preece at the Seppelt winery. Seppelt continues to release 'Hermitage' from its Great Western vineyards. The Seppelt Great Western Vineyards Hermitage 1984 was medium to full red in colour at time of tasting in late 1989. Its bouquet was a delicious amalgam of chocolate, spice and slightly smoky oak, while its palate of medium weight held a lovely balance of ripe maturing fruit and soft tannin. (17.5 pts) Ready to drink from 1990 but will hold for three to four years thereafter.

The other veteran of Great Western is Best's, famous also for its Hermitage. Its 1987 Great Western Hermitage, still a very youthful purple in hue in late 1989, showed light, almost subdued spicy berry fragrances on nose, but its palate was already open, revealing soft sweet fruit flavours and very acceptable in the mouth. (17 pts) Drink in 1991-93.

Perhaps 1987 was an atypically light year in Great Western, in that the customary black-pepper aromas and flavours seemed somewhat attenuated. In 1986, however, they were certainly all there as evidenced by the Montara Shiraz of that year. Tasted in August 1989, this was a wine of full red colour with the usual freshly crushed peppercorn nose. Its palate, though initially peppery in taste, became soft, full and round on mid-palate and finish. A ripe and complete red. (17.5 pts) Drink in 1991-94.

Cathcart Ridge also produced an excellent shiraz from 1986 vintage. Tasted when very young in May 1988, this showed that enigmatic eucalypt and mint character on nose, with a full ripe palate and good balance that promised good cellaring. (17 pts) Drink in 1991-94.

One other producer of excellent shiraz in this region is Mount Langi Ghiran, whose standards are extremely high. Seen in March 1990, Mount Langi Ghiran Shiraz 1988 held huge purple depths of colour, offering on nose predominant aromas of vanillan oak and crushed black peppercorns with no trace of eucalypt. On palate the wine revealed a complex integration of pepper, berry and spicy oak flavours with a slight tannic astringency on finish, which should hold the wine in good stead for four to six years' cellaring. (17.5 pts) Drink in 1994-96.

I must confess that shiraz from the cooler areas of Victoria has not excited me very much. Perhaps the wines seem too light and leafy without enough stuffing to see them through a few years' cellaring. In Geelong, Bannockburn produces the best of that area. In a sense it is gratifying to realise that our old workhorse variety does not succeed everywhere every year and that there are vineyard sites that in some years are just too cool for shiraz.

In the Yarra Valley, the same observation applies equally well, though here the vineyard sites seem definitely more varied than Geelong. Soil type and exposure to sunlight are as critical for shiraz as for cabernet sauvignon in this region.

The Yarra flavours of shiraz are usually those of berry and green leaf rather than the more concentrated black pepper and occasional eucalypt of central Victoria, though black-pepper characters are sometimes seen. Notable producers are Seville Estate, Yarra Yering (whose Dry Red No. 2 has a predominant proportion of shiraz, blended with other Rhône varieties), Bianchet and St Hubert's.

The Bianchet Shiraz 1986 was particularly pleasant drinking in late 1989, showing berry fruit and chocolatey oak aromas on nose and clean plummy flavours and balanced tannin and acid on finish. (17 pts) To be drunk in 1990-93.

St Hubert's Shiraz 1987 in April 1989 had a fine berry and black-pepper nose, and though 1987 was a cooler vintage than 1986 its palate showed typical crushed-peppercorn character and fine-grained finishing tannin. (17 pts) Drink in 1990–92.

The remaining strongholds of Victorian shiraz are the Goulburn Valley and the North-East—substantially warmer areas where shiraz has been known to ripen to excess, producing a generation ago huge wines so full of extract that they could support spoons standing vertically, or so the story went. Though the wines are certainly not lacking in strength, they are no longer a substitute for a three-course meal and a good cigar, as one critic once described them, but they still accept several years in cellar.

The southern end of the Goulburn Valley is well suited to shiraz, and here there are two makers of national repute, Chateau Tahbilk and Mitchelton.

Tahbilk of course is one of Australia's oldest continuing wineries, reflecting the traditions of Australian red wine making: ripe fruit and firm tannin. Tahbilk shiraz taste more of black pepper than berries and lack the eucalypt nuances of further west. In old age (ten years, plus) they resemble old Hunters, revealing leathery flavours though without the 'tar' of old Hunters. They always need at least five years in cellar, and in cooler years such as 1987 they reveal surprisingly fine fruit, though in warmer years the tannins reassert their authority and the wines, especially the show wines, which are always characterised by a bin number, need a correspondingly longer time in cellar, benefiting from ten years and more in some cases.

Mitchelton is more modern, in both architecture and shiraz style, avoiding the bigger-structured style of Tahbilk, though producing shiraz wines that certainly cellar well. The Mitchelton Shiraz 1987 produced from Nagambie fruit, tasted in June 1989, showed most attractive raspberry fruit on nose and a similar sweet fruit character on palate, made all the more harmonious by excellent vanillan oak. (17.5 pts) Drink in 1990–94.

Other winemakers producing shiraz in this region are Longleat and Walkershire.

The North-East of Victoria is in general extremely warm, and its shiraz wines reflect that warmth, being big, ripe and even slightly jammy on occasions. The best of them such as Brown Brothers at Milawa retain their youthful ripe warm earth flavours and their peppery wood tannins for a decade or more without seeming in the least aged. The Brown Brothers Victorian Shiraz 1986, tasted January 1989, is a typical example. A deep red-purple in hue, showing ripe fruit on nose and a youthful palate of more than ample dimensions, this wine needed at least five years in bottle to soften. (16 pts) Drink no earlier than 1995.

But shiraz in this part of the world is not all ripeness and warmth. Browns have in the past 15 years been responsible for a great deal of pioneering viticulture in the King Valley. During that time the Koombahla vineyard has earned a great deal of respect from winelovers everywhere, not in the least because of its shiraz. The Koombahla Shiraz 1986 is light years away from the bigger Milawa style. This wine, tasted at the same time, was medium red in colour with a distinct aroma of raspberries, showing on palate that same berry flavour and a touch of mint. A lighter elegant wine to be kept a shorter time. (17 pts) Drink in 1990–92.

Like Chateau Tahbilk, Bailey's has also preserved its shiraz traditions. Though the style is much less heroic than a generation ago, it still towers over the mere mortals of other areas. Bailey's Hermitage 1985, tasted in November 1988, was a dense purple-red in colour. Its massive nose was a concentration of crushed black peppercorns, ripeness and big American oak. Its palate was similarly huge and peppery, not only from varietal shiraz but also from tannin and alcohol. It was balanced and at the same time gargantuan, and as a postscript to my notes I wrote 'see again in ten years'. (16 pts) Not all the Bailey shiraz are as big. Tasted in December 1989, the Bailey Estate Shiraz 1987 reflects the cooler nature of the 1987 vintage. Purple-red in hue, this wine was subdued at first on nose, finally revealing attractive black-pepper aromas. On a tight-knit palate it was initially reticent, but after a little time in the glass it did open out showing pleasing pepper and spice flavours and noticeable tannins on finish. Very youthful yet, and in need of five years in cellar. (17 pts)

The shiraz of the Rutherglen–Wahgunyah district incline to extreme ripeness and in big years to overextraction, though in years such as 1987 overripeness becomes simply fullness of flavours. The wines of St Leonards, made at Brown Brothers by Roland Kaval, also include a shiraz. The 1987 St Leonards Shiraz, tasted early in 1989, was a full red-purple in colour with an excellent pepper and spice nose and ripe round palate in which American oak played an important but not a dominant part. This was an extremely elegant wine for the region which would certainly not suffer from three to four years' cellaring. (17 pts) Drink from 1993 onwards.

Other makers of robust Rutherglen shiraz are Buller Morris and Campbell, while All Saints (close to St Leonards) usually makes a lighter style which with bottle age can develop an appealing softness.

Shiraz is of course grown in the Victorian Sunraysia district, and there makes the soft current-drinking style that is found also in the South Australian Riverland and the MIA.

SOUTH AUSTRALIA

Arguably the most serious South Australian shiraz region, though not the most senior, is Coonawarra. Shiraz from this area when it is planted on the famous terra rossa soil, and not overcropped, can be classic, often as fine or finer than all but the best cabernet sauvignon. In flavour it is often difficult in Coonawarra to distinguish between the two, for each when picked in its mid-season has a distinct berry character on both nose and palate. It is only when each is picked late that the differences are easier to identify: pepperiness in shiraz, though never in Coonawarra as marked as in Victoria, and a more intense mulberry quality in cabernet sauvignon. The great disappointment in Coonawarra is that because of its cropping potentialities, which are usually 50 per cent greater than those of cabernet, it is treated as a second-rater, which it most certainly is not, and marketed accordingly. As a lover of Coonawarra shiraz I do not mind this in the slightest, for there have been some great bargains in Coonawarra shiraz, many more than in cabernet, but it does seem a pity to short-change the variety in the interests of cash-flow, when with care and selection some great individual shiraz wines could be made by the larger companies.

Amongst the bargains are Wynn's Coonawarra Hermitage, usually less than half the price of that same maker's cabernets. Such wines from years past have aged magnificently. I need only mention 1955 and 1958, both of which were very much alive in late 1988 and early 1989 respectively. These days the wines are made in a lighter style, for sprinting rather than marathon running, but they are usually of excellent quality and can live up to eight years if cellared well. 1986 may be one such. In October 1989, it was a full red-purple in colour with fresh, almost sappy berry fruit and smoky oak on nose. Its palate was full of those same berry fruit flavours, this time integrated with pleasant minty oak. (17 pts) Drink from 1990 onwards. Should live until 1995.

The 1987 Wynn's Coonawarra Hermitage was a similar style but lighter and more herbaceous as befits that cooler year. Here too was a wine, already very accessible to palate, that could be drunk from 1990 to 1992. (16.5 pts)

The Wynn's Coonawarra Estate Hermitage 1988 is also of top quality. Tasted in March 1990 this was a wine of big red-purple hues, revealing attractive berry and vanillan oak aromas. Palate was beautifully balanced, showing a firm but very harmonious concentration of berry flavours and fine-grained tannin that offered excellent cellaring prospects for three to five years. (17.5 pts) As usual, exceptional value. Drink 1993 onwards.

Of Wynn's associate company, Penfold's, I can only regret that its Coonawarra Bin 128 might now, with the current awareness of shiraz quality, have 'Grange' status if that company had not denigrated the quality of the wine. There were marvellous vintages of Bin 128 in the 1960s, 1965, 1966 and 1968 to name but three. Since then, for the sake, I presume, of necessary cash flow, Bin 128 has gone downhill. Its cause is not yet lost. Its former glory can be restored. All that is needed is a little of the old technique and an assurance to the consumer that here is a wine style that need not be consumed immediately but may be cellared with confidence for three to four years at least. Indeed it is not difficult to see Bin 128 on a par with the rarer shiraz styles of Penfold's such as Magill Shiraz, if not with Grange itself.

Of the other large companies, only Mildara produces a straight regional shiraz, usually of good quality. Its Coonawarra Hermitage 1987 was a light-to medium-weight wine of strawberry overtones on nose, and pepper and spice on palate. A useful wine, good early drinking and full-flavoured. (16 pts) Drink in 1990–91.

Other large companies of Coonawarra such as Lindeman and Katnook prefer to blend their shiraz with cabernet sauvignon; and fine wines they make, the Katnook Riddoch Estate Coonawarra Cabernet–Shiraz 1986 winning a Jimmy Watson Trophy in 1987, while the Lindeman Limestone Ridge Shiraz–Cabernet is a wonderful wine in most years, and Rouge Homme Coonawarra 'Claret' (a blend of predominantly shiraz and some cabernet) is consistent if not exciting drinking.

All of which leaves two small producers of excellent shiraz, Bowen and Brand.

Doug Bowen has consistently made excellent shiraz since his first vintage in 1975. His 1987 Shiraz was, in August 1989, full red-purple in hue with a nose full of ripe berry fragrances. On palate there were strawberry and spice flavours well balanced by good acidity and slightly astringent tannin. (16.5 pts) Drink in 1991–95.

Bill and Jim Brand took over from their father Eric a few years ago. Eric in his turn, like father-in-law Bill Redman, had been a Coonawarra pioneer, creating the first boutique winery in that region and making his debut as a winemaker with the wonderful 1966 vintage, which for me showed the true greatness of Coonawarra shiraz as a cellaring variety. Though ready to drink from the early 1970s, that wine seemed to become more velvety as the years went by, and it was only at the end of that decade that it was, most regrettably, all consumed.

Brand's Laira is still not a large winery, crushing less than 400 tonnes of their own fruit (and no other) each vintage and making two shiraz reds: Shiraz (simpliciter) from shiraz vines planted during the past 20 years, and Original Vineyard Shiraz from the fruit gathered from the veteran vines near Eric's house.

Both 1985 and 1986 Original Vineyard Shiraz were well in the classic cellaring mould, firm fruity well-balanced wines which will wear time as patiently and gracefully as great Coonawarra shiraz should. (Tasted January 1990.) (16.5 pts for each wine)

Little time need be spent on the shiraz of Padthaway, which has not been marketed separately by any company for some years. Nor would Langhorne Creek detain us unduly were it not for Bleasdale, whose shiraz wines are usually released at four years of age when almost, if not quite, ready to drink, soft fruity wines of good body which are very accessible to palate. This fruity softness is, however, much appreciated by the bigger wineries of South Australia, which purchase a great deal of Langhorne Creek shiraz for blending.

McLaren Vale is another story. Though lots of shiraz from this area finds its way into multi-blends, a good deal is still proudly bottled by local makers. One small maker who has consistently impressed me in recent years is John Hugo. His 1987 Shiraz still a very youthful purple-red, when tasted in October 1989, showed rather atypical (for the area) black-pepper aromas and smoky oak on nose, while palate offered an excellent fruit–oak integration and some richness. This was quite an elegant red for the McLaren Vale area, a wine of finesse inspired no doubt by both the coolness of the year and the quality of the making. (17 pts) Drink 1991 onwards.

Medium red-purple in shade, Hugo Shiraz 1988, tasted March 1990, offered deliciously sweet dark cherry aromas on nose and ripe berry fruit, spicy oak and firm tannins in a palate of excellent depth and structure. (17.5 pts) Drink 1992 onwards.

The Ryecroft McLaren Vale Hermitage 1987, tasted in September 1989, was paradoxically riper and firmer with typical berry–plum aromas and chocolate flavours. It was a more tannic style with less immediate appeal in need of three to five more years' cellaring. (16 pts) Drink 1994 onwards.

Norman's is another long-established company, with its present domicile at Clarendon in the hills above McLaren Vale. The Clarendon area is an interesting sub-area of McLaren Vale, distinctly cooler, with a fineness of fruit that sets this area apart, so much so that Norman's prefer the Adelaide Hills appellation for its Fine Hermitage 1987. When tasted in July 1989, this was a wine of a full red-purple colour with most attractive aromas of violets and black pepper. Its palate light and elegant but there was sufficient fruit weight, spicy oak and tannic drip to see harmonious cellar development for two years. (17 pts) Drink 1991 onwards.

Thomas Fern Hill made an excellent shiraz in that very friendly 1988 vintage. Tasted in March 1990, Thomas Fern Hill Shiraz 1988 held deep red-purple hues, offering on nose full ripe berry and pencilly oak aromas. On a full-bodied palate there was a very harmonious marriage of rich berry flavours, vanillan oak and firm but integrated tannins. (18.5 pts) A delightful red to be drunk in 1992–93.

Other makers of McLaren Vale shiraz whose wines are well worth a detailed inspection are, alphabetically, Coriole, Ingoldby, Scarpantoni, and Woodstock.

Though fortified wines are not within the purview of this book, it would be remiss of me not to mention the great shiraz vintage 'ports', released from time to time by the Hardy Wine Co. and its subsidiary, Reynella. They too, like the shiraz dry reds of the area, have been fined down somewhat during the 1980s and now show a certain elegance of fruit and spirit rather than the blackberry bulk of yesteryear.

It is a fair observation to say that shiraz has not been amongst the most keenly sought varieties recently planted in the northern part of the Adelaide Hills (or the Barossa Ranges, if you prefer). This is obviously because the upsurge in new plantings that has occurred in that area in the past

20 years has not coincided with a shiraz popularity phase. Certainly the variety is quite suited to the Eden Valley and surrounds, as was amply demonstrated by a most instructive tasting that I attended in June 1988. This was a vertical tasting of eight Henschke Mount Edelstone reds (100% shiraz) dating back to 1967. As Mount Edelstone and, for that matter, Hill of Grace must be among the most popular reds in this country with a respectable cellaring tradition, my notes are set out below:

Mount Edelstone 1967: mature brick-red in hue, ripe chocolate shiraz nose, also mature. Dark chocolate and roasted nuts flavours on palate, rich, ripe and appealing. Mature. (17.5 pts)

Mount Edelstone 1978: still a bright red in colour though starting to brown about the edges, ripe fruity berry nose with some bottle age showing, soft warm excellently balanced palate. Very pleasant drinking, but will hold for two to three years. (18.5 pts)

Mount Edelstone 1980: very full red colour still with some density, very good for an eight-year-old red. Nose of berries, recalling cabernet sauvignon. Soft entry to palate, which in turn is soft and ready to drink. Great balance but not quite as impressive as the 1978. (17.5 pts) Will last two to three years more.

Mount Edelstone 1982: very youthful full red colour with hints of purple. Aroma of berries on nose, though needs to open up slightly. Palate again is beautifully balanced showing youthful fruit. Lovely red. Needs further time. (18 pts) Drink from 1991.

Mount Edelstone 1984: huge red-purple tones, excellent berry and vanilla nose, palate very elegant with lighter fruit than 1982. Drink, but will hold for two to three years. (17 pts)

Mount Edelstone 1985: full red-purple colour, limpid, clean berry nose, like a lot of the 1985s a little subdued. Palate also slightly closed, berry flavoured with some tannic astringency. (16.5 pts) Needs four to five years. Drink 1994 onwards.

Mount Edelstone 1986: huge purple tones, very clean nose with subdued pepper and berry aromas. Full young palate of similar flavours. Soft, ripe tannins. Quite a mouthful, but lovely balance. (18.5 pts) Drink in 1993–98.

Mount Edelstone 1988 (cask sample): huge purple colour, youthful nose dominated by sweet American oak. Massive ripe palate. Very impressive, but not pointed as it was not a bottled wine.

Another excellent producer of Eden Valley shiraz is of course Tollana. Shortly after the Henschke tasting I had the opportunity to taste Tollana Eden Valley Hermitage 1986. It too underlined the excellence of that year. Full red-purple in hue, black pepper on nose was also evident on palate, as were round soft tannins. Will age well. (17.5 pts) Drink 1991 onwards.

Other producers of shiraz in the Eden Valley region of excellent repute but not tasted recently by me are Grand Cru (of Karl Seppelt) and Holmes at Springton.

The Barossa Valley is teeming with shiraz, but not all of the wine made originates there. That need not worry us as the best of the local shiraz is greatly prized by small local makers and some much larger ones such as Lehmann.

The Peter Lehmann Barossa Valley Shiraz 1984, a very cool Barossa vintage, is possibly atypical, but in March 1988 it did show medium-weight pepper and spice aromas and flavours and was certainly worth cellaring for two to three years. (16 pts) Drink in 1991–93.

Its younger brother of 1986 was in June 1989 riper and more forward, revealing berry and pepper aromas on nose and a spicy palate that would be *à point* in about 1991. (16 pts)

Basedow's is another member of the Peter Lehmann family of wineries that also produce Barossa shiraz wines of good quality, soft, fairly forward styles that do not require overmuch time in cellar.

Another smaller maker of lighter accessible shiraz is Elderton. The Elderton Hermitage 1986 in September 1989 showed delicious raspberry characters both on nose and palate while sweet oak flavours gave an added complexity to a wine which might otherwise have been oversimple. (16 pts) Drink in 1991–92.

The Elderton Command Shiraz 1985 is another fine wine showing how accommodating the Barossa Valley can be to shiraz. When tasted in March 1990 this wine was just entering its maturity phase. Medium to full red, it offered on nose mellowing fragrances of berries and vanillan oak, while palate was long, revealing intense blackberry fruit, spicy oak and firm but not obtrusive tannin. A classic bigger but smooth style. (18.5 pts) Drink 1991 onwards with great pleasure.

A bigger style of shiraz is made by St Hallett off its Old Block, a veteran vineyard which always produces shiraz of size yet softness, deceptively generous wines which have the versatility of being able to be consumed when three years old yet have the staying power to develop well over eight to ten. Old Block 1986 is just such a wine. Tasted late 1989, it was a deep red in hue, still with purple tints. On nose there were rich berry and vanillan oak aromas, while palate was rich and powerful yet soft enough to be drunk within two years. (17.5 pts) Will cellar well. Drink in 1992–98.

There are many other makers of shiraz in the Barossa Valley, both large and small. The bigger makers such as Blass marry their Barossa shiraz components with shiraz from other areas, creating excellent standard blends which vary little from year to year. The Blass Brown Label Hermitage is such a wine. Leo Buring follow a similar approach, as do Saltram and Yalumba.

The giant of the valley, Penfold's manages not only three regional shiraz, Kalimna Bin 28, Magill Estate (from the remaining part of the Magill vineyard in the eastern suburbs of Adelaide) and Kaiser Stuhl Red Ribbon, but also the impeccable cellar blends such as Grange and St Henri. Kalimna is rarely less than good, but Magill Estate has in recent years proved an exciting addition to the Penfold range.

Magill Estate Shiraz 1986, tasted October 1989, offered extremely attractive aromas of black pepper and charred oak on nose with a medium-weight palate of similar flavours. This was a red of great harmony and style, but not a blockbuster. (17.5 pts) Drink in 1992–94.

The ensuing year of this wine, 1987, was equally impressive, showing a distinct black-pepper nose and an open palate of excellent fruit and oak integration. (17.5 pts) Drink in 1993–95.

Kaiser Stuhl Red Ribbon Shiraz 1986 was a classically ripe Barossa shiraz, full red-purple in hue with an explosive nose of berries, pepper and vanillan oak. Palate flavours were full and round, again recalling berries though with chocolate oak textures. (17.5 pts) Drink in 1992–94. (Tasted October 1989.)

There must be great pressure placed upon winemakers from time to time to make earlier-maturing red wines, especially from wine company marketing personnel who see their opposition stealing a march on them in this niche or that, and also from accountants to whom cash-flow is always paramount. To Penfold's credit, the shout of commercial expediency has never echoed around Grange. As Penfold's chief winemaker, John Duval, said in February 1989, 'Penfold's will not change Grange style. It will not become softer or more approachable, though seasons will play a differing role.' At that dinner to celebrate the release of the 1983 Grange, four vintages were tasted: 1977, 1980, 1983 and 1986. My tasting notes follow, but I am also adding my notes on the 1962, a famous old Grange, the 1982, a superb softer Grange (if 'soft' and 'Grange' are not contradictions in terms), and the 1984.

Grange Hermitage 1962 (tasted in December 1989): bottle ullaged to low neck; dense brick-red in hue with brown edges, old ripe berries, camphory oak, bottle age, a hint of mushroom and a slight lift made for a very complex nose. Its palate was beautifully ripe and sweet, very deep and long with cedary wood flavours and a very lingering finish. A veteran now, has probably been ready for five years but has held well. Still worth a gold medal. (18.5 pts)

Grange Hermitage 1977: dense deep red in hue. Very fragrant berries and American oak nose, starting to open out. Palate too showed full berry flavours and peppery wood with slight tannic astringency on finish. (17.5 pts) Not quite ready. Drink 1991 onwards.

Grange Hermitage 1980: full deep red in colour, oak-dominant nose masking a light berry character. Palate also oak dominant at that stage and rather tannic. Needs at least eight to ten years to open out and soften, but is balanced and will mature well—ultimately. (18 pts) Drink in 1998–2005.

Grange Hermitage 1982 (tasted June 1988): deep red in hue, with a lovely open nose of berry fruit and new sweet oak. Very deep and long berry flavours on palate with surprisingly soft tannins. Marvellously harmonious. A very alluring wine. A Venus de Milo—with arms! (19 pts) Should be ready by 1995. Drink 1996 onwards, but be in no hurry.

Grange Hermitage 1983 (tasted February 1989 and October 1989): very dense black-red colour. Deep concentrated nose of mint, berry and spice. Huge undeveloped palate showing sweet minty fruit and firm tannins. (18.4 pts) Drink 1998 onwards.

Grange Hermitage 1984: someone once described Beethoven's Fourth Symphony as being 'a Grecian maiden between two Nordic giants'. There certainly are parallels between Beethoven's Fourth and the 1984 Grange. Though both are unmistakable in style, they are lighter than one would normally anticipate. Between the weight of 1983 and the massive concentration of 1986, the comparative accessibility of 1984 Grange comes as something of a shock. Tasted in May 1990, it was a deep dark red in shade, with some density but not as strongly hued as one expects. Its nose was very slightly subdued, but still managed clean berry fruit and spicy vanillan oak aromas, which would doubtlessly develop as the years go by. On a palate of good weight, length and balance, there were lightly concentrated berry and spice flavours and a firm tannin finish. An excellent Grange, which should be drinkable in three years instead of the usual ten. (17.5 pts) Drink in 1993–98.

Grange Hermitage 1986 (to be released 1992; tasted February 1989): a dense purple-black in hue, almost opaque and hardly a hint of red. Concentrated fruit–oak nose, closed almost clamped shut. Palate also is big, tannic and tight-structured. (17.5 pts) Needs at least 10 years. Drink in the year 2000.

Grange is of course a cellar style (that is, a blend of South Australian shiraz, still mostly from Penfold's Barossa vineyards). Uncharitably, perhaps one might say it is made according to a recipe, but though the ingredients may vary slightly in origin from year to year according to individual vintages, it is made with unwavering skill and certainly justifies the title of Australia's Premier Cru.

Penfold's remaining cellar-style shiraz red of great distinction and cellaring capacity is St Henri Claret. The pity of St Henri is that it has been totally overshadowed by Grange.

St Henri Claret 1966 (tasted December 1989): brick red and browning when nearly 24 years old, fading berry fruit and tannin showing on nose, similar tannin dominant palate. Can still be drunk. (15.5 pts)

St Henri Claret 1983 (tasted June 1988): medium full purple-red tones, well-balanced berry and vanillan oak nose. Nicely integrated berry and oak flavours on palate. Firm tannin finish. (17 pts) Drink in 1991–97.

St Henri Claret 1984 (tasted August 1989): full red hues, hints of purple. Aromas of leaves and berries, very attractive. Berry fruit and spicy oak palate nicely balanced by soft tannin—a very elegant wine. (18 pts) Drink in 1991–96.

The shiraz of the Clare Valley is, in a word, vigorous. Two more appropriate words might be 'ripe' and 'flavoursome'. Quite inappropriate are 'coarse' and 'flabby'. 1988 turned out to be a particularly fine year for Clare shiraz, highlighting, as it did, the typical black-pepper characters of the variety. Two fine examples were made by the Jesuit Brothers at Sevenhill and former Stanley winemaker Tim Adams, now practising on his own account.

Sevenhill Shiraz 1988, tasted in October 1989, was deep red purple in hue with a slightly subdued nose at first, later opening to reveal attractive aromas of crushed black peppercorns and vanillan oak, while palate reflects nose, showing intense pepper flavours and firm tannin. (17.5 pts) Drink in 1994–98.

Tim Adams Clare Valley Shiraz 1988, tasted in October 1989, was huge purple-red in shade with aromas of freshly ground pepper and spicy oak. Palate was of large dimensions with intense black pepper once again dominating flavours, firm but balanced tannin. (17 pts) Drink in 1995–2000.

Clare shiraz, though perhaps not the flavour of the 1980s decade, has inspired some excellent boutique winemaking in recent years. Jane Mitchell in the Clare Valley proper (both for herself and for Skillogalee), Tony Brady at Wendouree, Neil Pike, and that other Neil, Paulett, at Polish Hill River to the east of Clare all employ Clare shiraz to its maximum beneficial effect, while bigger makers such as Leasingham and Taylor's also make good shiraz at very fair prices.

1988 was a magnificent year for Clare and for Clare shiraz in particular. Arguably the best shiraz from Clare in that most generous of vintages was the 'Armagh' of Jim Barry Wines, a single-vineyard wine named after its vineyard. Dark red-purple in hue, Armagh 1988, tasted in May 1990, offered a deep nose of great complexity in which black pepper, ripe berries and spicy, minty oak were most compelling components. On palate the wine was rich and long, showing a marvellous balance of berry–pepper fruit, excellent oak integration and firm but not extractive tannin. (18.5 pts) 'Armagh' is the flagship of the Barry line, expensive but of effortless quality. Drink in 1995–2000.

WESTERN AUSTRALIA

In all its various styles, shiraz is also very much at home in the West from the warm-area, ready-drinking, sweet fruit styles of the Swan Valley to ultra-cool, peppery wines of Mount Barker–Frankland River, which rival the best wines of south-eastern Australia in their intensity.

The Swan Valley is undeniably hot, generating temperatures in most years that do not favour the steady ripening of any variety, including shiraz. Its shiraz are accordingly forward. The Evans & Tate Gnangara Shiraz has been a great commercial success as a ready-drinking style but is not recommended for cellaring for any length of time.

On the coast north of Perth, Paul Conti at Wanneroo makes Mariginiup Hermitage, a ripe berry and vanillan oak style, which makes attractive drinking after one or two years in bottle. The Mariginiup 1987 is a typical example of this reliable style. (16 pts) Drink in 1990–91.

The same tuart sand country that nurtures Paul Conti's vines at Wanneroo also supports shiraz at Leschenault near Bunbury and a similar early-drinking style is produced.

Nearby Capel is home to Peter and Diana Pratten's Capel Vale estate, where the vineyard soil is a deep loam. The Capel Vale Western Australian Shiraz 1987, tasted August 1989, was full red-purple in colour with a nose showing light black-pepper characters and a clean fruity palate with excellent tannin and acid balance. (17 pts) Drink 1992 onwards.

Shiraz is also made on the south-west coastal plain at Peel Estate near Baldivis.

It can be said with total justification that the Margaret River region finds much more time for cabernet sauvignon than for shiraz. Leeuwin Estate even grafted over its shiraz in the early 1980s to sauvignon blanc. There are, however, enough surviving vines and indeed prospering wines in the region to pass a favourable verdict on Margaret River shiraz.

The leading maker in the district is the redoubtable Cape Mentelle, whose 'Hermitage' (the Hunter term shows no sign of going out of fashion) is a blend of just over 80% Margaret River shiraz and the rest Donnybrook grenache, added for complexity and softness. The resultant 1987 vintage was medium-full red in colour with a most pleasing nose of plums, berries and smoky oak. Its palate was also attractively ripe but full-flavoured and well balanced enough to ensure a good cellaring life. (17 pts) Drink in 1992–96. (Tasted August 1989.)

Erland Happ also makes a very enjoyable shiraz. His 1986 vintage showed a full dense purple-red hue, when tasted in August 1989. Its slightly subdued nose was peppery in aroma, a characteristic that persisted on a well-balanced palate made more complex by smoky oak. A fairly soft forward style to be drunk in the early 1990s. (16 pts)

Sandalford is the second largest winery in Western Australia, and it too is firmly esconsed in Margaret River with the largest single vineyard in the region, 140 hectares. Though lack of water and wind exposure are sometimes problems in that vineyard, Sandalford made a very successful Margaret River Shiraz in 1987, characteristically deep red in colour with attractive black-pepper aromas on nose, and a most enjoyable medium to full palate with abundant berry and pepper flavours. (17.5 pts) Drink in 1992–97. (Tasted August 1989.)

If the inhabitants of Margaret River merely tolerate shiraz, those of Mount Barker-Frankland River show no such reluctance, for shiraz in that area has exhibited all the classic qualities that make this region as favourable a site as the central highlands of Victoria.

The area is undoubtedly cool, so cool in fact that in cold years late-ripening varieties such as cabernet sauvignon may find difficulty in achieving

Pinot Noir grapes on the vine, Doonkuna Estate, Canberra.

Cabernet sauvignon grapes on the vine, Camden Estate, New South Wales.

Chardonnay leaves, Leeuwin Estate, Margaret River, Western Australia.

Merlot vine, Wyndham Estate, Lower Hunter, New South Wales.

full maturity, but then this is a hurdle always faced by winegrowers in such areas. Winter and spring rain is usually quite generous, but irrigation needed from spring onwards presents serious problems because of a high water table and salinity. So highly prized is sweet water that new plantings such as those of Goundrey at its Langton Estate have totally self-contained irrigation systems which are self-cleansing, so that the water may be used again.

Goundrey indeed is a good place to commence this review of regional shiraz. The Goundrey Windy Hill Shiraz 1988, tasted August 1989, was profoundly purple in hue. Its bouquet was intense and redolent of crushed black peppercorns, though excellent ripening conditions had added a nuance of berry. On a perfectly balanced palate, flavours were full, round and chocolatey with soft but persistent tannin and acid adding the backbone needed for good cellaring life. A shiraz of great intensity. (18.5 pts) Drink in 1995–2000.

The shiraz off the Chatsfield vineyard of Ken and Joyce Lynch is also made at Langton. The Chatsfield Shiraz 1988, tasted at the same time, was very similar to the Windy Hill, deep in its red-purple tones with a ripe nose of berries and peppercorns and a soft almost velvety palate of great depth. This was a wine of very great potential. (18.5 pts) Drink in 1995–2000.

Vintage 1987, cooler than its ensuing year, produced correspondingly lighter shiraz, but they were still a great success. The Plantagenet Shiraz 1987, tasted July 1989, showed more typical black pepper on nose without the ripe berries of 1988. Palate flavours, again of black pepper, were long, full and very satisfying. (18 pts) Drink in 1994–98.

Another 1987 of excellent quality, though this time from the more westerly region of Frankland River, is Alkoomi Shiraz. This wine, tasted in August 1989, was full red-purple in shade with the typical black-pepper aromas of the region. Its palate is full with soft fruit on middle palate and a good balance of tannin and acid on finish. It is a wine that offers good medium-term cellaring prospects. (16.5 pts) Drink in 1992–94.

Elsewhere in Australia, shiraz has received a charisma bypass. The Tasmanians by and large feel that chardonnay, pinot noir and cabernet sauvignon are much more exciting, and who can blame them, though the leafy cabernet sauvignons of the Apple Isle rarely hold out much hope of satisfactory maturity.

Perhaps Stanthorpe in Queensland's Granite Belt offers greatest promise as Australia's next new shiraz area and not only because of its 'nouveau' styles. Serious shiraz from that area have deep colour and great volumes of fruit on nose and palate, but such wines will be from the 1990s.

Other areas of promise for shiraz will be the Hilltops region of the South-West Slopes of New South Wales, and there may be more in Western Australia.

But more important for shiraz is the newfound respect in which it is held by winemakers throughout Australia. Australia's 'native' variety has thrown off its wearisome workhorse image and with each ensuing year of winemaking skill looks more like a racehorse. And so it should!

MEDIUM AND FULL-BODIED, FIRM FINISH

CABERNET SAUVIGNON

Like chardonnay, cabernet sauvignon has so universally proved its merit that it threatens 'native' varieties around the world. In the political terms of a generation ago, it has become a viticultural imperialist, completely dominating the interest of consumers wherever it is grown. It is the archetypal varietal wine.

There seems little doubt that its home is the Bordeaux region, though there is little mention of grape varieties there until the sixteenth century, when 'la Bidure' receives literary attention for the first time. Though this may be the same vine as 'la Vidure', is it the vine mentioned by the Roman agricultural writers as 'Biturica', the vine of the Bituriges, the inhabitants of Burdigala (present-day Bordeaux), or is it simply (and more prosaically) an elision of the words *vigne dure* (hard vine)?

Either way, from the beginning of the eighteenth century it was mentioned with increasing interest in viticultural despatches and by the early nineteenth century had begun to be recognised as a major contributor to the premium wines of the Medoc and Graves. About the same time it perhaps commenced its international career, being exported to Australia in the Busby Collection in 1832. It may have done this even earlier, who knows, for seeds of the 'claret grape' arrived with Governor Phillip in the provisions of the First Fleet. There is no doubt, however, that by the middle of that century it had found its overseas feet with substantial plantings taking place not only in Australia but also in California.

Since then it has found its way to all winegrowing countries of the world with the exception of the coolest and the most northerly. In all of them it makes at the very least a sound wine. In a select few, it is capable of exciting the senses of wine lovers anywhere. California, where 'varietal' trends commenced, Italy, Spain, certainly Australia, and perhaps even New Zealand, South Africa and Chile each have their winemaking regions where cabernet sauvignon is a showcase variety. In France, where in content it accounts for more than 50 per cent of the matchless wines of the Medoc and Graves, there are about 23 000 hectares, and it has found its way to the South especially Provence, where quite legally it 'improves' the local wines.

Though it is grown in the north-east of Italy, it is not as widely encountered there as its cousin, cabernet franc. In Tuscany, however, it is playing havoc with the *denominazione* laws. There, as an often-illegal ameliorant to the widespread Italian variety sangiovese, cabernet sauvignon is adding style, body and greater finesse to the wines of the Chianti region, as well as making stunning appearances in more northerly wines such as Sassicaia. In Spain cabernet threatens local varieties in the Penedés where Torres and other makers are producing marvellous cabernet-dominant reds.

In Australia there were 3662 hectares of cabernet sauvignon as at mid-1988, nearly 60 per cent of that area (2113 hectares) being cultivated in South Australia alone. In cabernet production, though not in quality, New South Wales (607 hectares), Victoria (483 hectares) and Western Australia (230 hectares) most definitely bring up the rear.

As a variety, cabernet sauvignon is vigorous in growth (given a reasonable viticultural environment), but fairly low yielding in non-irrigated areas (6–10 tonnes per hectare). Its leaves are five-lobed and quite deeply indented, frequently cut into the veins at the base of the petiolar sinus. Its bunches, deep purple in colour, which ripen late mid-season, tend to be thin and conical, sometimes with one shoulder. In areas where vines are hand-pruned, it is usually cane-pruned, certainly justifying its old French synonym *vidure* (hard vine) in the minds and hands of both pruners and harvesters, though ideal because of its toughness for mechanical harvesting.

In the research stations it has also been the subject of much clonal selection. Notwithstanding the fact that in the early days of the wine boom much cabernet was propagated merely because of its availability, later plantings have been more circumspect, greater attention being paid to more suitable clones.

In the vineyard it usually sets its fruit quite well, perhaps because of its later flowering avoiding the windiest weeks of spring. It is resistant to downy mildew (though not so to the fungal disease oidium) and bunch rot in wetter years. In the disastrously wet vintage of 1971 it was the only red grape in the Hunter Valley that made red wine not rosé. In dry years, however, its yield per tonne is often reduced even more than other varieties because of the thickness of its skins.

Cabernet sauvignon in the winery is also quite versatile, being made into rosé, carbonically fermented light red, the full range of red styles from light and leafy, to heavier skin-contacted 'berry' wines and also into 'port'.

Though in New South Wales it was an important variety in the Hunter Valley in the nineteenth century (Dalwood Cabernet being sold at premium prices in London in 1870), it was eclipsed by economics in the 1930s, being reduced by the 1950s to odd vines in the declining vineyard area of that period until resuscitated by Max Lake at his Folly and McWilliam's at Mount Pleasant in the mid-1960s.

Cabernet sauvignon has always had a more certain home in South

Australia and to a lesser extent in Victoria. In the latter state it was planted extensively by Hubert de Castella at Yering in 1857 and by John Pinney Bear at Chateau Tahbilk the following decade. It did indeed go into extinction in the Yarra Valley in the 1920s, but its history at Tahbilk has been continuous.

SOUTH AUSTRALIA

In South Australia cabernet sauvignon began with Joseph Gilbert at Pewsey Vale in the late 1840s and was quite widely planted in that state for the rest of the century, managing a last hurrah in the 1890s at Clare and in the Penola Fruit Colony (Coonawarra). Though it certainly declined in the first 30 years of this century, there was never any real danger of extinction.

Thus cabernet sauvignon survived in all the leading areas of South Australia until the red wine boom of the 1960s. Since then it has been widely planted in all winegrowing areas of the state. Coonawarra and Padthaway have the largest cabernet vignoble (719 hectares as at mid-year 1986), Coonawarra being, by common consent, the area for cabernet excellence. Rarely does a firm-finish wine that does not contain or consist entirely of Coonawarra cabernet win a major 'full-bodied, firm-finish' trophy—though to prove me wrong, an elegant Hardy blend of Padthaway and McLaren Vale cabernet did win the Jimmy Watson Trophy in 1988.

During the 1970s, however, Coonawarra had a rather rough ride on the rollercoaster of fashion. Firstly the white wine boom gripped Australia, causing (Coonawarra notwithstanding) some consumer neglect of our best red areas. At the same time, red wine fashion switched in favour of warmer-area reds dominated by new oak maturation, leading such wines to dominate the show ring for several years. Though Coonawarra red is quite compatible with such wood, as is quite plainly shown today, it does need longer bottle maturation than 'warmer' styles such as that of Blass.

Then from 1976 onwards there was the 'cassis' fad, a taste reaction which led to cabernet wines almost cordial-like in flavour. Indeed the 'cassis' revolution provoked a great deal of discussion amongst winemakers and judges as to the 'correct' flavour profiles of Australian cabernet. Should they be vegetative, 'green and grassy' like capsicum, ripe like 'berries', or seemingly overripe and tending to jamminess like 'cassis'? Coonawarra seemed well able to produce all three. Since the early 1980s Coonawarra cabernets have been complex indeed, often showing a little of all three characters in the same wine. Nevertheless the quality has been maintained, though hopefully 'blackcurrant jam' wines will not trouble the district again. The cause of this 'cassis' character has never been properly explained. Some critics have blamed mechanical pruning, which leads to uneven flowering and hence to uneven ripening of the fruit, which when picked mechanically presents the winemaker with a mishmash of immature, mature and supermature fruit impossible to separate. Others point out that this characteristic was present even before mechanical pruning and harvesting became common in the district.

Another explanation offered for 'cassis' is the release of a chemical compound called dimethyl sulphide by a yeast then in common use. A subsequent change of yeast has produced wines with little of that character.

In March 1989 I was fortunate enough to taste both the Lindeman's St George Vineyard cabernets and the Mildara Coonawarra cabernets from 1984 to 1986 inclusive and also some older cabernets from each company. My notes follow.

1984:

Mildara Coonawarra: still dark red in hue with some density, this wine has a harmonious nose of capsicum and 'berry' with deft use of subtle oak. Medium-bodied, the wine shows the same flavour characteristics on palate as on nose. It is an elegant style which will improve in bottle for one or two years more. (17 pts)

Lindeman's St George: medium to dark red in colour, with a distinctly 'leafy' nose. On palate, there are slightly unripe 'green stalk' characters and hints of oak, all of which need more time to come together—a very complex palate in which I would like to see more depth of fruit. Drink from now until 1992. (17 pts)

1985:

Mildara Coonawarra: deep red in colour with hints of purple, the wine shows on nose some 'wintergreen' character but otherwise was closed, a feature that I also noted on the palate. In size the palate is full enough, but it seems to lack generosity. It may well be undergoing a development phase, prior to revealing its fruit. It is certainly worth waiting three to five years more. (16.5 pts)

Lindeman's St George: deep and dense in its red-purple robe, this wine also shares the slightly closed nose of the Mildara, though the Nevers oak used in maturation has been very well handled. The nose needs yet to develop fully, but the palate is beautifully formed, showing marvellous harmony in its integration of 'berry' fruit and good wood. This is a classic cabernet, which will benefit greatly from four to seven more years' bottle age. (18 pts)

1986:

If on the whole, 1985 is a 'sleeper' year, 1986 is abundant in its depth of fruit and 'openness'.

Mildara Coonawarra: still carrying considerable depths of purple in its colour, the wine reveals an open and pleasant nose of berries and cassis. There is also good depth of fruit on the long, clean, flavoursome palate, which finishes with a little peppery tannin. A well-crafted wine with good cellaring potential for three to five more years. (18 pts)

Lindeman's St George: its purple-red hue is massive and dense, and the wine has a deep and concentrated berry nose. On a very stylish palate there are both capsicum and berry flavours with a peppery tannin/oak finish. It is a wine of size yet of elegant flavour and balance, which should be kept a further five to seven years. (18.5 pts)

There are two other Lindeman's St Georges that might be encountered from time to time. These are the 1982 and the illustrious 1980. The former is still developing well in bottle, showing a clean and attractive loganberry nose. As for the palate, it is ever so slightly austere, but the clean berry flavours that it does have harmonise beautifully with the clever wood handling. It will develop further in the next two years. (18 pts)

If the 'cassis' invasion produced anything worthwhile, it must certainly have been the St George Cabernet Sauvignon 1980, winner of the Jimmy Watson Trophy in 1981, and nearly nine years old at the time of my tasting in March 1989. Obviously more mature in colour, with browns starting to creep into the rim of the glass, the wine on nose is more restrained though still with marked cassis character. I do not object to this; it was present in the one bottle of Château Palmer 1961 that I have ever tasted, surely a suitable precedent if ever there was one. The remarkable thing about the St George is its palate: fresh, full and deep in fruit, worthy of at least five more years in cellar. (18.5 pts)

Arguably the most successful exponent of cabernet sauvignon style in Coonawarra in the modern era has been Wynn's. Since the creation of its Coonawarra Estate label, in design as fresh today as it was 35 years ago, Wynn's Coonawarra Estate cabernets have always provoked great interest among wine lovers and even the occasional spark of controversy.

The great years have been 1954 (the first, still drinkable though certainly fading in November 1988), 1955, 1959, 1960, 1962, 1970, 1975, 1976 (the Jimmy Watson winner in 1977), 1979, 1982, 1984 and most certainly 1986. As may be seen from this list of years, there have been periods when either Coonawarra or the winemaking has been at fault. There were serious problems with volatility in the 1960s, years such as 1971 when most of Coonawarra succeeded and Wynn's inexplicably did not, but generally Wynn's are justifiably regarded as the saviour of Coonawarra in the latter half of the twentieth century.

The line of Coonawarra Estate Cabernet Sauvignons will undoubtedly continue to provide some of the best such wine in the region. Great Coonawarra years produce great cabernets, and in the great year of 1982 Wynn's had a marvellous idea. Why not commemorate John Riddoch, the founder of the district, by placing his name on the very best cabernet made in that vintage. Thus the John Riddoch Limited Release Cabernet Sauvignon was created, the first of such being the 1982. Still deep red in hue (very youthful for its age), this wine shows a generous, yet complex, blackberry and vanilla nose. The palate is full and soft, and overall the wine is beginning to drink very well indeed. Be in no hurry. The sweet fruit and oak harmony is still evolving, and the wine can easily wait until its tenth birthday and well beyond. (18.5 pts)

So poor was 1983 vintage because of botrytis that no 'John Riddoch' was bottled that year, but 1984 certainly made up for that deficiency. Being a very cool year, the 1984 differs quite markedly from the 1982. Typical cool, capsicum aromas, heightened by a touch of peppery wood, greet the nose, while on a medium-weight palate the wine shows capsicum–berry flavours. About three more years will bring the wine to its peak. (17.5 pts)

In common with many other writers, I hailed the 1985 vintage . . . initially. I now have certain reservations. Even in Coonawarra the cabernets are a little closed on nose and a trifle austere on palate. Will they fill out? The 'John Riddoch' of that year is also a little closed on nose, showing just a touch of oak. On palate there is a reserved mintiness, often seen in cabernet. Though the wine should age quite well, at the time of tasting it lacked a little generosity. (17 pts)

The same certainly cannot be said of the hugely coloured purple-red 1986. On nose there were all the aromas of the ripeness spectrum, a trace of capsicum, a fullness of berries, all highlighted by a touch of cassis. The palate is full, ripe and loaded with sweet cabernet fruit. Importantly, there is also the necessary firmness of fruit and oak tannin and balancing acidity, which will assist a long and successful bottle maturation. (18.5 pts) Drink in 1996–2000. The John Riddoch line (1982–86) was tasted in April 1989.

Wynn's John Riddoch Cabernet Sauvignon 1987 also has the same aristocratic manners as the other members of the family. When tasted in April 1990 it was an intense ruby-purple in the glass, offering on nose profound aromas of berry and cassis fruit and pencilly oak, while palate presented long berry cassis flavours, assertive but harmonious oak and an excellent tannin–acid balance. (18.5 pts) Most definitely a cellaring style to be drunk not before 1994.

Other Coonawarra cabernets include the excellent St Hugo range of Orlando and also Jacaranda Ridge, a superb 1982, released in 1988, which has become the precursor of a line of super-cabernets, much in the same way as Wynn's John Riddoch. Jacaranda Ridge Coonawarra Cabernet Sauvignon 1986 was released in May 1990. At that time it held a maturing medium to full red hue, while on an attractive nose it showed rich aromas of ripe berry fruit and complex vanillan and charred oak. Its palate also offered a wealth of deep berry cassis flavours well integrated with spicy oak. Soft and forward, this is a delightful cabernet which should be drunk between 1991 and 1994. (18 pts)

Besides St George, Lindeman's have Rouge Homme (with Wynn's Coonawarra Estate, the ancestor of all Coonawarra cabernets). Though the quality is usually very good, one cannot escape the feeling that Rouge Homme these days sits on the back burner, firmly set in the mid-market price bracket and perhaps a repository for Coonawarra cabernets, which finish 'a close second' in company tastings. Even so, 'a close second' in that company's scheme of things is usually A1 quality anywhere else.

Katnook, the winemaking arm of the Coonawarra Machinery Company, one of the largest growers in the region, has also made a cabernet name for itself since the early 1980s, producing richly flavoured wine, in vogue when first made but in the latter part of the decade a little old-fashioned in style.

Two Hunter Valley companies, Hungerford Hill* and Rosemount, have vineyard holdings in Coonawarra. Hungerford Hill in particular has produced Coonawarra cabernets of some distinction since 1975. Though made in far-off Pokolbin these wines always showed the classic Coonawarra berry flavour and tannic structure, which ensure a good cellaring life. Particularly good years were 1980 and 1982. In 1983, however, after a takeover battle, the company lost its original Coonawarra vineyards to the Coonawarra Machinery Company, retaining only a five-year grape-supply contract. Hungerford Hill made good use of that intervening period to develop its Abbey vineyard 1 kilometre north of Penola, first crops being vintaged in 1988. Given a few years for its vines to mature, Abbey should be an outstanding cabernet vineyard.

Rosemount too has a young vineyard close to Penola, and only one cabernet has yet been released, but knowing that company's dedication to quality and its skilled winemaking supervised by Philip Shaw, I have no doubt that Rosemount will produce a notable line of Coonawarra cabernet wines in the years to come if the first Kirri Billi Cabernet Sauvignon is any guide. Rosemount Kirri Billi Cabernet Sauvignon 1986 (tasted April 1990) was full red in colour, showing delicate cassis fruit and spicy oak aromas on nose. In flavour its palate reflected the nose, adding a soft round ripeness and a well-integrated tannin–acid balance. (16.5 pts) Drink in 1991–93.

Of the smaller makers, totally resident in Coonawarra, Brand's Laira is one of my favourites. Never subject to the extremes of cabernet fashion, Bill and Jim Brand go on making good cabernets with proved cellaring capacity. They too have suffered winemaking problems such as volatility and mercaptan over the years, but in recent vintages are right back to top form. The 1971 (the first 100% cabernet), 1976 and 1982 have proved excellent vintages. The 1986 may be the best of all, but wait until 1994 at least (1986 was tasted in October 1988 and again in March 1989). (17.5 pts)

Bowen, Haselgrove and Leconfield are other good makers, all with wonderful cabernets from time to time, while Redman, one of the most exciting names of the late 1960s and the early 1970s, proves rather inconsistent these days. Certainly, there are more exciting cabernets in the region today, but I console myself (and my guests) with the occasional magnum of 1972 Redman Cabernet Sauvignon, now quite mature but drinking well and showing no signs of the slippery downhill path.

Other exciting Coonawarra names, such as Petaluma and Hollick, also

---

* Hungerford Hill was purchased by Seppelt in June 1990. Coonawarra fruit will subsequently be vinified at Seppelt's Great Western winery as Seppelt wine.

produce great cabernets, but these wines are more often blended with varieties such as merlot. (They will be reviewed in the chapter on cabernet blends and blenders.)

If tradition has the slightest scintilla of meaning, cabernet sauvignon will remain the premium red variety of Coonawarra, though the increasing popularity of merlot in the district will undoubtedly lead to many more cabernet–merlot blends. Let us hope, however, that some Coonawarra winemakers at least will always regard 100% cabernet sauvignon wine as a winemaking priority, for Coonawarra cabernet sauvignon in good years deserves a place in anyone's list of national treasures.

To the north of Coonawarra is the Padthaway region—for cabernet not quite as meaningful, though of course a predominantly Padthaway cabernet of 1987 vintage won the Jimmy Watson Trophy for Thomas Hardy in 1988. Here the wines are usually lighter with less body, without the staying power of their more southerly brothers. As such they usually need the structural support of bigger wines from warmer areas. Alternatively they may add a degree of elegance to commercial cabernet blends. Their elegant berry fruit character will always be very useful to winemakers.

Besides the Hardy Wine Company, which uses substantial amounts of Padthaway cabernet in its Collection and Bird Series Cabernets (both area blends), companies such as Seppelt and Lindeman find Padthaway cabernet of great worth in regional cabernet blends: Seppelt in its excellent Black Label Cabernet Sauvignon, and Lindeman in its export Bin 45 Cabernet Sauvignon. Lindeman ceased marketing a Padthaway regional cabernet sauvignon in 1989. Another significant producer who finds this region of great importance in its cabernet calculations is Seaview, whose top-selling Seaview Cabernet Sauvignon always contains fruit from this area.

Though it is a hotter region, Langhorne Creek produces cabernets of much the same commercial purpose, avidly sought by winemakers to add a warm suppleness to cellar blends, but rarely seen in their own plumage.

From Dr Alexander Kelly's time (130 years ago), cabernet sauvignon has been a permanent resident of McLaren Vale. It is still an important variety there, producing rich minty berry flavours, sometimes with a touch of 'chocolate', typical of good warm-area fruit. Historically Thomas Hardy has dominated the area, building also a great reputation for McLaren Vale cabernet along the way. Though a straight varietal wine is made in most years, these days substantial cabernet supplies from Padthaway offer more blending options to that company. Seaview, part of the Penfold realm for several years, is also a famous name which still grows cabernet in the region. No longer, however, is Seaview Cabernet Sauvignon exclusively from McLaren Vale. These days it is a much more diverse blend, based as mentioned above, primarily upon Padthaway fruit.

Most of the smaller makers of McLaren Vale include cabernet sauvignon in their vinous repertoire, and though it may seem inappropriate to label Chateau Reynella as such, it is indeed when compared to its giant parent, the Hardy Wine Co. Chateau Reynella sources its local cabernet from vineyards at Reynella close to home. Its Cabernet Sauvignon 1987, tasted in July 1989, was full red in hue, delightfully aromatic on nose with fragrances of mulberries, cassis and nutty oak. A medium-bodied wine it showed a delightful harmony of berry and nutty oak flavours, being fine and supple in the mouth. (17 pts) Drink 1991 onwards.

Other makers in the region make bigger, more youthfully tannic styles. The Norman's Adelaide Hills Cabernet Sauvignon 1987 and the Ryecroft Cabernet of the same year are two such, which given three to four years in cellar will soften those tannins and become quite harmonious. (16.5 pts for each wine) Drink 1993 and after.

Another young wine at the same tasting, which completed an attractive quartet of cabernets, was Ingoldby Cabernet Sauvignon 1987. Full red-purple in hue with a concentrated berry and vanilla nose, this wine showed a similar power and harmony on palate, promising an extremely pleasant cabernet about 1993. (17.5 pts)

Any list of makers of good cabernet in McLaren Vale is deservedly quite long, but should usually include, besides those I have already mentioned, Coolawin, Coriole, Daringa, Marienberg (whose cabernets are released usually with 4-5 years bottle age), Mount Hurtle, Pirramimma, Thomas Fernhill, Wirra Wirra and Woodstock.

The vinous link between McLaren Vale and the Barossa Valley is of course the Mount Lofty Ranges, though for cabernet sauvignon it is a tenuous one. At its southern edge in the hills above McLaren Vale there are some excellent cabernet vineyards, but as the countryside gains in altitude the vineyards high in the ranges to the east of Adelaide are planted predominantly to the earlier-ripening varieties, chardonnay and pinot noir. This area may prove to be just too cold for cabernet.

At the far north of the range, in the hills to the south-east of the Barossa Valley, there is no doubt that cabernet prospers. In the Eden Valley names such as Pewsey Vale and Tollana have proven the excellence of the area, while small estates such as Mountadam are capable of cabernet of the highest quality. The cabernets of this region are indeed complete wines, those from long slow-ripening years showing the 'green leaf' character of their altitude, and those from hotter years reflecting the chocolatey qualities of warmer climes.

One of those warmer years was 1986. The Pewsey Vale Cabernet Sauvignon of that year (tasted in November 1989) was still quite a youthful purple-red in hue. Its nose was typically leafy with a light touch of capsicum adding a pleasant note of complexity. On a well-balanced palate long flavours were dominated by spicy capsicum, enhanced by a suggestion of cassis. This was a ripe wine aging well, which should reach maturity by 1992. (16.5 pts)

The following year (1987), in contrast, showed just how cool the Eden Valley could be. Cyril Henschke Cabernet Sauvignon 1987 was medium red-purple in shade without great density. Its nose showed delightful leafy berry aromas, quite classical, while its palate was medium-bodied, lightly blackberry in flavour with finely interwoven acid and tannin on finish and very stylish oak handling. This was an elegant wine which should be ready for the table about 1993. (17.5 pts) (Tasted November 1989.)

Tollana is fortunate enough to have 60 hectares of vineyard at Woodbury in the Barossa Ranges. Its cabernet sauvignon style is always extremely fine. Recent vintages tasted included the 1984 and the 1986. The Tollana Eden Valley Cabernet Sauvignon Bin TR 222 1984 is splendidly constructed. When tasted in March 1989 it still held purple tints in a full red robe. Dominant mint plus suspicions of cassis and vanillan oak made up a very complex nose. On a medium-weight palate, berry flavours and soft tannin were well integrated. In all, a lovely cabernet style to drink from 1990 onwards. (17.5 pts)

Its younger brother of 1986 showed the typical family heritage. Full red-purple colour, 'berry' and vanillan wood nose, and a long 'berry and spice' palate with more flesh than the 1984. (17.5 pts) Drink 1992 onwards.

Warmer climes certainly do exist on the Barossa Valley floor, though cabernet here is often quite diverse. The spectrum varies from soft wines which can be drinkable fairly early, to bigger 'berry' wines with lots of body that can live for years. Kalimna is an example of the latter style. With the exception of Peter Lehmann, very few straight Barossa cabernets are made by the larger companies. For the true style of the valley, dark coloured and berry-like on nose and palate, one must look to smaller makers.

The Peter Lehmann Barossa Valley Cabernet Sauvignon 1987 held a bright red-purple colour, when tasted in December 1989. On nose there were attractive berry–cassis aromas. Its berry-flavoured palate was quite long and ripe, with soft tannins and acid ensuring a clean finish. A medium-bodied style, it should be drinking at its best in 1991–93. (17 pts)

Smaller makers who also take pride in their Barossa cabernets are Basedow and Rockford, while a much larger maker, Leo Buring, a subsidiary of Lindeman's, also has a 100% Barossa cabernet on its list from time to time, though Barossa/Coonawarra cellar blends are more often seen.

In the Clare region, cabernet vies with shiraz as the district's widest-grown grape variety. Stanley Wine Company showed remarkable varietal foresight when it planted cabernet sauvignon and other quality cultivars such as rhine riesling in the 1950s, ensuring that the company got off to a flying start in the red boom a decade later.

The Clare style, like that of the Barossa, varies from year to year and from maker to maker, but in the main is epitomised for me by the wines of Tim Knappstein and Mitchell, wines of a dense deep red, of minty 'berry' sometimes spicy fragrances, and firm palates of good balance and structure that can live for years. On the whole they are never as soft as those of the Barossa, yet are tighter and more tannic than the cabernets of Coonawarra. Clare is capable of producing massive cabernets with huge closed palates that need years to open up, if they ever do. Yet the best cabernets of the district manage to keep their fruit open to the palate, without ever being light or nondescript. Clare is a classic cabernet area without perhaps the ultimate finesse of Coonawarra.

In the preparation of this book, I was fortunate enough to taste recent cabernets from both makers, the only disappointment being the Mitchell Cabernet Sauvignon 1985, broken in transit.

Tim Knappstein Cabernet Sauvignon 1987: full red-purple in hue, leafy, capsicum and cassis aromas on a very youthful nose. Lovely open berry and green leaf palate with soft tannins, elegantly balanced. (18.5 pts) Drink in 1990-95.

Tim Knappstein Cabernet Sauvignon 1986: full red-purple colour. Big berry and cassis nose. Palate dominated by berry/cassis flavours, but well balanced with fine tannins. A wine to cellar for four to five years. (18 pts) Drink in 1994-97.

Tim Knappstein Cabernet Sauvignon 1985: still a deep red in shade, this wine was rather subdued on nose, though there were slight berry aromas. Palate similarly was rather closed with a firm tannin finish. (16.5 pts) Try again in 1992. May be ready in the mid-1990s.

Tim Knappstein Cabernet Sauvignon 1984: full red in colour still. Berry aromas dominated a slightly subdued nose, while similar flavours were revealed on an austere palate, which was ready to drink. (16.5 pts)

Tim Knappstein Cabernet Sauvignon 1980: a deep red still, though with touches of brown, this one showed a most harmonious berry and vanillan oak nose. Its palate was still big and flavoursome with an excellent balance of fruit and wood and a firm but not aggressive tannic finish. (18 pts) Drinking well in late 1989 and should go on for at least two years thereafter.

Mitchell Cabernet Sauvignon 1987: deep red-purple with some density, this wine offered a subdued mintiness on nose and a youthful fresh palate with warm mint and spice flavours the predominant features. A wine of good balance with well-integrated tannin to be kept in cellar for at least three to four years. (17 pts) Drink in 1993-95.

Mitchell Cabernet Sauvignon 1986: still youthful in hue with reds and purples predominant, this wine showed ripe berry aromas on nose and a full soft minty palate with *sotto voce* tannins. Another wine of good cellar potential. (17 pts) Drink in 1993-96.

Mitchell Cabernet Sauvignon 1984: medium to full red in colour, this was a wine that presented a most attractive leafy, cedary bouquet. Its palate was virtually mature and offered delightfully soft berry and cedar flavours.

A most accessible wine and a marvellous mouthful in late 1989. (18.5 pts) Drink in 1990–92.

Mitchell Cabernet Sauvignon 1983: a wine of an unusual (for its age) deep red hue still hinting at purple, showing an undeveloped rather closed nose and a yet quite young and spicy palate. It certainly needs more time in bottle, three years at least. Would have been huge on release. (16 pts) See again in 1993.

Mitchell Cabernet Sauvignon 1982: medium red and maturing in colour, this cabernet showed most complex aromas of capsicum, cedar and even a hint of mushroom in a mature bouquet. Palate, however, was still fresh, combining ripe berry flavours with spicy wood and soft tannin in a most harmonious way. (18 pts) Drink from 1991 onwards.

Though at the time of writing this book I had not tasted the Tim Knappstein or Mitchell Cabernet Sauvignons of 1988, other 1988 Clare cabernets had come my way by late 1989. Sevenhill Cabernet Sauvignon 1988 is a dense purple-black in hue, with berry, mint and eucalypt aromas all present in a vigorous nose. Its palate also was young and vital with a great depth of minty fruit and peppery tannin which will need at least five years to soften. (17.5 pts) Drink not before 1995.

Pike's Polish Hill River Estate has also succeeded with cabernet in 1988, but even allowing for a 15% addition of cabernet franc and merlot it is a much softer and more forward wine than the traditionally big Sevenhill. In late 1989 it was of full red colour, showing an open berry nose and an accessible medium-weight palate with berry and spicy wood flavours pre-eminent. (16.5 pts) Drink in 1990–94.

Other Clare makers of exciting cabernet sauvignon include Jeffrey Grosset and, in a traditional but no less exciting way, Wendouree. Larger makers of good well-priced cabernets from the region are Taylor's, and Leasingham formerly Stanley, whose Bin 49 Cabernet Sauvignons of the late 1960s and 1970s have been solely responsible for Clare's fame as a cabernet area. Regrettably the Bin 49 of 1988 was rather light and inconsequential.

Other cabernet makers of the region whose cabernets are often of excellent quality are Jud's Hill (Brian Barry) and Jim Barry.

The Riverland regions of South Australia, in common with similar areas of New South Wales and Victoria, produce in general simple fruity cabernets of light to medium body. Such wines are supple, take oak quite well and usually become extremely pleasant drinking within two to three years of vintage. They should not, unless in exceptional cases, be kept beyond that.

The one remaining region of South Australia where cabernet is grown is the Adelaide Plains north of Elizabeth. Its main claim to fame is that it is the home of Roseworthy Agricultural College. The area as a whole is exceptionally warm, and the cabernet wines grown here reflect this. Only in cool years such as 1984 is cabernet of any real distinction.

VICTORIA

In recent years Victoria has assumed a very high wine profile. It has declared with a good deal of conviction to the rest of Australia and indeed to the world that Victorian wines are somehow superior to others. The truth is of course that they are not. Its climates (macro and micro) are as diverse in their effect on the grape as those of the rest of the nation. Perhaps the reason for this surge of enthusiasm or chauvinism, if you are a non-Victorian, is that Victoria was for a long time reduced to so few wine areas that the renaissance of the vine in areas famous in the nineteenth century has caused an overreaction. Certainly the state's cabernets are as varied as those in any other state, whether as a result of climate or of winemaking skill.

It is fashionable these days—and I suppose that one should take due note of fashion, however fickle it may prove to be—to regard the Yarra Valley as the pacesetter for all but the richest of Victorian wine styles. Cabernet of course is no exception. The bouquets and flavours of cabernet sauvignon vary greatly amongst the Yarra Valley's microclimates and soils, though they generally encompass that part of the fruit and vegetative spectrum that commences with 'green leaf' and 'capsicum', goes through ripe 'berry', and finishes with 'cassis'.

Paradoxically its cabernet mentor is Dr John Middleton, who does not produce a straight cabernet sauvignon. Middleton is convinced that cabernet sauvignon requires the other Bordeaux varieties, cabernet franc, merlot and malbec, to supplement its palate. Several other Yarra makers have taken note of his 25 years' experience with the variety, including his former medical partner, Dr Peter McMahon, at Seville Estate. Middleton believes that cabernet should be mouthfilling, and that implies a full middle palate and a finish with a good tannin grip.

Other makers in the area insist that both cabernet sauvignon blends and straight cabernet are perfectly viable alternatives for the region. Oakridge is one such, producing a phenomenally good straight 1986 cabernet sauvignon and also a good blend of cabernet shiraz and merlot, the reason for this being the volcanic soils in the cool and undulating Seville area.

David Fyffe of Yarra Burn also makes excellent cabernet. In August 1988 his 1986 wine was a very dark red with profound depths of purple. On nose there was a fascinating complexity of cassis, berries and leaves, while the palate offered the same gentle but generous berry flavours. It was a ripe wine but, faithful to its cool area of origin, showed slight herbaceousness on finish. It is a wine to be drunk about 1992-93. (17.5 pts) The 1987 is also a wonderful wine. (18 pts)

Another excellent wine cast in that same Yarra mould is Coldstream Hills Lilydale Cabernet Sauvignon Four Vineyards Blend 1987. This wine displayed a deep red-purple robe with a complex nose of capsicum, cassis and beautifully handled wood. On palate there was an intriguing amalgam of sweet berry fruit, soft green capsicum character and spicy wood. Though the wine looked big in glass, it was not so on palate, proving elegant and almost delicate. A fine well-balanced wine, worth three to four years more in cellar. (18 pts) (Tasted late 1988.)

Yarra Valley cabernets are deceptively fruity; some critics even go so far as to affix that unflattering epithet 'light', but not I. Within that outstanding fruit they are extremely complex. Their tannins are soft, hardly ever obtruding. Most well-made wines have the capacity to age well over five to ten years. After that, the finest of them come into their own.

The Yarra cannot be left without mention of that off-shoot one-vineyard area, Wantirna South, where lawyer/winemaker Reg Egan vies in cabernet experience with the Yarra's John Middleton. The cabernets of Wantirna have been the downfall of many a blind taster, myself included.

Like the Yarra, Mornington Pensinula is manifold in its variety of soils and microclimates. Unlike the Yarra, Mornington is as yet minute. Already, however, it has shown an aptitude for cabernet, producing wines of huge colour, which exhibit the usual cool-climate aromatic spectrum of green-leaf capsicum through 'berry' to cassis with impressive fruit weight on palate. There seems no doubt that cabernet will thrive in maritime Mornington.

Geelong too produces cabernets of substantial worth. Bannockburn, Hickinbotham Winemakers and Zambelli are all names that have polished the cabernet image of the district.

Mornington and Geelong are but the centrepieces of that cool-climate coastal arc of Victoria. The eastern end, Gippsland, cannot yet be said to have proved its cabernet reputation, though winemakers such as Ken Eckersley continue to persevere. The western tip, Drumborg (north of Portland), pioneered and still owned by Seppelt, has shown the cabernet lover several vintages of ultimate quality. Here cabernet fights a climatic battle at the extremities of its season, suffering problems of berry-set in spring because of prevailing gales, and sometimes simply running out of warmth in autumn. But when the spring is still and the autumn is warm, a superb vintage is the result. Not every autumn is so kind.

The northern edge of the Great Divide is a natural frontier of Victorian viticulture, separating the generally warmer northern, north-western and north-eastern areas of the state from the cool fastnesses of the Victorian Alps, the Central Highlands and its truly temperate and often downright chilly southern regions.

The Bendigo area sits on the north-western edge of the Great Divide and is the centre of a pot-pourri of microclimates that produced famous red wines during the 1880s. It regained its fame during the 1970s for the same reason and that because of one vineyard, Balgownie, the creation of Stuart Anderson, an unashamed Bordeaux enthusiast. From 1973 onwards, Anderson has made classically structured, long-lived cabernets

Verdelho vines, Willespie Wines (foreground) and rhine riesling vines, Sandalford Margaret River Estate (background), Margaret River, Western Australia.

ABOVE: *Netting is draped over the chardonnay vines to protect the grapes from the birds at Happ's, Margaret River, Western Australia.*

BELOW: *Traminer bud burst, Lindeman Padthaway, South Australia.*

which develop well for a decade or more in bottle. Though he sold Balgownie to Mildara Wines in 1984, the wine styles continue under his tutelage without compromise. These are the wines that have consistently demonstrated his prowess as a winemaker. Put simply, the Balgownie cabernets are complex, evolving wines, at their best exhibiting the depth and style of vintages such as 1975 and 1980. Not all of them go on to such heights, but all are worth cellaring. As for more recent vintages, though 1986 was full-bodied and concentrated, 1987 will be one of the 'cool-area' Bendigo cabernets that Anderson has made. It is a harmonious wine of 'leafy', minty aromatics, with a palate characterised by clean 'berry' flavours, which precede a firm tannic finish and is certainly a wine to be kept in cellar for at least five years. (17.5 pts) (Tasted June 1989.)

Other noteworthy cabernet makers on the warmer westerly side of the Bendigo are Blanche Barkly and Passing Clouds; to its east, Chateau Le Amon also has an excellent reputation.

To the south-east of the city in that arc between Heathcote and Castlemaine are generally cooler climes. Here is shiraz country *par excellence*, though Heathcote Winery and Mount Ida make cabernets of more than passing interest.

Though generalisations are dangerous, Bendigo cabernets are on the whole deep in colour, displaying bouquets of peppermint and sometimes eucalyptus. Their palates, which tend to 'berry' flavours, have great depth and usually excellent texture and develop extremely well over a five- to ten-year term.

The cabernets of Macedon have some similarities to those of Bendigo. What they lack in size they make up for in 'minty' elegance, though at times Macedon cabernet may not ripen fully because the area is largely too cool for the variety. As a consequence the district's shiraz reds seem to overshadow the cabernets.

To the north-east of Macedon is the Goulburn Valley, where Chateau Tahbilk, long a solitary outpost of Victorian cabernet and the showplace of the region, still makes its traditional styles. There are usually two: a 'commercial' release of fairly recent vintage, three or four years old, and a 'show' wine, more expensive and distinguished by a bin number, often six or more years of age. The 'commercial' wines are uniformly well-balanced reds showing some mint characters on nose and palate, but fairly simple and 'unshowy' by modern-day cabernet standards. They accept bottle age gracefully and are usually at their best six to ten years after vintage. The 'show' wines, however, are a race apart. Inevitably the wines are very full in colour even on release at six or more years of age, with rather deep, even unexplored bouquets, sometimes hinting at old wood or leather ('cassis' and 'capsicum' noses are rarely found in Tahbilk style). They are invariably full-bodied and tannic on palate but harmonious within that immensity. Needless to say they are built for the long haul, and they do in fact improve markedly with extended bottle age (10–15 years), which brings together the massive fruit, the tannin 'elbows' and the slight sulphide characters sometimes present. If any vineyard has created and mastered its own cabernet genre, it is Chateau Tahbilk.

Another showplace, though of a more modern architectural style, is Mitchelton, discernible for kilometres by its tower, for all the world like a witch's hat. Cabernet is sourced both from Mitchelton's own substantial vineyard and from local growers. As well the company sometimes casts its cabernet net as far afield as Coonawarra and even Mount Barker. Both local wines and inter-regional blends are produced. A local cabernet of excellent standard is produced each year of a finer, more elegant style than other makers in the area. The 1986 Mitchelton is a typical example. (16.5 pts)

The third important cabernet 'name' lies high above the Goulburn Valley in the Strathbogie Ranges. The view from the 500-metre-high Mount Helen vineyard of Tisdall is spectacular, and so were the first straight cabernets made in 1979 and 1980 by then-winemaker John Ellis. The last straight Mount Helen cabernet sauvignon was made in 1983, a year of fire and drought throughout Victoria. Since 1985, during Jeff Clarke's time as winemaker, cabernet–merlot blends have been produced, which are reviewed in the chapter on cabernet blends. 1984 was the last cabernet sauvignon so called (it contained 20% merlot), and when tasted in March 1989 was a harmonious wine with an excellent balance of 'berry' fruit and wood on nose. The softening palate showed medium-bodied fruitiness and well-integrated soft tannins. (17.5 pts) Though it will certainly last longer, it should be at its peak in 1991.

The North-East of Victoria is undoubtedly one of the warmest wine regions of the state and arguably worst equipped to produce cabernets of the finely grained texture that are acclaimed today. Wines of strength and longevity? Yes! Wines of delicacy and finesse? No! Well, in that *Pinaforean* phrase, hardly ever! At least not before vineyards began to take over the King Valley from that dreadful weed, tobacco. With one exception, the vineyards of Rutherglen and Wahgunyah should be left to their sublime muscats and tokays. That exception is Brown Brothers St Leonard's Vineyard, set on the bank of the Murray River and as hot as any other vineyard in the district. Yet for their area, these are surprisingly delicate cabernets, of medium body and good fruit, which cellar staggeringly well.

All the St Leonard's wines are made at Brown's Milawa winery. The Brown family, now in their third generation and second century of active involvement with Milawa wine, pioneered this region and since its foundation, cabernet sauvignon has usually figured in their plans.

The cabernets of Milawa origin are, when young, deceptively rich in body. They are never unbalanced or extractive, and they accept cellaring well. In 1989 the Brown Brothers Family Reserve Cabernet Sauvignon 1976 was beautifully mature. (17 pts)

For the cabernet enthusiast who is attuned to current developments in the variety, the winds of change have long been blowing in the North-East uplands. The cabernets of the King Valley are even more exciting than those of Milawa. Here Browns have once more been pioneers, encouraging and counselling the planting of vineyards. As a consequence, new names like Koombahla and Meadow Creek have in the past decade sprung to the fore as quality cabernet areas. These wines have body and depth and all the elegant attributes of more southerly climes—and well they might, for what they lose in latitude they acquire in altitude. Though at present no cabernet sauvignon is planted there, Whitlands, high above the King Valley, is the latest pioneering venture of Brown Brothers. It is undoubtedly the most significant viticultural development in north-east Victoria this century.

As I have mentioned, away from Milawa and the King Valley, the other cabernets of the region have often been too thick, viscous and alcoholic, assuming the vast dimensions of wines which should perhaps be fortified or left to spend 25 years in cellar.

Though they are so dissimilar to their French counterparts, the curiously named Victorian Pyrenees also overlook vineyards. In this case, the twin regions of Avoca–Moonambel. Cabernets here, as elsewhere in the warmer areas of central and western Victoria, are distinguished by mint/eucalypt flavours on palate and sometimes by a superabundance of tannin, which often leads to imbalance. Cool years such as 1984 seem not to produce such aggressive tannins, leading to increased fruit on palate and a better-balanced wine.

Dominique Portet made his first Taltarni cabernet in 1977. Huge wines followed until the early 1980s, but with 1982 came a slightly softer tannic imprint, as Dominique came to terms with the Moonambel *climat*. Indeed the winemaking careers of Portet and Cape Mentelle's David Hohnen have run closely parallel since the mid-1970s, when both worked together at Taltarni. Each seems much influenced by the other. Each holds cabernet in high regard. Each has Californian experience and believes in the importance of tannin and new oak. Each seems now to be appreciating the equally great importance of fruit and balance. Nonetheless, each still makes cabernets for the long haul. In early 1989 the Taltarni Cabernet Sauvignon 1986 was of huge colour, rather closed on nose and palate but with a suspicion of regional mint/eucalypt and a firm tannin finish. Given time and patience the wine will reward the taster. (17.5 pts) Drink 1995 onwards.

Dominique Portet makes no bones about disliking 'eucalyptus' in his cabernets and works hard against it, even to the extent of once grafting over a cabernet vineyard with pronounced 'eucalypt' to white grapes which do not reproduce the same trait. Dominique feels that this character is imparted by the soil of vineyards recently cleared of long-established forest and for that reason always declines to plant cabernet sauvignon in such country.

Other makers such as Mount Avoca, Redbank and Warrenmang make cabernets of similar style to Taltarni, showing that same 'eucalypt' character, though Dalwhinnie makes a somewhat lighter and more elegant style.

Though cabernet figured prominently in the marvellous Great Western red blends made by Colin Preece over a generation ago, curiously enough in these cabernet-conscious days, it does not dominate the red vignoble of that area. Make no mistake, it is certainly well represented, but only a few makers of the region such as Seppelt and Mount Langi Ghiran make a speciality of it—and even then Seppelt, although producing exceptional cabernet wines, do not for some reason bottle a Great Western cabernet every vintage. Perhaps corporate wisdom feels that quality in some years and quantity in others does not justify it.

Whatever the reason, exceptional Great Western years are worth waiting for. In March 1989 I tasted both 1980 and 1984 Great Western Cabernet Sauvignon. Though it had long since disappeared from retail shelves, 1980 is reviewed for interest and as an indicator of cabernet development potential in that area: medium dark red and beginning to brown, though still with some density, the wine showed a complex bouquet of berry–cassis aromatics and harmonious bottle age. The medium-weight palate was quite soft on entry with well-integrated berry fruit and smoky wood flavours. The wine was quite ready to drink at that stage, though no haste was necessary. (18 pts)

At the same time, its younger brother, Great Western Cabernet Sauvignon 1984, was about to be released. This wine was a dense full-red in colour with no sign of aging brown. Its bouquet was extremely impressive, combining green leaf and berry aromas with elegant vanilla oak, while a medium-bodied palate was highlighted by a lively integration of capsicum, berry and spicy wood flavours in well-balanced harmony. A cool year, 1984 displays Great Western cabernet style to perfection, medium-bodied, fruity without excessive extraction, yet with two or three years' cellaring potential ahead of it even though released at five years of age. (17.5 pts)

TASMANIA

I have mentioned the kindness that autumn in cool areas sometimes extends to cabernet. In Tasmania, cabernet perforce relies on such acts of grace. There, aspect and shelter are critical in spring, and soft warm 'Indian summers' essential in autumn. Even when comparative ripeness is achieved, the variety retains a leafy green character which often recalls the cabernet wines of the Loire, another cabernet frontier. So only when the mainland of Australia suffers excessive heat does Tasmania experience optimum ripening conditions, and cool years on the mainland are usually disastrous on the Apple Isle.

WESTERN AUSTRALIA

Providing there is moderate protection and an absence of salt-bearing winds, a maritime environment seems to be highly beneficial to cabernet sauvignon. I suppose I need only quote the Medoc vineyards as an example, but there are others such as Hawkes Bay in New Zealand which are also famous for cabernet and our own Mornington region. Our maritime region that is most experienced in the variety is Margaret River, where virtually all the vineyards are within 15 kilometres of the Indian Ocean.

The region's main disadvantage is that it has practically no winter. This of course means that new buds often burst in July, leading to an extended berry-set period. Thus these tender shoots are exposed for much longer than elsewhere in Australia to climatic risks such as salt-bearing winds, heavy rains and frosts. Cabernet sauvignon is well able to cope.

The area's cabernet types vary from maker to maker—'capsicum' from vines with profuse foliage, 'berry' from those with less dense canopies, and also 'cassis' from riper styles. Some makers such as David Hohnen at Cape Mentelle use differentiated pickings of cabernet to achieve complexity of nose and palate, starting at ripenesses as low as 11° Baumé and going through to 12.5° Baumé, producing wines which, as David says, may be drunk at five years of age but are bred to last 20. Other makers in Margaret River, as more merlot and cabernet franc become available, blend in small quantities of such varieties to gain greater softness and to fill out 'holes' in the palate of cabernet sauvignon.

Though Cape Mentelle has established its reputation as the region's top cabernet producer virtually beyond doubt (two Jimmy Watson Trophies in 1983 and 1984 have seen to that), there are several other noteworthy makers whose wines are always fascinating to examine in any cabernet context. Approaching Cape Mentelle in firmness, but usually softer and more accessible to the palate, is Moss Wood whose cabernets exemplify the soft but full 'berry' aromas and flavours which can always be achieved in the region. More elegant and supple styles include Vasse Felix and the Redbrook cabernets of Evans & Tate, while those of Leeuwin Estate are also sometimes forward, but due more to extended bottle aging before release than initially light fruit weight. Though Cullen's Willyabrup have not made a straight cabernet since 1982 (all cabernet now being blended with merlot), those made before that year have aged particularly well despite the fact that Di Cullen, as winemaker, feels they were too straightforward in palate. Another local maker whose fine cabernet wines are undeservedly little known outside his native heath is Ian Lewis of Cape Clairault—big-coloured 'berry' wines made with care and skill and meant to last.

Notwithstanding the great cabernet names of Margaret River such as Cape Mentelle, Mosswood and Leeuwin Estate, it would be curmudgeonly of me not to mention the superb Willespie Cabernet Sauvignon of 1987. Tasted in August 1989, it was an imperial purple in hue, showing a most harmonious nose of ripe berries, capsicum and well-handled French oak with ripe berries, soft tannins and vanillan oak highlighting a most attractive palate. This was a wine of marvellous balance which should age exceptionally well. (18.5 pts) Drink in 1995–2000.

At that same tasting of Western Australian cabernets in late August 1989, I caught up with several other excellent Margaret Rivers of 1987, including Moss Wood, Evans & Tate, Cape Clairault and Cape Mentelle, which also showed its 1984 Jimmy Watson Trophy winner, the 1983 Cabernet Sauvignon.

Moss Wood Cabernet Sauvignon 1987: full red-purple in hue, rather subdued berry nose, well-balanced softly accessible berry palate. (17.5 pts) Will mature well. Drink in 1992–97.

Evans & Tate Margaret River Cabernet Sauvignon 1987: deep purple-red in shade with a very pleasing nose of berries and vanilla, this wine showed sweet berry fruit and excellent balance on palate, but is inclined to be forward. (17 pts) Drink in 1991–94.

Cape Clairault Cabernet Sauvignon 1987: medium full red-purple colour, typically harmonious nose of berries and vanillan oak, lovely palate of similar flavours, beautifully balanced. (17.5 pts) Will age extremely well. Drink 1994 onwards.

Cape Mentelle Cabernet Sauvignon 1987: a big purple-red in tone, with a subdued nose showing just a hint of berry fruit, this wine was also a little closed on palate, which nevertheless was big and firm. (17 pts) Needs at least three to five years to open out.

Cape Mentelle Cabernet Sauvignon 1983: still a full dense red in colour with a berry nose beginning to unfold, this wine also had a big firm palate with good balance of tannin and acid. A tightly structured cabernet needing another three to five years at least. (18 pts)

As this book was about to go to print, the first of the Margaret River cabernets of 1988 was released. The Evans & Tate Margaret River Cabernet Sauvignon 1988 was full red-purple in shade, showing a ripe nose of berries and cassis, rich but not overdone. On palate there were full berry flavours with rather sappy tannins in good balance. A bigger style than usual from this maker, which should be cellared for three to four years. (18 pts) Drink 1994 onwards.

Cabernet also flourishes in what is still officially called the Lower Great Southern Region, but which its winemakers prefer to call Mount Barker–Frankland River. Its chief town is coastal Albany, cool, wet and verdant green in winter. Though there are vineyards within a few kilometres of the town and indeed a winery (Galafrey) at its centre, the chief viticultural outposts are Mount Barker, Denmark and Frankland River. In the Frankland River area, Alkoomi established a distinguished reputation for cabernet as long ago as the late 1970s. Classically structured, these wines require a mandatory ten years in cellar. Even then they are only just reaching maturity.

Much closer to Mount Barker is the Forest Hill vineyard, the pioneer vines of the region. Its wines, together with those of Plantagenet and Howard Park, were made until recently at the Plantagenet winery in Mount Barker by winemaker John Wade, a master of cabernet, whose skill and craftsmanship can be no better illustrated than by the Wynn cabernets made at Coonawarra during the early 1980s. 'Howard Park' is the winemaker's own premium label, a cabernet (and a rhine riesling) made in very small quantities from local fruit of surpassing quality. The Plantagenet cabernets are 'leafy' wines of medium weight, berry/cassis in flavour and some elegance. Future vintages of Forest Hill cabernet will be made at Vasse Felix in Margaret River.

Mention must also be made of the excellent Goundrey wines made at Denmark by Mike Goundrey until 1987, then by Rodney Hooper in 1988 and 1989, and also of the impressive new Langton winery built by Goundrey much closer to Mount Barker and intended to crush 500 tonnes by the early 1990s. The largest grower in this area (indeed the largest grower in the whole state) is Houghton, whose Netley Brook vineyard is also amongst the oldest. The Houghton Frankland River cabernets are medium-bodied with that capsicum–berry flavour profile common to the district and usually age well over the medium term (three to five years). New vineyard developments throughout this region will ensure that Mount Barker–Frankland River cabernets will have a much greater national impact by the year 2000.

I tasted several fine cabernets from both Mount Barker and Frankland River in late August 1989. My notes follow.

Goundrey Mount Barker Cabernet Sauvignon 1985: full red in colour with aromas of berries and charred oak, this wine was just starting to mature, showing clean sweet fruit on mid-palate and a very good acid and tannin balance on finish. (17.5 pts) Will age well for two to three years yet.

Alkoomi Frankland Cabernet Sauvignon 1987: full red-purple colour with a typical capsicum and berry nose, this one is firm on palate but promises well for the future. (17 pts) Drink 1995 onwards.

Howard Park Cabernet Sauvignon 1987: a deep purple-red in colour, this young cabernet needed at least four to five more years in bottle at time of tasting, though its berry and vanillan oak nose was certainly most alluring. Its palate showed restrained berry fruit and excellent balance, but more cellaring time was certainly needed. (17.5 pts) Try after 1995.

Howard Park Cabernet Sauvignon 1986: a sumptuous wine, this one offered harmonious ripe berry fragrances on nose and full berry flavours on a ripe and weighty palate. Excellent balance. (18 pts) Drink not before 1993.

Houghton Frankland River Cabernet Sauvignon 1987: full red-purple in colour with a light berry nose and a soft medium-weight berry-flavoured palate.

(16.5 pts) Forward style. Drink in 1991–93.
Houghton Frankland River Cabernet Sauvignon 1986: similar comments to those for 1987, except that the palate is riper and a little more forward. (16.5 pts) Drink in 1990–92.
Plantagenet Mount Barker Cabernet Sauvignon 1987: medium to full red-purple in hue, berry-dominant nose, medium to full palate weight, berry flavoured, well balanced. (17 pts) Drink 1994 onwards.

Castle Rock Estate also produces well-structured cabernets from its Porongurups vineyard east of Mount Barker. 1986 and 1987 are both good wines which will benefit from three to four years in cellar. 1987 in particular has lovely berry fruit on nose and palate, good balance and well-integrated tannins. (17.5 pts) Drink 1994 onwards.

Elsewhere in Western Australia the cabernet vista is not so exciting. The variety is grown on the tuart sands of the south-west coastal plain; this country, like sandy soils anywhere, produces light, forward, flavoursome cabernets of low tannin, one-dimensional wines without much depth of palate. The wiser makers of this long drawn region stretching from north of Perth as far south as Busselton find it necessary to add complexity to the supple local cabernets by adding cabernet from other districts such as Margaret River.

Undeniably hot, the Swan Valley and its northern extension, Moondah Brook near Gin Gin, produce cabernet reds of softer, sweeter, simpler style, which do improve in the short term (one to three years). The variety here also makes some of Australia's best rosés.

NEW SOUTH WALES

Though it is the ancestral home of Australian cabernet, New South Wales faces stiff competition from more southerly states in its efforts to maintain its status as a leading cabernet producer. With few exceptions the cabernets of the Hunter Valley are solid rather than spectacular, depending more on the nuances of wood than exceptional fruit for style and intricacy. Only in great years such as 1986 and 1987 does the variety shine, though in damp vintages (and these frequently occur in the Hunter Valley) it does have the capacity to resist the elements rather better than shiraz.

Max Lake (together with McWilliam's) was the pioneer of the cabernet renaissance in the Hunter Valley. I remember well Lake's Folly Cabernet 1967 more than once being mistaken for a good-year Bordeaux at blind tastings. Subsequent years did not show up quite as well, with worrying hints of mercaptan sometimes present on nose, while on palate oak sometimes outweighed fruit. With age the effect is more often old Hunter rather than old cabernet, though in early 1990, the Folly Cabernet 1987 was an impressive wine.

McWilliam's, that other precursor of Hunter cabernet, have similarly experienced the vicissitudes of this intriguing variety over the years. The first vintage, 1966, was magnificent, though minute in quantity (it was never commercially released). It still marches on, in marvellous condition as recently as September 1988. The vintages of the mid-1980s under the control of winemaker Phil Ryan have been of excellent quality. In March 1989 I was fortunate to taste six vintages up to and including 1988, the latest of which, because of McWilliam's admirable policy of releasing reds with a degree of bottle age, will be available in the early 1990s.

Mount Pleasant Cabernet Sauvignon 1983 (released in 1987) was a brown-edged red in hue, just about mature. Its nose showed the regional traits of 'berry' and 'tar', while the palate was soft, ripe and ready to drink. It is a style, however, that should maintain its flavour platform for several years without any sudden 'dives'. (16.5 pts)

As for 1984, what this wine lacks in ripeness on palate, compared to its immediate predecessor, it makes up in its complex leafy capsicum nose and its light and immediately accessible palate. (17 pts)

1985 was the first of a trio of good Hunter years. The Mount Pleasant Cabernet of that year also has a maturing colour, is slightly closed on nose, but full flavoursome and well balanced on palate. It should be ready for consumption about 1993. (16.5 pts)

The following vintage is, paradoxically, more open and softly fruity on nose. Its palate reflects the nose, very agreeable in March 1989 and certainly ready to drink in 1990–91. (17 pts)

As for the third of the trio, 1987, this Mount Pleasant Cabernet is the most promising of all. Minty on nose and palate, of medium weight and elegant length, this 'cool-year' cabernet should be ready by 1995. (17.5 pts)

The youngest wine, 1988, was at the time of tasting incomplete, though its light characters suggested that it would be a forward wine.

One of the most interesting styles of cabernet in the Hunter is that of Saxonvale made by Alasdair Sutherland until 1989 and thereafter by John Baruzzi. Sometimes high-cassis in nose and palate (a style in itself old-fashioned in wine-show terms), the wines are for that reason both distinctive and attractive. Cassis character, however, does tend to be aggressive when a wine is young and for that reason should be left to age. 1985 Bin 1 Cabernet Sauvignon is a typical example. In August 1988 it still held a dark red-purple hue, with a huge nose of complex cassis and spicy oak. Similar huge flavours riveted the attention of the palate. It is a style that positively demands to be left alone for three to four years. (17 pts)

Since its foundation in 1970, Brokenwood has always been especially interested in cabernet sauvignon, and even though I am part of Brokenwood, good wines whatever their provenance should be brought to the attention of wine lovers everywhere. Earlier good cabernet years have included 1975, 1977, 1979 and 1980, but since 1983 there has been a Graveyard Cabernet Sauvignon each year, an individual-vineyard cabernet made in very small quantity (often only five or six hogsheads), which is a true *tête de cuvée*.

1987 was for the Hunter an exceptionally cool and dry year, which rewarded all varieties and certainly cabernet. In March 1989 the Graveyard Cabernet of 1987 was a vivid red-purple in colour with lively mint aromas on nose, while a rich palate showed ripe 'berry' and oak flavours in complete harmony. It was an elegant cabernet of much promise to be held in cellar for four or five years more. (17 pts)

Other Lower Hunter makers whose repertoire occasionally includes outstanding cabernet sauvignon are Briar Ridge (formerly the Robson Vineyard), Drayton, Little's, Rothbury Estate, Simon Whitlam, Tamburlaine, Terrace Vale, Tulloch and Wyndham Estate.

Of the bigger makers of the Upper Hunter, Rosemount confines its cabernet attention to area blends, while Arrowfield/Mount Arrow makes cabernet of good local standard. The one maker of the region who relies solely on cabernet for red and rosé is Callatoota, whose wines are regrettably unknown to me.

Though Mudgee lies on virtually the same line of latitude as the Hunter Valley, the two areas are quite dissimilar in both climate and cabernet. Mudgee, higher, drier and more continental in climate, generally begins its vintage up to a month later than the Lower Hunter. The cabernet styles of the region are generally more intense in colour and firmer in body than those of the Hunter, often nevertheless possessing considerable grace when made by the area's old cabernet hands, Huntington and Montrose. The best Mudgee cabernets, like those elsewhere, are made in years free of drought stress, and trickle irrigation is therefore virtually a necessity in this area. Even so such wines on release at about two years of age require at least four more years in cellar.

At Huntington, Bob Roberts generally shortens this cellaring time by releasing his wines three to four years after current vintage. His Huntington Estate Cabernet Sauvignon Bin FB16 of 1984 reflects that cool vintage perfectly. In hue the wine is full red, having shed its youthful purples, though retaining some density. On nose, herbaceous capsicum aromas are very evident, while the palate encounters 'sweet' fruit of similar flavours and spicy wood on finish. All in all, a straightforward but appealing wine, really accessible to the palate. (18 pts) Drink in 1990-92.

A rather more complex Mudgee cabernet from 1984 is the Montrose wine, made by Carlo Corino. Medium full red in colour with some density, this wine on nose exhibits a fascinating mix of light 'capsicum' and fresh 'coffee', far removed, however, from the 'old coffee' aromas of oxidation. Its palate, full and soft, held a slight berry sweetness, reinforced by an intricate coalescence of capsicum and herbaceousness. At five years of age it was very good, having the potential to develop great complexity over two to three more years. (17.5 pts) Drink in 1992-93.

1985 is perhaps a more typical Mudgee year for cabernet. Both the Huntington and the Montrose were very youthful in colour still, a little closed on nose, and berry-flavoured. They were both good styles to cellar for three to four more years.

Another excellent Montrose cabernet sauvignon was made in 1986. A big red-purple colour, this wine had an attractive 'berry' and 'vanilla' bouquet with an ever so slight touch of capsicum. In a ripe palate the flavours of the wine were all smooth 'berry', finishing in soft well-integrated tannin. A well-made cabernet with a cellaring future of three to four more years. (The Mudgee cabernets described above were tasted in April 1989.)

Other makers in the district making reliable cabernet wines are Thistle Hill (an outstanding newcomer), Miramar, Botobolar and Amberton.

The cabernet banner of course flies elsewhere in New South Wales. In Port Macquarie, the Cassegrain Winery (mentioned also in connection with Pokolbin cabernet) made excellent Hastings cabernet in 1985 and 1986. There are of course many cool viticultural regions in New South Wales quite capable of producing top cabernet sauvignon. The Hilltops area near Young, Bungendore east of Canberra, and Orange in the Central Tablelands are but a few. Many have yet to be discovered.

MULTI-AREA BLENDS

What certainly has been discovered in Australia is the premium cabernet sauvignon blend, the 'cellar style', where cabernet wine from various areas of Australia is blended to make a premium style. It is a practice that is illegal in other countries, especially France. In Australia, winemakers and legislators seem to think more laterally, reasoning that a superior wine of multi-area origin is preferable to an inferior wine from one area. There is no reason why, given winemaking integrity, multi-area origin cannot coexist with single-area wines most peacefully in this age of glasnost. Such wines are archetypal brand styles, existing across the whole price spectrum of cabernet sauvignon.

In the Hunter Valley, Rosemount markets a very fine multi-sourced cabernet as part of its Diamond Label series. Brokenwood also has produced a two- or three-area blend since 1983. It is a legitimate approach to quality cabernet winemaking. In Victoria, Mitchelton has adopted the same approach, while also producing a single-area cabernet from its own region. And Lindeman's at Karadoc in the North-West blend multi-area cabernets from their own vast resources.

In South Australia, the practice is even more widespread. Leo Buring (a subsidiary of Lindeman), Seppelt with its Black Label and Gold Label brands, Blass and Yalumba all blending cabernets from various areas. The resultant wines are of good quality and affordable price, and they cellar well for a few years if that is required which it rarely is these days.

In the case of Penfold's, however, really superb quality (and a premium price) is usually achieved with Cabernet Sauvignon Bin 707. The 1986 was a Barossa–Coonawarra blend of exemplary style. In October 1989 I noted it as follows: dense purple-red in hue, rich and complex but youthful nose of berries and charred oak, very attractive. A huge palate with an intense concentration of berries, vanillan wood and soft tannins. Cellar till 1995 at least. Drink till 2005. (18.5 pts)

Penfold's Cabernet Sauvignon Bin 707 1987 was, in April 1990, a vigorous full purple-red in hue, revealing deep aromas of raspberry, mint and cedary oak in a delightful nose. On palate the wine was most complex, offering a huge range of flavours of which capsicum, cassis, cedar and tobacco were but a few, while a firm but balanced tannin finish would ensure that the wine lasts well in cellar. (18.5 pts) Drink 1995 onwards.

Another popular member of the Penfold circle is Seaview Cabernet Sauvignon, good quality, early drinking and always reasonably priced. Other cabernets of multi-area blend and decent quality are Kaiser Stuhl and Killawarra.

The remaining Barossa Valley giant with a large-selling multi-area cabernet is Orlando, its RF Cabernet Sauvignon being culled from diverse regional sources within south-eastern Australia (according to Orlando's export label, but without more specific area information). This is always pleasant easy drinking in the mainstream of the commercial blended style.

Krondorf also, though Barossa-based, sources its cabernet fruit from the Barossa, Coonawarra and McLaren Vale, the resultant high-quality wines being released under both its top label, Burge & Wilson, and its standard Krondorf label.

This has been a brief statement of Australian cabernet sauvignon in the late 1980s. If asked the question 'Which area produces the best cabernet sauvignon?'—and do not forget that I am talking about cabernet sauvignon per se (that is, 100%, or at the very least 80%, in accord with Australian law)—I must unhesitatingly answer 'Coonawarra'. The track record is there, the runs are on the board, name your own cliché, but Coonawarra is undoubtedly it, and it is Coonawarra not only because of fruit quality, length of palate and softish tannins but also for good old-fashioned depth of palate, 'extract' if you like (an unfashionable word these days), but very necessary if your cabernet sauvignon is to be really worth five years' and more patient cellaring.

And other areas? Perhaps Margaret River holds promise of the greatest consistency, warm enough to ripen cabernet sauvignon properly in most years, and most rewarding on palate after seven to ten years if my experience of older wines from Cullen's and Leeuwin Estate is anything to go by.

And then possibly the Yarra Valley in warm years or warmer parts of the Yarra Valley. Nor am I playing with words, for the Yarra will always be the viticultural front line for cabernet sauvignon weatherwise, and the front line is a dangerous place even if you are winning. Mornington and Geelong are similarly very cool for the variety, and Tasmania too cold in general, unless you adore Loire cabernet franc wines such as Chinon and Bourgeuil, to which Tasmanian cabernet often has a marked resemblance.

Of the rest of Australia, Mount Barker (WA) and Eden Valley (SA) also take my fancy, but the valleys in the shadow of Mount Lofty do seem too cold for cabernet sauvignon, however great their potential might be for pinot noir and chardonnay.

All of which leaves a sizeable chunk of higher, cooler Central Victoria unmentioned. Bendigo (Balgownie) takes my vote, while farther west Taltarni at Moonambel and Seppelt at Great Western both make local cabernets with sufficient 'stuffing' and style for the long haul.

Clare and Mudgee lead the remaining areas, most of which are too warm generally for great cabernet sauvignon. The North-East of Victoria, the Swan Valley, even the Hunter Valley, except in cool years take more from cabernet sauvignon than they seem to contribute to it. Firmness and tannin are no substitute for fruit flavour. That is why in such areas a variety such as merlot, which seems to retain its soft supple fruitiness in most climates, should be planted in greater profusion. The resultant merlot–cabernet blends should be well worth tasting, and it is to cabernet blends and blending varieties that we will now turn.

CABERNET BLENDERS AND BLENDS

Merlot

Merlot, that most useful of all blending varieties, is exactly that—except in Pomerol where the cabernet cousins, franc and sauvignon, become 'useful' in their own turn and are blended with it. The exception is Château Petrus where merlot making has become the finest of fine arts, and cabernet franc (or bouchet as the locals call it) is never added. Or is it? We must leave that mystery for another day.

Certainly merlot is by far the most widely grown red variety in the greater Bordeaux area. It is popular also in other parts of southern France, in north-eastern Italy where it makes pleasant light- to medium-bodied reds, in Hungary and in what old-fashioned authors call the Balkans, Yugoslavia and Bulgaria.

As a personal assistant to cabernet sauvignon, it has followed dutifully to most New Wine World countries, though in South Africa consumers apparently prefer their cabernet sauvignon straight. In Washington State and California it is made as a straight varietal, but even in California, the heartland of varietal wines, its worth as a natural softener for cabernet sauvignon is slowly being realised. In Chile also, the two varieties are being blended most harmoniously (perhaps ultimately to the detriment of our own exports, as Chilean costs seem much cheaper than our own); and finally to that other long narrow nation of the Pacific Rim, New Zealand, where its natural home would seem to be Hawkes Bay, source of New Zealand's biggest cabernets.

In Australia, merlot was introduced as recently as the 1960s by the Commonwealth Scientific and Industrial Research Organisation (CSIRO) in its search for 'new' varieties of promise. It is perhaps the only major world variety that was not aboard Busby's boat in 1832. But that is logical, for in Bordeaux it was hardly known until the late eighteenth century, its own rise to some prominence occurring a century later with the growth in popularity of the cheaper clarets from the right bank of the Gironde, St Emilion and Pomerol.

Historically the chief function of merlot in Medoc and Graves has been to assuage the firmer and more astringent tendencies of cabernet sauvignon and to fill the well-known hole in the cabernet doughnut—that dip in mid-palate of cabernet sauvignon which occurs after initial entry to palate and before what is usually a tannic finish—in much the same way, though with different mid-palate flavour, as Australian winemakers used shiraz before the 'discovery' of merlot a decade ago.

Conversely the wholly merlot wines of Pomerol and St Emilion, which from time to time needed more backbone if they were to age well, were firmed by the addition of a minor proportion of cabernet franc or more rarely cabernet sauvignon; the ability to age well over a decade or more is, even today, a highly regarded virtue of Bordeaux reds, for wine consumers are certainly willing to be patient if they know that such patience will be rewarded by a well-aged, cedar-scented, smooth-palated berry-fruited red which caresses the tongue and lingers gracefully on, long after it has been swallowed.

There are signs that Australian winemakers are taking note of this French tradition, and there is no reason for them not to, for cabernet sauvignon in this country also suffers the doughnut effect. Equally, in an era when wine lovers are enjoying younger softer reds of two to three years of age, there is no reason why merlot should not thrive as a single varietal, either as a 'nouveau' style such as that of Cassegrain or as a fuller dry red to be drunk after two years in cellar. Indeed more and more examples of this latter style will be seen during the 1990s as new vineyards come into bearing.

It is still by no means a statistically important variety in Australia, only 316 hectares planted as at mid-June 1988 and only 1321 tonnes produced for winemaking purposes, but that need not trouble us, for it is growing in public esteem, and as always, the popularity horse will draw the statistical cart.

Cabernet Franc

Cabernet franc may have entered Australia on the Busby passport, perhaps as 'Carbenet a petits grains' (small-berried cabernet) listed in the catalogue with 'Malbek' and 'Verdot' as varieties '... almost exclusively cultivated in the vineyards of Medoc, and the Carbenet à petits grains and Carbernet Sauvignen are alone to be found in those of highest reputation': James Busby, *Journal of a Tour*, 1833, p. 119. Note that there is absolutely no mention of merlot in the Medoc, nor of St Emilion or Pomerol, in the 1830s mere outposts of Bordeaux. Perhaps even then in the Medoc, carbenet à petits grains was planted only as a supplement to cabernet sauvignon in the proportion of one vine to five or six, as it is today. Assuming this practice was followed in Australia at that time, it is little wonder that carbenet à petits grains (cabernet franc?) may have disappeared in the mists of viticultural time, but malbec and verdot survived, being mentioned by Sir William Macarthur in the late 1840s, verdot only seeming to die out in the 1930s.

Like merlot, neither cabernet franc nor malbec yet loom large in the viticultural scheme of things. Malbec indeed seems to have reached its zenith of popularity (as at mid-year 1988, 203 bearing hectares with only 9 hectares unbearing), while cabernet franc shoots up in winegrowing esteem (122 hectares in bearing with 73 hectares yet to bear). As for verdot, it is not yet separately listed, though planting interest is increasing.

Outside Australia, cabernet franc is widely planted in Bordeaux and also in the Loire Valley, where it alone is responsible for the fresh fruity 'Beaujolais' cabernets of Chinon and Bourgueil. It is also grown in north-east Italy and Central Europe. In the New World, it is of course grown in California, but there too it is regarded as subservient to cabernet sauvignon.

Malbec

Malbec also is grown quite widely in France from the Loire to Bordeaux and in the south-west, where it is most famous for its contribution to Cahors. Elsewhere it is most favoured in Argentina, where it is the leading red variety.

FLAVOUR CHARACTERS OF THE BLENDERS

What are the flavour characters of these varieties? When ripe, cabernet franc (like cabernet sauvignon) has berry flavours, but they are less well defined, softer perhaps and less insistent. When not at optimal maturity, it has similar leafy grassy flavours, but both have considerable tannin and seem a more suitable partner for merlot than each other.

Malbec offers berries and spice, but again the flavour is not as incisive as merlot 'plums'. The role that each should play must be one of support for a cabernet sauvignon–merlot blend or, if needs be, for a blend in which merlot is dominant.

Either way, merlot shows great promise in warm and cool areas alike.

The blends

NEW SOUTH WALES

In the Hunter Valley, merlot is used to very good effect by Wyndham Estate in its Bin 888 Cabernet-Merlot: softening, otherwise rather tannic wines with a beguiling plumminess in ripe years such as 1986, adding a definite fruit elegance in 1987, and building up what otherwise might have been a rather thin cabernet sauvignon in damp years such as 1988. Wyndham has certainly started a line worth following and cellaring for several years.

Hungerford Hill also made good cabernet merlot blends during the 1980s.

Brokenwood also releases a merlot blend from time to time when quality demands, the last being a rich Merlot-Cabernet Sauvignon 1986 under its Cricket Pitch label.

Elsewhere in the Lower Hunter Valley, merlot is as yet rarely used, though Murray Tyrrell does release a pleasant blend of cabernet and merlot under the 'Old Winery' label. Indeed shiraz is in that area still the preferred blending medium for cabernet sauvignon, if cabernet is to be blended at all—Brokenwood making a shiraz-cabernet from year to year and Drayton's making a consistently good cabernet–hermitage. The 1987 Drayton Cabernet Hermitage (tasted October 1989) was deep red in colour with an initially shy berry nose which opened out well a few minutes later. A firm palate revealed long fruit flavours and excellent tannin and acid balance. A good red to be cellared for two to four years. (16.5 pts) Drink in 1990–92.

Most of the Lower Hunter makers blend cabernet and shiraz from time to time to very good effect, though with the rising popularity of merlot it is unlikely that Hunter cabernet-shiraz blends will ever be as frequent as they have been in the past.

In the Upper Hunter, blends of cabernet and merlot are presently non-existent, though Arrowfield, now renamed Mount Arrow, did release an excellent McLaren Vale merlot from the 1986 vintage. That wine, tasted October 1988, showed full red in colour with berry and plum aromas on nose. Palate revealed lovely soft elegant fruit and light well-integrated tannin. (17.5 pts) Drink in 1990–92.

Merlot has also been employed to good effect at Mudgee, where Bob Roberts at Huntington Estate first made a cabernet-merlot blend in 1981. In 1984, a remarkably good year in most places (except the lower Hunter) but especially in Mudgee, Bob made three blends, a cabernet–merlot, a merlot–cabernet and a shiraz–cabernet.

Huntington Estate Cabernet–Merlot Bin FB(full-bodied)32 1984: dark red in hue with very pale brown starting to appear on the edges. A lovely nose of leafy cabernet and minty oak. Open palate with lively fruit of berry and mint flavours and excellent body. (18 pts) Drink 1994 onwards.

Huntington Estate Merlot–Cabernet Bin FB31 1984: full red in colour, no browns. Plummy nose, attractive and fruity. Lively fresh fruit on palate, though without the body of FB32 and consequently will mature earlier. Still a very good wine. (17 pts) Drink in 1992–94.

Huntington Estate Shiraz–Cabernet Bin FB20 1984: dark red, yet quite bright and without browns. Peppery berry nose with a touch of smoke or tar. Peppery fruit dominates palate, but an 'inky' complexing character pervades the finish, perhaps a peculiarity of Mudgee shiraz. Should live well, but I had a few reservations about that finish. (16 pts) Drink 1993 onwards. (The three above were tasted in January 1990.)

As in the Lower Hunter, numbers of other Mudgee makers offer cabernet–shiraz or vice versa. The best of them usually are, in alphabetical order, Botobolar (St Gilbert), Burnbrae, Craigmoor, Erudgere, Montrose and a newcomer, Thistle Hill.

In the Murrumbidgee Irrigation Area merlot is also grown, though I doubt whether in that area it will ever amount to much more than current drinking. Still, I await the pleasure of being proved wrong.

The Bungendore area of New South Wales, adjacent to our national capital, Canberra, is home to the region's best vineyard, Lark Hill. That estate's Cabernet–Merlot 1987, tasted twice in March 1989, showed typical cool-area cabernet leafiness and plummy merlot fruit on nose. Its palate in that year was fine and elegant, and while it was not a big wine it had sufficient weight and balance to make a very good bottle in the early 1990s. (16.5 pts) Drink in 1992–94.

Elsewhere in New South Wales the only other producer of merlot was Cassegrain at Port Macquarie, where it is used in a refreshing nouveau-style red and in a cabernet–merlot blend of usually very good quality.

VICTORIA

As in New South Wales, the cabernet–shiraz (shiraz–cabernet) blend is frequently encountered in Victoria, where there are also rising numbers of cabernet–merlot and even more complicated 'Bordeaux' blends, especially in cooler areas. The Yarra Valley is currently inspiring widespread interest in merlot, cabernet franc and even petit verdot; and it is from that Valley with its various microclimates that many a fascinating blend will come during the 1990s.

Putting the crystal ball aside, there is no doubt that the Yarra Valley has already produced some lovely blends. With a few exceptions, they cannot be said to be full-bodied wines. Flavourful is a more suitable term, especially for Yarra wines such as Diamond Valley Cabernets 1986, a blend of cabernet sauvignon (50%), merlot (30%), cabernet franc (15%) and malbec (5%). Tasted in August 1988 this wine was deep red in hue with a complex berry, redcurrant and capsicum nose. Its highlight was its palate, which revealed long sweet berry flavours, excellent use of French oak, and soft tannins so well integrated with fruit that they were difficult to recognise at all. (17.5 pts) Drink in 1991-93.

This all accords with David Lance's policy that fruit should subsume wood and never be dominated by it.

The Diamond Valley Cabernets 1987, tasted January 1990, was purple-red in colour, with light berry capsicum aromas on nose, obviously the product of a cooler year. On palate there were berry and capsicum flavours, spicy oak and more tannic weight than the 1986 but excellent persistence. This too was a wine to keep in cellar for two to three years. (16.5 pts) Drink in 1992-93.

Lighter still than Diamond Valley are the cabernet-merlots of St Hubert's. Tasted in March 1989, the 1986 St Hubert's Cabernet-Merlot, medium to full red in colour with purple tints, offered capsicum aromas on nose and similarly flavoured fruit and soft tannins on palate. This was a forward style to drink from 1991 to 1992. (16 pts)

If St Hubert's tends to be of lighter style, Oakridge Estate, judged by its 1986 vintage, most certainly is not. Oakridge is set apart from most other Yarra vineyards, except Seville Estate, by its magnificent red volcanic soil, which gives to the Oakridge reds a marvellous fullness of flavour without heaviness or extraction. Though the 1986 Cabernet Sauvignon was an exceptional wine by any standards, the Oakridge Cabernet-Shiraz-Merlot 1986, tasted September 1989, was also a superb wine. Medium to full red-purple in shade, this wine offered a beautifully balanced nose of berries and subtle oak, while its palate was replete with ripe berry flavours and soft tannins, very harmoniously integrated. It was deceptively open and accessible to palate and could even have been drunk at that time, but certainly will age well into the 1990s. (18 pts) Drink in 1990-96.

The one winemaker who has seen the renaissance of the Yarra and who indeed invented the term 'Cabernets' as a convenient abbreviation for that Bordeaux brotherhood of grape varieties (which when spelt out in full makes labels read like phone books) is Dr John Middleton of Mount Mary. His simple justification for using a Bordeaux blend of 50% cabernet sauvignon, 20% cabernet franc, 25% merlot, 3% malbec and 2% petit verdot is that it works in an area where ripening, say, a 100% cabernet sauvignon wine would often be very difficult. He is also fascinated by the fragrances and flavours of these varieties, describing the aroma of cabernet sauvignon as 'violets' and sometimes 'cassis' (less favourably, for it may then be overripe), the nose of cabernet franc as 'mulberry' and that of merlot as 'cherry, plum and earth'. And their common factor? A cedary character which becomes more noticeable as the wines age. For him, 1988 is one of the best Mount Mary Cabernets of recent memory.

At Coldstream Hills, James Halliday has wasted little time in adding a cabernet–merlot blend to that company's exciting repertoire of wines. What a marvellous red the Coldstream Hills Cabernet–Merlot 1988 is! Tasted in March 1990 it was rich and deep in its purple robe. On a most complex nose the wine offered attractive berry–plum and vanillan oak aromas, while on a round yet elegant palate, berry–plum and minty oak flavours married most harmoniously with soft oak tannins. A delicious red to be cellared until 1994. (18.5 pts)

Other Yarra makers of cabernet–merlot blends of excellent repute are Yarra Yering (Dry Red No 1) and Yarra Ridge.

Lou Bianchet is another Yarra maker who follows the Italian tradition, making a 100% merlot wine. The Bianchet Merlot 1987, tasted in January 1989, was medium to full red in colour with the typical 'sweet plum' nose of merlot and a medium-weight, easily accessible palate of plum and tobacco flavour. The wine was forward but well structured and would cellar well for one to three years. (16 pts)

By any standards the Mornington Peninsula is still minute, though beginning to grow rapidly, 160 hectares of vines at the end of 1989. One outstanding cabernet–merlot from this region is that of Dromana Estate. Its 1988, tasted in March and October 1989, was a very youthful purple in hue, revealing a complex nose of plums, tobacco and capsicum. Its palate was medium-weight, repeating the aromatic components as flavours but adding a great length and lovely sweet oak characters. A really outstanding 1988, which could almost have been drunk in 1989. That, however, would have been a pity. (18.5 pts) Drink 1994 onwards.

Another Mornington cabernet–merlot, tasted in September 1989, was Elgee Park 1987. Medium to full red in shade with some youthful purples, this wine presented berry–tobacco aromas in a light elegant bouquet. Berry fruit dominated its medium-weight palate, which was finished by soft tannin and good acidity. A fruity, pleasant red and typical of the cool 1987 year. (16.5 pts) Drink in 1990–93.

Mornington is an exciting area and great things are bound to happen there during the nineties.

On the Western shores of Port Phillip Bay lies the Geelong region, an area that has already proved most suitable for pinot noir and chardonnay. Geelong's renaissance as a winegrowing area owes much to Daryl and Nini Sefton, whose Idyll Vineyard curiously grows neither pinot nor chardonnay, but produces a very consistent cabernet–shiraz blend. The Idyll Cabernet Sauvignon–Shiraz 1986, tasted March 1989, held a full red-purple hue at that time. Dominant characters on nose were the black pepper of shiraz made more complex by a slight gamey aroma, while cabernet berry flavours and soft tannins harmonised well on a balanced palate. (16 pts) Drink in 1991-93.

To the north-east of Mornington is East Gippsland. Names to note here for cabernet-merlot blends are Nicholson River and McAlister Vineyards.

Within sight of Mount Buller and the Victorian snowfields is Delatite, whose extremely cool vineyards produce lighter-style reds in most years. 1988, however, was not one of those years, ripening the Delatite Bordeaux red varieties to perfection. Devil's River 1988 (a blend of 45% merlot, 30% cabernet sauvignon, 20% malbec and 5% cabernet franc), tasted December 1989, was an imperial purple in hue with an excitingly aromatic nose of berries, plums, mint and spice. Velvety soft on palate, this was a wine with a wealth of berry and plum flavours on palate and lovely fruit-tannin balance. (19 pts) Drink in 1990-94.

Another mountain vineyard in Central Victoria is Mount Helen, on top of the Strathbogie Range above the Goulburn Valley. Dr Peter Tisdall has done more than most towards the development of viticulture in that often-harsh environment, and there is no doubt that the cabernet-merlot blends and the straight merlot varietal wines from this pioneering vineyard are of consistently high quality. My notes of Mount Helen Merlot from 1984 to 1988 follow; 1986 is missing because no straight merlot was produced that year.

1984: full red in colour, delicate bouquet of plums. Soft fruit entry to palate, full middle palate, good length and soft tannins on finish. Excellent example of variety. (17.5 pts) Drink 1991 onwards.

1985: full red in hue with traces of purple, subdued slightly berryish nose, ripe fruit, peppery oak, firm tannins on finish, needs more time to open out, a little lacking in balance. (15.5 pts) Drink in 1992-94.

1987: medium to full red with tints of purple, good nose with typical plummy-tobacco aromas, medium-weight palate, slightly lifted berry flavours. Forward style. (16.5 pts) Drink in 1991-92. (The above three wines were tasted in September 1989.)

1988: medium to full red in colour, with typical 'plums' and smoky oak aromas. Soft rich palate with a slight dominance of oak but overall well balanced. (17 pts) Drink in 1992-94. (Tasted December 1989.)

The Mount Helen Cabernet-Merlot blends are usually composed of 75% cabernet sauvignon and 25% merlot. 1985 was the first of the line. A dense deep red in shade with some purple tints, this wine (like the straight merlot of the same year) was subdued on nose, though some breathing of the bottle brought forth some oak aromas and light berry fruit after a few minutes. Its palate was deep and full with slightly lifted berry and oak flavours and firm tannin backing. (17 pts) Drink in 1993-96.

Mount Helen Cabernet–Merlot 1986: deep red with hints of purple but not as profound as 1985. Its nose was merlot-dominant at time of tasting, showing generous plummy aromas and harmonious wood. Its medium-weight palate also offered a pleasant coalescence of plummy merlot and spicy oak. A soft and generous wine. (17 pts) Drink in 1991–93. (Both the above were tasted in March 1989.)

Mount Helen Cabernet–Merlot 1987 (70% cabernet sauvignon, 30% merlot): medium-full red–purple in tone with berry cabernet and spicy oak aromas in the ascendancy in a subtle nose. On a soft palate there were sweet berry fruit flavours and soft well-integrated tannins. A fairly forward elegant wine. (16.5 pts) Drink in 1992–93. (Tasted January 1990.)

Tisdall's Jeff Clarke also wears another winemaking hat, that of Mount Ida in Heathcote. This is again a Central Victorian vineyard of great quality, whose shiraz–cabernet blends are always of an excellent standard. In June 1989, I tasted Mount Ida Shiraz–Cabernet 1985. This wine was still a vigorous red-purple in colour with intense aromas of berries, pepper and vanillan oak. On a most complex palate, ripe berries, sweet oak and soft tannins created a most pleasing harmony. (17.5 pts) Drink in 1991–96.

In the same area Jasper Hill also makes very good shiraz–cabernet blends from year to year.

West of Bendigo, Passing Clouds shows the typical mint and berry flavours of this blend, adding for good measure some regional gumleaf.

Traditionally, Australian blends of varietal reds have relied on cabernet sauvignon and shiraz, but occasionally a little malbec was added if available. Though the label does not disclose it, such a blend is still made at Virgin Hills near Kyneton in Central Victoria. During the 1970s and early 1980s I tasted several of the wines made prior to that time. 'Huge' was a fair description, for colour, nose and palate were all larger than lifesize. As Virgin Hills 1979 had spent nearly a decade in my cellar, I looked at it again early in January 1990. A full dense red in colour, browning very slightly at the edges, it revealed dominant aromas of pepper (Central Victorian shiraz once more to the fore) and vanillan oak. Only the slightest trace of berry (cabernet?) was present. Its palate was austere, showing lively woody spicy flavours, which were quite long but lacking in softness. It was still very alive and developing, but its lack of flesh was disappointing. (16 pts) Drink 1992 onwards.

In a sense, that wine bridged the gap between old Australian blends and new. Though it was obviously built to live and certainly has done so, has the wait for it been worthwhile? Yes and no. Yes, in the educational sense. Virgin Hills 1979 is austere but alive and drinkable in 1990. No, because it does not seem generous enough; or is it that my own tastes have changed during the wait?

A winemaker of a new estate who makes just one wine, and that intended for ten to fifteen years' cellaring, faces a predicament. Does he or she have a loyal enough purchasing public who will cellar a wine for the intended length of time, or will their tastes change in the meantime?

The Virgin Hills style of the late 1980s seems lighter than before, certainly if 1987 vintage is typical. The wine of that admittedly cool year, when tasted in February 1989, showed full red-purple in colour with herbaceous and berry aromas that spoke of a long slow ripening. Flavours on palate were again in the leaf–berry spectrum but were soft and clean, with oak, acid and tannin nicely in balance. (17 pts) Drink 1994 onwards.

In the Victorian Pyrenees two makers deserve mention: Chateau Remy for its blend of cabernet sauvignon, shiraz and merlot which it calls Blue Pyrenees; and that other varietal blend of the region, Taltarni's Reserve des Pyrenees, a blend of cabernet sauvignon and malbec.

The Blue Pyrenees Estate 1986, tasted October 1989, was a deep red-purple in hue, showing a complex nose of plums, black pepper, berries and spicy oak, while its long palate was not as generous as the bouquet, offering regional peppery flavours and a firm tannic finish. (16 pts) Drink 1994 onwards. After a somewhat inconsistent start, Blue Pyrenees, an estate wine from Chateau Remy's own vineyards at Avoca, becomes more reliable each vintage, growing in quality as the percentage of merlot increases. 1988 Blue Pyrenees is also an exceptional wine.

Reserve des Pyrenees is a lighter red, intended perhaps in the Taltarni scheme of things to be drunk while the maturity of its estate-grown Cabernet Sauvignon and French Syrah are awaited—by saying this, I certainly do not imply that the Reserve is in any way inferior. It can age very well in cellar for short to medium term (two to four years). Tasted in January 1990, Reserve des Pyrenees 1986 showed berry and spice aromas on a ripe nose, avoiding (perhaps because of the absence of shiraz) the black-pepper gumleaf character that is to be seen in other regional wines. On palate there were soft, ripe berry flavours and well-integrated tannins. Though a harmonious wine, it was restrained and would cellar well for two to three years. (17.5 pts) Drink 1993 onwards. Taltarni also produces a straight varietal merlot from time to time.

At Great Western, good cabernet merlot blends are made by Dr Graeme Bertuch at Cathcart Ridge and by Trevor Mast at Mount Langi Ghiran, both in regrettably small quantities.

In the North-East of Victoria, merlot does not as yet seem to be making much of an impression except in the King Valley, where Brown Brothers produce a usually successful blend of that variety and cabernet franc. As the 1986 King Valley blend of these varieties showed, the wine can be quite light, with light to medium red hues, leafy tobacco aromas and herbaceous palate flavours producing a forward-drinking style. (15.5 pts) Drink in 1991.

Other Brown Brothers blends concentrate on the more traditional blending varieties of the region, shiraz and mondeuse, a variety native to the northern Rhône and Savoy, whose Australian circulation is virtually confined to the North-East. The Browns have been blending these varieties for many years, usually with shiraz as the dominant partner. Brown Brothers Shiraz, Mondeuse & Cabernet 1986, tasted March 1989, was typical of the blend. Deep in colour, a little austere and closed on nose, this wine showed good fruit on palate, but lacked fullness. (16 pts) Such wines do soften in bottle after about five years, but sometimes retain a hot spirity finish which I ascribe to the warmth of the area preceding vintage. Drink in 1992-96.

St Leonard's also makes good cabernet-merlot blends, which often include some cabernet franc. The 1985, seen in January 1989, was a very elegant style, now unlikely to be found on sale.

Chris Killeen of Stanton and Killeen also makes reliable cabernet-shiraz blends. His Cabernet-Shiraz 1983, tasted March 1989, was showing a mature garnet-red in colour, but soft attractive berry fruit aromas were delightfully present on nose, while its palate offered rich flavours, surprisingly restrained for the area. (16.5 pts) A nicely balanced red to be drunk in 1991-92.

Another very small maker of exciting cabernet blends is Giaconda at Beechworth east of Wangaratta, very definitely in the North-East but higher and cooler than most other vineyards in the area save those of the King Valley.

Like the North-East, the Goulburn Valley produces traditionally sturdy cabernet-shiraz blends. Smaller vineyards to look for are Osicka, Longleat and Walkershire—not forgetting one of the bigger inhabitants of the region, Mitchelton, which markets a cabernet-shiraz-merlot blend under its Thomas Mitchell label.

SOUTH AUSTRALIA

While the cabernet blends of Victoria will be crucial in some cooler areas to the making of a complete 'cabernet' wine, Coonawarra winemakers whose cabernet sauvignons are usually complete have welcomed merlot to the vinefold most enthusiastically. Bigger makers such as Lindeman and Mildara have now had five years' experience of what I once called 'modern multi-varietal mouthfuls': blends of cabernet sauvignon, merlot, cabernet franc and malbec. Mildara indeed produces two blends at different market levels, Alexanders (a 'Bordeaux' blend) and Jamieson's Run, in which shiraz also has the major part, with the Bordeaux varieties playing supporting roles.

Lindeman's Pyrus, indeed, has to date been the most egalitarian of all these blends, with equal amounts of cabernet sauvignon, cabernet franc, merlot and malbec being employed in the first two wines of that line.
Lindeman's Pyrus 1985 (tasted July 1987): purple-red in hue with some density. Full berry and spice aromas with underlying sweet oak, complex but fruit dominant. Palate flavours of berry cassis and smoky oak, full soft textures. Generous and slightly forward palate, but certainly complex.

Should age well for four to five years. (17.5 pts) Drink in 1991–93.
Lindeman's Pyrus 1986 (tasted March 1989): deep red-purple in shade, aromas of mulberries, ripe plums and smoky oak. Good depth of soft berry fruit and smoky oak flavours. Tannins very soft and almost unnoticeable. Forward ripe style. (16.5 pts) Drink in 1991–93.

If the Lindeman's Pyrus blend has not yet (despite its Jimmy Watson Trophy in 1986) quite proved itself, that other Lindeman's classic, Limestone Ridge Shiraz–Cabernet, most certainly has. Made with but a few interruptions since 1971, notable years have been 1976, 1978 (which I tasted in magnum in June 1988, marked at 17.5 pts, noting a full red hue, an open berry nose and long mature berry flavours), 1982 (seen May 1989 and noted at 18.5 pts, being medium red in tone, with berry fruit and vanillan oak on nose and long berry and spice flavours on palate, still to be kept in cellar for two to three more years and to be drunk in 1992–93), 1984 and 1986. The 1986, last seen in October 1989, very deep in its red-purple hues, has an intensity matched by the abundant berry fruit and charred oak aromas on nose, revealed rich mint and mulberry flavours on palate. (18 pts) Start to drink sparingly 1993 and on.

What can one say about a wine named 'Alexanders'? Though called after one of the early vineyard 'blockers' of Coonawarra, whose land Mildara now owns, the name conjures up all sorts of impressions. Will it be a conquering hero or a ragtime band? Certainly my first thoughts inclined to the heroic rather than the jazzy, for Mildara Alexanders 1985, full red in colour with light purple hues when last tasted in March 1989, showing on nose a light touch of capsicum against a counterpoint of pencil-shavings French oak, certainly looked like a wine for the longer haul. Its palate was well structured for just that purpose, full but not excessive fruit, perhaps a slight wood dominance even a touch of austerity, its style recalling a young Medoc and needing at least five years more to open fully. Showing great promise. (18 pts) Drink 1995 onwards.

Alexanders 1986 was deeper in its purple-reds than 1985, showing on nose very harmonious capsicum and berry aromas. On palate there was a plethora of ripe fruit, beautifully balanced by soft well-integrated tannin and good acidity. It was a most complete but youthful wine. (18.5 pts) Cellar from five to seven years. Drink in 1995–98. A most exciting wine.

On the other hand, I was not quite so impressed by Alexanders 1987, tasted August 1989. This was a very youthful red-purple in colour with a complex lifted nose with berry, cassis and vanillan oak all striving for attention. Palate was of medium weight with berry fruit flavours initially on palate, then a hole in flavour and a firm tannin finish. (15.5 pts) Not quite in the class of its predecessors, but it may come together given time. Drink 1994 onwards.

More cheaply priced than its elder brother Alexanders (logically, I suppose, because of its shiraz content and the lesser quantities of the Bordeaux blenders forming part of it), Jamieson's Run is of excellent quality also. The lesson to be learnt is that Coonawarra shiraz, although a generous bearer by the standards of other varieties in the area, is very much an upper-crust variety on the terra rossa soils of the region. It may lengthen a blend but it hardly ever lessens it. In recent years, only in 1989 vintage was Coonawarra shiraz of uneven quality and then because of botrytis assisted by mid-vintage showers.

Since its first vintage in 1985, the varietal content of Jamieson's Run has varied according to season, in line with Mildara's policy of making a forward-drinking style of quality. Nearly always, in any critique of this line, will you find the words 'excellent value'.

Jamieson's Run 1985 (70% shiraz, 20% cabernet sauvignon, 5% merlot and 5% cabernet franc): medium to full red in hue with purple tints, full nose of berries and sweet oak in harmony, berry and vanillan oak flavours in good depth on a well-balanced, medium-bodied palate. (16.5 pts) Drink in 1992-93.

Jamieson's Run 1986 (80% shiraz, 7% cabernet sauvignon, 7% merlot and 6% cabernet franc): full red-purple hue, intense berry cassis aromas in a very ripe fruit-dominant nose against a counterpoint of sweet oak, berry–cassis flavours on a medium-bodied palate with excellent acid and fine tannin on finish. Elegant wine. (17 pts) Drink in 1991-93. (Both 1985 and 1986 were tasted in February 1989.)

Jamieson's Run 1987 (content similar to the 1986): medium to full red in colour, very attractive nose showing complex aromas of capsicum, berries and vanillan oak, berries and sweet vanillan oak flavours, and soft tannins on a medium-bodied palate. (17.5 pts) Excellent value. Drink 1991-93.

Jamieson's Run 1988 (content similar to the 1986): deep purple-red in shade, rich berry–plum nose with a touch of charred oak, outstanding aromatics, soft fruit entry to palate, long flavours of berry–plum fruit and spicy–dusty oak which needed a year or so more to integrate fully with fruit, soft balanced tannins and acid. Marvellous prospects for intermediate-term cellaring (four years). (18.5 pts) Drink 1994 onwards. (1987 and 1988 both tasted late 1989.)

Though Petaluma has made a Coonawarra red each year since 1979, it is fair to say that not until 1985 was the style finally settled. In 1984 there had been a Petaluma Cabernet–Merlot, but there was also a straight Cabernet Sauvignon made in the same year. In 1985, a watershed year for merlot in Coonawarra, and not only in the hands of Petaluma, it set the cabernet–merlot blend as its future course in that region. Vintages 1985 to 1988 will provide the benchmarks for the style. In early January 1990 I tasted the first three of those four vintages, 1988 being not then in bottle.

Petaluma Coonawarra 1985 (vintages 1985-87 all consist of 70% cabernet sauvignon and 30% merlot): deep red, still with hints of purple but just starting to mature in hue, restrained berry and French oak aromas in good balance, medium to full in body with good flesh and a firm backbone and finish. Dark berry flavours and good oak balance. A keeper. (18 pts) Drink in 1995–2000.

Petaluma Coonawarra 1986: deep purple-red in hue, though fractionally lighter than the 1985, aromas of plums and powder in a restrained nose and, after some minutes in the glass, berries. Riper softer berry fruit on palate than 1985, medium to full body, even with a slight touch of cassis. The wine is fruit-dominant on palate, but is well constructed, oak, tannin and soft acidity providing the necessary backbone for a good cellaring life. (17.5 pts) Drink in 1993–98.

Petaluma Coonawarra 1987: a youthful purple-red in shade, with aromas of leafy cabernet, plummy merlot, cedar and tobacco, providing an outstandingly complex nose, lighter fruitier more open palate than either 1985 or 1986, medium bodied but ripe with elegant flavours of plums and berries. Perhaps more forward than prior wines but is still beautifully balanced and will age well. (18.5 pts) Drink in 1994–98.

Petaluma Coonawarra 1988 (70% cabernet sauvignon and 30% merlot): when tasted May 1990 it held a very youthful purple-red shade. On nose its youth was once again quite evident, offering ripe berry, chocolate and char oak aromas, while a long cabernet-dominant palate revealed profound berry and spicy oak flavours and firm but balanced tannin. Though this wine had quite a big palate, it was not massive and unapproachable, merely in need of five more years of cellaring patience before it even approaches its peak. If Bordeaux–Coonawarra comparisons have any validity whatsoever, this is Petaluma's Mouton, perhaps only to be surpassed by 1990—not yet tasted but by reputation a superb Coonawarra vintage. (18.5 pts) Drink in 1995–2000. The 1989 Coonawarra red vintage will be the first to be missed by Petaluma.

Perhaps the only gap in the smile of Wynn's existence at the time of writing is the lack of a cabernet–merlot blend of a quality to compare with the John Riddoch. It must assuredly come before Wynn's rivals steal too big a march. In the meantime there is only Wynn's Cabernet-Hermitage, which, though a perfectly respectable red, just does not have the chutzpah to rank with the complex multi-blends of Mildara and Lindeman.

Another cabernet–shiraz blend that surprised its makers and showed once more how good Coonawarra shiraz can capture a blend is the Riddoch Estate Cabernet–Shiraz 1986, the second label of Katnook Estate and the winner of the 1987 Jimmy Watson Trophy. A blend of 75% cabernet sauvignon and 25% shiraz, this wine, tasted in late 1988, was a deep red-purple in tone, revealing capsicum–berry aromas on nose. Its full-bodied palate offered rich soft berry fruit flavours and harmonious tannin. (18.5 pts) Drink in 1992–96.

All arguments aside, Penfold's is Australia's leading red wine making company with extensive vineyards in Coonawarra—without even considering those considerably larger holdings of its associated company, Wynn's. It is disappointing therefore to note that Penfold's only vintage-to-vintage red from Coonawarra is Bin 128 Shiraz. Good though Coonawarra shiraz is and it can be extremely good, as is Bin 128 in most years, one can only wonder why more use hasn't been made of cabernet sauvignon on a regular basis. Certainly some marvellous special bins of Cabernet–Shiraz have emanated from the Penfold's vineyards, witness Bin 620 from 1966 and Bin 820 from 1982, but why hasn't the attempt been made on a regular basis to make wines like Bin 820 since 1982? Surely fruit of sufficient quality was available during the 1980s even though the best of it may have been used to fulfil the demands of wines such as Cabernet Sauvignon Bin 707?

The smaller vignerons of Coonawarra such as Bowen, Brand and Hollick are enjoying well-deserved success with their blends of cabernet sauvignon and merlot.

Bowen Cabernet–Merlot 1987 (90% cabernet sauvignon, 10% merlot) tasted August 1989: full red purple hues, sweet dark berry and leaf aromas on nose, rich harmonious berry and sweet oak flavours, good length and excellent balance. Lovely red. (18.5 pts) Will age well. Drink 1994 onwards.

Brand's Cabernet–Merlot 1986 (70% cabernet sauvignon, 30% merlot) tasted March 1989 and January 1990: deep red-purple in shade, red- and blackcurrant aromas dominating light oak on nose, berry–cassis flavours most attractive on a long palate, well structured for aging medium-term. (17 pts) Drink in 1991–94.

Hollick Cabernet–Merlot 1985 (96% cabernet sauvignon, 4% merlot) tasted August 1988: medium red-purple hue, attractive minty–leafy aromas, herbaceous–berry flavours, good body and oak balance on palate. (17 pts) Drink in 1992–94.

Hollick Cabernet–Merlot 1986 (90% cabernet sauvignon, 10% merlot) tasted twice in March and April 1989: a generous red-purple in hue, ripe aromas of leaf, mint and plum in an attractive nose, soft full berry and plum flavours on a fairly forward palate. (17 pts) Drink in 1991–93.

Hollick Cabernet–Merlot 1987 (90% cabernet sauvignon, 9% merlot, 1% cabernet franc) tasted August 1989: full red in colour with some density, subdued nose with slight tobacco aromas, herbaceous–berry flavours with good oak and tannin backbone. (16 pts) Drink 1992 onwards.

Straight merlot varietals are still fairly rare in Coonawarra, though the Brands reserve small quantities each year of merlot (and sometimes malbec) for cellar-door sales. Rosemount, however, made a promising merlot-dominant red in 1986 from the young vines of its Kirri Billi estate just north of Penola.

Rosemount Kirri Billi Coonawarra Merlot 1986 (85% merlot, 15% cabernet sauvignon) tasted December 1989: medium to full red in hue, this wine was initially subdued on nose but then opened, revealing aromas of plums and tobacco. Palate flavours were soft and plummy with good depth of fruit and a pleasing balance of tannin and acid on finish. May be kept two to four years. (17 pts) Drink in 1991–93.

Merlot is also grown at Padthaway, and Seppelt felt that its 1987 Padthaway Cabernet–Merlot was too good to submerge in any of its bigger multiregional red blends. So did I.

Seppelt Padthaway Cabernet–Merlot 1987 (80% cabernet sauvignon, 20% merlot) tasted December 1989: medium to full red in colour, this wine offered a pleasing coalescence of berries and spice on nose. Berry flavours were also present on a medium-bodied and nicely ripe but balanced palate. (17.5 pts) Drink in 1991–93.

Malbec is a popular variety in the vineyards of Langhorne Creek, producing warm spicy berry-flavoured wines of short- to medium-term cellaring potential. Winemakers of note here are Bleasdale and Temple Bruer, which also makes a cabernet–merlot blend.

Merlot is grown in small quantities in the Riverland region of South Australia, and there as part of the Renmano range, Chairman's Selection Merlot Bin 540 is usually of good quality and very reasonably priced.

It is McLaren Vale that has provided the setting for several very interesting varietal blends in recent years. Former Hardy winemaker Rob Dundon at Beresford has made a speciality of Coonawarra cabernet sauvignon and McLaren cabernet franc blends. The pairing is fascinating, matching the more intense 'berries' of sauvignon with the lighter more leafy 'berries' of franc. Beresford Cabernet Sauvignon Cabernet Franc 1986 is a case in point: blended from 76% cabernet sauvignon and 24% cabernet franc, this wine was medium to full red in shade, with berry and leaf aromas. Palate flavours revealed soft berry fruit and firm leafy characters on back palate, which added an austerity to the wine and highlighted a green stalkiness which may be varietal or the effect of fruit off young vines. (16 pts) Drink in 1991–92.

Chateau Reynella, now a subsidiary of the Hardy Wine Company, also uses local merlot and malbec in conjunction with cabernet sauvignon. These are firm wines which usually need at least three years in cellar.

Former Chateau Reynella winemaker Geoff Merrill also uses about 20% McLaren Vale cabernet franc in his Cabernet Sauvignon wine. Its effect, as Geoff says, is to add a floral complexity to the wine which is quite noticeable in its younger years, although it is absorbed into nose and palate by more dominant cabernet sauvignon berry characters as the wine gains bottle age.

Geoff Merrill Cabernet 1986 (80% Coonawarra cabernet sauvignon, 20% McLaren Vale cabernet franc) tasted March 1989: deep red in shade, offering attractive redcurrant and raspberry aromas against a canvas of pencilly oak, this wine reveals ripe berry-cassis flavours and a very good tannin-acid balance on finish. (17.5 pts) Drink in 1993–97.

Wirra Wirra was one of the first wineries in McLaren Vale to make consistent use of merlot in a red blend. That wine was Church Block, now one of the most sought-after reds on restaurant lists, and no wonder: it is generally medium-bodied and very easy drinking. Church Block Cabernet–Shiraz–Merlot 1988 is no exception. An attractive limpid red in hue, this wine offered a complex nose of fresh mulberries, sweet oak and a touch of chocolate. On a medium-bodied palate there were fresh berry flavours and soft well-integrated tannins. (16 pts) Forward. Drink in 1991–92.

Other makers of good varietal blends in McLaren Vale are Scarpantoni, Shottesbrooke and Thomas Fernhill, not forgetting the giant of the region, Thomas Hardy, whose fruit is both local and from Padthaway.

What is the future of the Bordeaux varieties in the Adelaide Hills? Certainly cabernet sauvignon has been a long-standing variety in the vineyards of the warmer northern limit, having been first planted more than 140 years ago in the first Pewsey Vale vineyard and re-established by Yalumba in the same location in 1961. In the cooler locales of the southern and central Hills, in cool years such as 1987, cabernet sauvignon faces serious difficulties in ripening on that chill and often windswept terrain. Proper vineyard siting and exposure to sunlight are critical to all varieties in these areas, and the presence of the earlier-ripening merlot is crucial in any local vineyard, if a complete 'cabernet' red is to be made. As a local grower and winemaker for his own estate, Stafford Ridge, as well as for Hardy's, Geoff Weaver well realises this—the differences between the cabernet vintages in 1987 and 1988 being very marked in that area.

Heggies was the second substantial vineyard investment made by Yalumba in the slightly warmer Eden Valley area of those northern Hills. Here cabernet sauvignon, merlot and cabernet franc ripen well but still show on occasions those leafy characters that usually identify cool-area cabernet blends. In September 1989, I tasted Heggies Cabernets 1985, 1986 and 1987, each a blend of 75% cabernet sauvignon, 15% cabernet franc and 10% merlot.

Heggies Cabernets 1985: medium to full red and still purple-tinted, berry aromas on nose but a little subdued and needs to open out, soft berry fruit flavours on palate with good tannin balance. (17 pts) Drink in 1992–93.
Heggies Cabernets 1986: medium-full purple-red, nose offering ripe berries and a touch of smoky oak. Ripe full berry flavours and soft integrated tannin. Attractive forward-drinking style. (16.5 pts) Drink in 1991–92.
Heggies Cabernets 1987: youthful medium purple-red in shade, complex aromas of berries, plums and green leaf, subtle oak background, medium-bodied with flavours of capsicum and berries, very elegant and well balanced, soft tannin. A lovely soft-fruited wine. (18 pts) Drink in 1992–94.

'H' also stands for Henschke, long-term winemakers of Eden Valley fruit. The Henschke Keyneton Estate Shiraz–Cabernet–Malbec is perhaps a blend of a former age, but in the skilled hands of Stephen Henschke this blend is by no means old-fashioned. Keyneton 1987, tasted December

1989, was medium to full red in colour with hints of purple, offering complex aromas of pepper, spice and berries with minty oak also in train. Palate was of medium body dominated by spice and peppery oak flavours but well balanced. (17 pts) Drink in 1991–93.

The vineyard area of the Adelaide Hills seems virtually to grow by the day, and the 1990s will undoubtedly see the present trickle of cabernet blends grow, if not into a flood then certainly into a steady stream, into which I will be only too delighted to dip at any time in the future.

Without any shadow of doubt, the most outstanding cabernet–merlot blend that I have seen recently from the Barossa has been the 1987 vintage of St Hallett. This wine, tasted in December 1989, was an attractive full red-purple in hue, revealing on nose most delightful aromas of plums, vanilla and tobacco. Its palate offered soft, almost sweet fruit flavours against a canvas of vanillan oak and well-balanced tannin. It was a most generous wine, rich and youthful, in need of a cellar for two to four years. (18.5 pts) Drink in 1992–94.

Other makers of cabernet merlot blends of good quality are Elderton, Charles Cimicky (formerly Karlsburg), and Lakewood.

Also tasted in September 1989 was the Merlot 1988 of Grant Burge. This was full red in colour, with a nose of excellent plum and tobacco fragrances. Its palate was quite full and open, showing a lovely harmony of plum and vanilla oak flavours. Though made to be drunk quite early, it certainly had the structure to age well for two to three years. (17 pts) Drink in 1991–93.

Two Barossa winemakers of major importance also require mention: Penfold's for its Bin 389 Cabernet–Shiraz blend, in which Barossa fruit plays a key role, and Wolf Blass for his company's multi-area blends of cabernet sauvignon, shiraz and now occasionally merlot, the most notable of which are those appearing under the Black Label. Current releases of such wines at time of writing were the 1986 vintage of Bin 389 and the 1984 of Black Label.

Penfold's Cabernet Shiraz Bin 389 1986: medium to full red in hue, this wine showed a very subtle harmony of berries and spicy oak aromas. Palate was very smooth and sophisticated, combining supple berry and spicy oak flavours extremely well. (17 pts) It was not a profound palate, but it was as usual very accessible. Drink in 1991–92.

Wolf Blass Black Label Cabernet Sauvignon–Shiraz–Merlot 1984: a maturing garnet-red in hue, this wine was a model of harmony in bouquet, spicy, cedary oak and plummy fruit making an almost Bordeaux-like contribution to aroma. Its medium-weight palate was no whit inferior to its nose, revealing full soft berry and plum flavours and delightful oak integration. (18.5 pts) A top multi-area multi-varietal blend that may mellow longer in cellar for two to three years. Drink in 1992–94. (Both wines tasted October 1989.)

No matter how attached one may be to red blends of a favourite area, Blass blends are never lacking in interest.

Seppelt also produces a 'Dorrien' cabernet blend from time to time, which is always of premium quality, and a most reliable 'Premier Vineyard' cabernet–merlot–malbec blend.

On the rather warm Adelaide Plains, the Primo Estate of Joe Grilli produces remarkably delicate wines for that area. Amongst them is an often excellent cabernet–merlot blend. The Primo Estate 'Joseph' Cabernet Sauvignon–Merlot 1987, tasted October 1989, was medium to full red in colour. Berry and vanillan oak aromas highlighted the bouquet, while similar flavours were pleasingly noticeable on palate. A well-balanced blend of good style. (17 pts) Drink in 1992–93. I am informed that 1988 was also an excellent vintage for this blend.

Another blend recently seen which was produced in this area was the Roseworthy Cabernet Merlot 1987. Tasted in April 1989, this very youthful purple-red blend was pungently herbaceous on nose, showing dominant capsicum aromas. Its palate, however, was more complex, unfolding capsicum berry flavours and finely textured tannins. (16.5 pts) Drink in 1992.

The Angle Vale winery of the Berri–Renmano Group also makes good cabernet blends from time to time under its Lauriston label. A good recent example was Lauriston Cabernet–Shiraz–Malbec 1985, which when tasted in October 1989 was a maturing red in hue, ripe and sweet on nose with aromas of old wood, and softly and richly flavoured on its well-balanced palate. (17 pts) Drink no later than 1992.

The cabernet sauvignon of Clare has occasionally been accused of being too firm and unyielding, and that is why merlot and cabernet franc and to a lesser extent malbec should be 'naturals' for the area in most years. Malbec of course has veteran status in the region, having been used for many years in cabernet blends by Stanley and Wendouree. Merlot and cabernet franc, though newer to the region, show much promise, nowhere more than at Penfold's Clare Estate.

The first Clare Estate red, a blend of 40% merlot, 29% cabernet sauvignon, 28% malbec, and 3% cabernet franc made in 1985, when tasted in mid-1988 was full red-purple in hue with a deep nose of plums and berries and complex oak handled in the usual immaculate Penfold's fashion. Its palate was ripe with berry cassis flavours uppermost, lovely oak integration and fine-grained tannins providing an elegantly soft finish. (17.5 pts) At its best in 1992.

Its successor, Clare Estate 1986, was also merlot-dominant (41%) with the supporting players malbec (33%), cabernet sauvignon (12%) and cabernet franc (14%). In the glass in March 1989 it was a deep red with a purple wash, spicily aromatic, showing a fine balance of plums and vanillan oak, and full, ripe and soft on palate with a lovely harmony of plums and spicy oak. A most alluring red. (18 pts) Drink in 1992-94.

Tim Knappstein is a vastly experienced winemaker in the Clare region. His Cabernet-Merlot blend, made in a more forward-drinking style than his Cabernet Sauvignon, contains 15% merlot (his Cabernet Sauvignon also has a 7% merlot constituent). In August 1989 I tasted a range of four Knappstein Cabernet-Merlots from 1985 to 1988.

1985: full red in hue, berry-oak aromas balanced but subdued on nose, palate flavours, predominantly of berries and spice, quite firm with noticeable tannin on finish. A bigger Clare style. (17 pts) Drink in 1994.

1986: full red-purple in colour, ripe berry-dominant nose, open and pleasing beautifully balanced berry-spice and plum flavours on palate, soft and accessible but has sufficient tannin to keep well until 1993. (18 pts)

1987: medium to full red in shade, soft berry-plum-tobacco aromas in a forward nose. Soft elegant leafy berry flavours. Ready quite soon. (16.5 pts) Drink in 1991-92.

1988: medium to full red in colour, touches of purple, rich plummy nose, full soft ripe palate with soft well-integrated tannins. (17.5 pts) Drink 1994 onwards.

Tasted also were a range of cabernets (the later vintages of which included the 7% merlot content). The differences were obvious. The cabernet sauvignon range was firmer, more tannic and destined for a longer life—hardly a function of the 8% merlot difference in the wines, a more likely cause being a difference in winemaking technique, such as longer cabernet skin contact or use of cabernet pressings. Whatever the cause of the difference, Clare merlot did the wines no disservice at all.

Though clerical orders have a certain reputation for conservatism, Brother John May of the Jesuit Brotherhood at Sevenhill has embraced both cabernet franc and merlot almost with a religious zeal. In August 1989 I tasted the Sevenhill Merlot-Cabernet Franc 1987. Deep red-purple in colour, with fresh minty aromas on nose and a long palate showing a very harmonious liaison of dark berries, plums and charred oak, this wine was very new regime and quite the antithesis of the traditionally heavy Clare style. (17.5 pts) Drink in 1991-92. From year to year Sevenhill also make an excellent cabernet-malbec blend.

While discussing such blends, mention must be made of the Bridgewater Mill Cabernet-Malbec 1987. Though I have not discussed second-level or commercial labels in any length in this book unless they are of outstanding quality, it is precisely for this reason that the Bridgewater Mill wine now qualifies; also because this red, sourced from Clare, will become a regular release. When last tasted in October 1989 it was a youthful purple-red, with mint, spice and vanilla aromas on bouquet. Its long full-bodied palate, highlighted by mint and peppery oak flavours, finished quite firmly, but all was in good balance. (17.5 pts) Drink 1994 onwards.

The wines from the Skillogalee vineyard are made by the Mitchell winery under contract. Skillogalee Cabernet 1988 was 85% cabernet sauvignon with an unascertained 15% of cabernet franc and malbec (both varieties being picked and crushed together). Tasted in December 1989, this was another wine of very youthful deep red-purple hue, showing on nose aromas of mint berries and leafy cabernet. On a long palate, predominant flavours were of ripe berries and minty wood, finishing with quite firm tannins. A rich but not overextractive red, showing the firmness and length that cabernet sauvignon with even a small addition of cabernet franc can give to a wine. (17 pts) Drink in 1994–96. Seen at the same time was a very good Skillogalee Shiraz–Cabernet, also from 1988 vintage.

Other makers of interesting cabernet sauvignons, sometimes with a small percentage of merlot, cabernet franc and/or malbec, are Jeffrey Grosset, Jim Barry Wines, Jud's Hill (Brian Barry), Neil Paulett, Andrew and Neil Pike, Leasingham, whose Cabernet–Malbec Bin 56 (with those of Wendouree) probably aroused the blending interest of many winemakers and consumers alike in the 1960s and 1970s, Wendouree and the Wilson Vineyard.

WESTERN AUSTRALIA

When a new wave of pioneer vignerons began to explore the viticultural boundaries of the West 25 years ago, cabernet sauvignon was one of the first varieties used to assess the qualities of those then-unknown areas, Margaret River and the Great Southern (Mount Barker–Frankland River). Not surprisingly, since sufficient planting material became available in the early 1980s, interest has also greatly increased in its Bordeaux cousin, merlot, especially in Margaret River where merlot is being employed not only in its traditional role as softener for heavier and sturdier cabernet sauvignons, but also more infrequently as a single varietal red. Interest in merlot is still growing, as might be expected in the Great Southern and also in the Perth Hills (or Darling Ranges as they used to be).

Cabernet franc presently has a lower profile, but is also planted in Margaret River and to a much smaller extent in the Great Southern.

Malbec, however, as in South Australia, is quite a veteran of Western Australian viticulture, though nowhere planted in vast tracts.

Chittering Estate is a recent adornment to the northern edge of the Perth Hills. There winemaker Steven Shapira makes a firm cabernet–merlot style, designed, as he says, in the European style to be kept a while. The Chittering Estate Cabernet–Merlot 1987 (85% cabernet sauvignon and 15% merlot), tasted in July 1989 and again the following month, was deep and dense in its purple-red hue, showing cassis, berries and smoky oak aromas on nose. Concentrated berry flavours dominated palate, which was long and firmly tannic on finish. A *vin de garde* as the French would say, hard to taste at that time, due to tannin, but certainly with sufficient fruit. (16 pts) Do not drink before 1995.

Other makers of this classic Bordeaux blend in the Perth Hills are Darlington Vineyard and Hainault.

In Margaret River, Cullen's Willyabrup (now in the skilful hands of Vanya Cullen, who succeeds to the faithful and equally skilled stewardship of her mother, Di) moves on ever growing in strength. The Cullen's Cabernet–Merlot 1987, when tasted in August 1989, was a prominent red-purple in shade with some density. Its nose showed delightful berry–vanillan aromas and an attractively long palate of berry flavours, some skinsy tannins on finish and overall a great integration of wood and fruit. (18 pts) Keep until 1993.

Evans & Tate make both a cabernet sauvignon with a merlot content and a straight merlot from their Margaret River fruit. The Redbrook Cabernet Sauvignon 1987 (84% cabernet sauvignon, 10% merlot, 6% cabernet franc) was medium to full red-purple in tone, with cedary berry aromas on a very pleasing and elegant nose. Clean berry flavours on palate were long and soft though persistent, and the wine finished with light and well-integrated tannins. (17.5 pts) Drink in 1991–93. If there is any criticism to be made, it is that the wine is perhaps a little too light for long-term cellaring (that is, four years or more), but any winemaker is entitled to choose his own style. (Tasted August 1989.)

The Evans & Tate lighter touch is also quite evident in the Redbrook Merlots, four vintages of which I tasted in April 1989.

Redbrook Merlot 1983: a very full dense red in hue even at six years of age, clean full slightly lifted aromas of plums and tobacco, a varietally faithful nose, berries and hint of straw on a long palate, soft tannin finish. Good structure, depth and style. (17.5 pts) Drinking well at that time, though would hold for one or two years longer.

Redbrook Merlot 1984: full red in tone with brown edges, berry and tobacco aromas on nose, supple medium-weight well-balanced palate, berry flavours, pleasant drinking at that time, lighter than the 1983, will hold one or two years longer. (17 pts)

Redbrook Merlot 1985: developing red-brown colour, lifted tobacco nose, lifted edgy palate. Drink up. Not pointed, because of volatility.

Redbrook Merlot 1986: medium to full red in hue, with aromas of ripe plum on a very pleasant nose, medium-weight palate, plummy flavours, supple easy-drinking, deceptively forward. Between 1984 and 1983 in weight and cellaring potential. (17 pts) Drink in 1991–93.

Like Evans & Tate, Erl Happ makes both a cabernet–merlot blend and a 100% varietal merlot. The Happ Merlots are also very true to variety, making soft full fruity reds of immediate appeal.

Happ's Merlot 1986 (tasted July 1988): full red in colour and slightly subdued on nose, this wine showed typical plummy flavours on a soft and supple ready-drinking palate. (16 pts) Drink in 1990–92.

Happ's Merlot 1987: medium to full red in shade, bouquet was highlighted by plums, while a very accessible palate showed soft and full berry flavours. (17 pts) Drink in 1991–93.

Happ's Cabernet–Merlot 1986 (tasted August 1989): medium to full red in shade with some purple tints, this wine showed quite complex berry plum and capsicum aromatics, while its soft palate was dominated by berry-capsicum flavours and finished with well-integrated tannin. (16.5 pts) Drink in 1992-93.

On the strength of the Redbrook and Happ merlots, showing especially in the case of the older Redbrooks that the variety has the capacity to age well in bottle over a medium term (three to four years), producing in that time a soft though serious-drinking red, merlot would appear to have a bright future in the Margaret River region. Nevertheless, winemaking skill is needed to avoid unidimensionality.

Dominant merlot (60%) and cabernet sauvignon (40%) comprise the Ribbon Vale Estate Merlot-Cabernet 1987. This wine showed Margaret River merlot close to its best. When tasted in July 1989, it was a deep red-purple in hue, with an attractive berry nose, a long firm berry and plum palate and a firm tannic finish. (17.5 pts) Cellar until 1993.

Peter Gherardi at Freycinet Estate employs both merlot and cabernet franc in his Cabernet Sauvignon. 1986 Freycinet Cabernet Sauvignon, when tasted in July 1989, was deep red-purple in hue, with a complex melange of cassis, berry and capsicum aromas on nose. Palate was full and firm showing good sweet fruit and well-integrated tannin. (17.5 pts) Do not drink before 1992.

The traditional Australian blend of cabernet sauvignon and shiraz shows to great advantage at Redgate. Its 1987 blend was particularly successful. Medium to full red-purple in colour, this wine revealed quite complex aromas of berries, cassis and black pepper on nose, while the palate disclosed leafy berry flavours beautifully complemented by cedary oak characters on back palate. (17.5 pts) Drink 1993 onwards.

Malbec too makes an occasional appearance in Margaret River, always as a blending variety. At Vasse Felix, the proportion of malbec contained in its Cabernet Sauvignon varies between 5% and 15%. The 1987 vintage contains 7%. Tasted in August 1989, the Vasse Felix Cabernet Sauvignon of that year was deep red-purple in hue, showing a lovely combination of berry fruit and peppery oak aromas on nose. Flavours too were quite harmonious, uniting those berry and pepper characters in an evenly balanced and long palate. This was a wine of good cellaring potential, elegant yet tightly structured. (17 pts) Drink 1993 onwards.

Perhaps it may be said of malbec that in Margaret River it complements cabernet sauvignon too well, surrendering its own lightly spicy fruit qualities to the more dominant aromas and flavours of regional cabernet sauvignon and small oak, without offering merlot's characteristic softening qualities.

Malbec is also grown in the Great Southern region—or Mount Barker-Frankland River, as its winemakers prefer to call it. Merv Lange at Alkoomi has made 100% varietal malbec for many years. Two Alkoomi Malbecs have come my way in recent times. The 1986, tasted August 1988, was then a very youthful purple-red in colour. On nose this wine showed typically spicy aromatics, with similar spice and light berry flavours revealed on a ripe palate. A full wine with intermediate cellaring potential. (16.5 pts) Drink in 1992. Its younger brother, the 1987, tasted a year later, was very similar, spicily aromatic on nose, medium weight on palate with clean, light berry and spice flavours, though without the fullness of the 1986. A good wine, which will cellar well in the short to medium term (two to four years). (16 pts) Drink 1993 onwards. Alkoomi also has plantings of merlot, which have already seen their first small crops (the Alkoomi Cabernet Sauvignon 1987 contains about 4% merlot). Coming vintages of merlot at Alkoomi should provide blending options of great interest.

At Frankland River, Houghton grow malbec which on occasions has been released as a separate varietal. More often it has been blended with shiraz, the 1987 blend of which was full red-purple in shade with strawberry and spice aromas and flavours. A pleasant, well-balanced soft-finishing red with short-term cellaring potential. (15.5 pts) Drink in 1992—though shiraz–malbec blends, like those of shiraz and merlot, while pleasant drinking from time to time incline towards the expedient rather than the classical. At least a significant proportion of cabernet sauvignon or cabernet franc seems to be required.

At Capel Vale, that very interesting winery of Dr Peter Pratten midway between Busselton and Bunbury, 'Baudin' is made. This is a blend of cabernet sauvignon, merlot and shiraz. Capel Vale Baudin 1987, tasted August 1989, was very young in colour, with a slightly lifted berry fruit and a medium-weight palate of berry-pepper flavours and a firm tannic finish. Perhaps more mid-palate fruit would have helped the wine, but it may fill out. (16 pts) Drink 1992 onwards.

Other blends of cabernet and merlot of good quality are to be found at Baldivis Estate near Mandurah.

In Western Australia, and especially Margaret River and Mount Barker–Frankland River, merlot has very great potential. Looking into that crystal ball of prediction for the 1990s decade, I foresee many exciting cabernet blends, especially from makers such as Cape Mentelle and Moss Wood, who are only very recently acquainted with the variety in their own vineyards.

As for cabernet franc, prospects seem as limited as in the eastern states. Its role seems to be confined to making cabernet sauvignon more complex, without necessarily making its palate more generous or accessible.

Likewise, malbec should play only bit parts, being blended with cabernet sauvignon in very small proportions and then only as a minor assistant to merlot.

OTHER REDS

There remain about 3000 hectares of red grape varieties grown in Australia for table wine production. The chief of these in quantity is grenache, used for rosé, bulk red and tawny port. It is hardly ever seen in its own right except for rosé, in which role it is eminently satisfactory in such areas as McLaren Vale, where Reynella and Mount Hurtle make very good everyday-drinking wines.

As for mataro or mourvedre, it is useful in bulk blends for its high tannic astringency, but is rarely seen these days on labels, if only because our winemakers are seeking fruit, not excessive tannin, in their wines.

Zinfandel is planted in minute quantity, being prized at Cape Mentelle in Margaret River where David Hohnen sometimes feels that it is the best wine of the vintage, producing Rhône-like reds of spicy berry flavours, which do have good aging potential. The variety is hardly planted elsewhere, but who knows, its day may come.

Another that may be destined to exist in only one Australian area is mondeuse, a variety of eastern France, for many years used at Milawa by Brown Brothers as a partner for shiraz and cabernet sauvignon.

There are Italian varieties (indeed, zinfandel may be one), barbera, sangiovese and nebbiolo. During his time as winemaker at Montrose, Carlo Corino, who returned to Italy in 1989, made some fine barberas.

Then there are the hybrids, both locally developed and imported: tarrango, an Australian very good for light fresh reds as Brown Brothers have proved; ruby cabernet, useful in providing cabernet-style wines in hot areas, where cabernet sauvignon produces indifferent wine; rubired, with its intensely coloured juice, a little going a very long way in colour improvement; and chambourcin, a hybrid bred for tougher damper conditions, yet managing to make very good shiraz-like red at Port Macquarie on the mid north coast of New South Wales.

There are also the other early-ripeners of central and eastern France: meunier, certainly a variety sought after by sparkling winemakers but sometimes made as a single variety red at Great Western or blended with pinot noir to make an acceptably soft forward-drinking 'Burgundian' red, as it was by Best's in 1988. And what of gamay noir à jus blanc, the true 'Beaujolais' variety? There is little planted in Australia. I have never tasted one, but it too may find a niche in one of our cool areas.

As the years go by and the regional requirements of the red varieties planted in Australia become better known, perhaps vignerons may be encouraged to plant only the variety or varieties most suitable for their region instead of the ubiquitous cabernet sauvignon and shiraz. Some of the lesser varieties may then be better grown—and known to wine lovers throughout the nation. It took the French more than 500 years. Here perhaps it may not take as long.

BOTTLE-FERMENTED

SPARKLING WINES

In the chapters on chardonnay and pinot noir, I wrote of the requirements for top Australian sparkling wine, not 'champagne', for that of course is made only in the Champagne region of France, a fact our makers of better-quality Australian sparkling wine are slowly coming to recognise. This chapter is about the best of our sparkling wines—that is, those made from chardonnay, pinot noir and perhaps meunier. Such wines are expensive, but I make no apology for that. Their expense may make them better appreciated. Of the rest, I will make no individual comment except that most of them are great for party quaffing or for mixing with orange juice.

Undoubtedly the palm for our best sparkling wines must be awarded to Australia's most experienced maker, Seppelt, who in the late 1970s realised that Australia could, indeed should, do better, much better in this field. They imported French expertise, in the person of Dominique Landragin. Though he had very little raw material of excellence to work with, quite early on the experimental wines began to show that Seppelt's effort was certainly not in vain, for the older Great Western vintage wines of the 1960s and early 1970s, excellent though they were, bore little resemblance to champagne, except in method. Landragin, while of course maintaining the method, began to apply the brushstrokes of the authentic taste. After Landragin's departure to Yellowglen, his successor, the ebullient Warren Randall, carried the work still further, blending truly great Australian wines like 1984 Salinger and 1986 Great Western Vintage Brut. The former wine is unlikely now to be found, but the latter wine, which I last tasted in August 1989, may still be available. Pale to medium yellow in hue, with a fine bead and a vigorous mousse, this wine offered most attractive creamy yeasty aromas in a delightful nose, while a long palate revealed an excellent balance of nutty fruit, creamy autolysis and a refreshing acidity. A superbly complex wine with loads of flavour. (18.5 pts) Drink from 1990 onwards, but it should age very gracefully to at least 1993 if cellared correctly.

Seppelt also makes Fleur de Lys, a range of medium-priced non-vintage and vintage sparkling wines of good quality, the vintage wine and a Chardonnay Brut vintage by the champagne method, the non-vintage by the transfer process. In style, the Fleur de Lys vintage Chardonnay tends to show more varietal character than a true blanc de blancs should, but for lovers of the creamy chardonnay taste it is a most suitable wine.

Another sparkling wine of excellent varietal chardonnay in a similar style is the Wolf Blass Chardonnay Cuvée of any given year. Indeed Australia seems remarkably well placed to make sparkling chardonnays of great quality in most years.

Yet since 1986 vintage, Seppelt has had a worthy rival for excellence at the top of our sparkling wine market: Croser, whether the wine delicately crafted at Bridgewater Mill from the best pinot noir and chardonnay that the Petaluma vineyards in the Piccadilly Valley can grow; or the man, a dedicated winemaker, totally convinced since the late 1960s that top-quality sparkling wine would be one of his more important missions in a very busy life.

Croser Pinot Noir Chardonnay 1987, tasted September 1989, was then pale yellow in hue, revealing a very fine bead and a vigorous mousse. Its bouquet showed an excellent integration of creamy chardonnay and cracked yeast aromas, while palate offered a delicious liaison of chardonnay 'cream' and restrained yeast flavours enlivened by that intense mousse. It was also a wine that seemed to have good potential for bottle development if properly cellared. (18.5 pts) Drink in 1990-92.

Bridgewater Mill Pinot Chardonnay Brut, a second-label sparkling wine, not necessarily made from Adelaide Hills fruit, is also a very fine aperitif style.

A very recent and innovative entrant to the Australian sparkling wine market has been Domaine Chandon: innovative not for any technical reason but for its marketing policy which dictates that it will make non-vintage sparkling wines from top-quality material from its own Yarra vineyard and other suitable Victorian, Tasmanian and South Australian areas, which it will sell in the upper echelons of Australian and overseas markets—a courageous strategy, considering the Australian equation of local non-vintage sparkling wine with downmarket mass-produced product. Domaine Chandon NV 87/1 is, however, a superb response to any such Jeremiac prophecies. Tasted in March 1990, this wine was pale to medium yellow in colour, finely beaded with a vigorous mousse. Persistent creamy-nutty aromas and flavours made for an exceptional bouquet and palate, while crisp acidity 'cut' the palate perfectly. (18 pts) Drink in 1990-93.

Another specialist sparkling winemaker is Yellowglen, founded by Ian Home in the early 1970s. This vineyard grabbed the spotlight when Dominique Landragin was enlisted as a shareholder and sparkling winemaker in 1982. Despite a national marketing strategy pitched at the middle and upper levels of the market, production was small and the company was purchased by Mildara in 1984. At the top of the Yellowglen list is Cuvée Victoria, a vintage sparkling wine made from the classic varieties, pinot noir and chardonnay, grown in Victoria and always worth tasting.

On his departure from Yellowglen in 1987 Dominique Landragin commenced making sparkling and other table wines on his own account. The upshot is a range of sparkling non-vintage wines of consistent quality.

Tasted in October 1989, Landragin Australia Reserve NV was pink-gold in hue, offering a complex nutty toasty pinot nose and also slightly herbaceous aromas, characters which with toasty yeast flavours were repeated on palate. A complex and delicate wine. (17 pts)

That Barossa maker of substantial stature, Yalumba, has been for years a vigorous participant in the lower and middle ranges of the Australian sparkling market, and since 1984 the producer of 'D', a champagne-method wine of chardonnay, pinot noir and meunier lineage. The 1986 'D', tasted in September 1989, was medium yellow in hue and finely beaded. On nose it revealed aromas of toasted nuts and developing creaminess, while palate showed a lively creamy mousse, fine balance and a clean acid 'cut'. (17.5 pts)

Strangely, the one crack in the huge megalith that is the Penfold's organisation is sparkling wine of excellence. To complement a range of superb reds such as Grange Hermitage, Bin 707 Cabernet Sauvignon and Wynn's John Riddoch Cabernet, a sparkling wine of superb quality is needed. That it hasn't yet eventuated is not so much a commentary upon winemaking skill as upon order of priorities. Certainly, though the Seaview Pinot Chardonnay Brut and Blanc de Blancs have shown great promise from time to time (the Seaview Pinot Chardonnay of 1984 was especially fine) and are quite consistent, they lack the brilliance of a top Seppelt Salinger or Great Western Vintage Brut. And wines such as Wynn's Edmond Mazure seem too prone to premature aging. However, given time and the undoubted collective skills of the organisation the Penfold megalith will triumph.

Like those of Penfold, Hardy's sparkling wines also seem to lack ultimate style. Good sound quality, yes! Excitement on nose and palate, no!

Another specialist sparkling winemaker is Chateau Remy, whose French parent company owns three famous Champagne houses: Charles Heidsieck, Piper Heidsieck, and the redoubtable Krug, the Rolls-Royce of champagnes (or should it be that Rolls-Royce is the Krug of motor cars?). Regrettably, the local scion has not yet reached those sublime heights, but the time may come when with top-quality chardonnay and pinot noir, Chateau Remy will produce sparkling wines of superb character, though perhaps not from the Avoca region of western Victoria.

That other French winemaker of the region, Dominique Portet, also makes sparkling wines. To the hypercritic, which I suppose I am, they are full flavoursome styles lacking a little delicacy, which will certainly be rectified when Taltarni's new Tasmanian vineyard comes fully into production in 1991.

While in Tasmania, mention must also be made of Heemskerk, of which Roederer owns fifty per cent. Here, too, there are increased plantings of pinot noir and chardonnay for sparkling wine production, though no wines have yet been released.

Sparkling wines of good quality are produced in most wine-producing regions of Australia. In the Lower Hunter Valley, Tyrrell's rely solely on pinot noir for a wine of great character. Hungerford Hill have shown that great sparkling wine was not the sole prerogative of cool areas, when it secured a trophy at the Royal Melbourne Wine Show for a 1986 Chardonnay Brut.

In the Upper Hunter, both Rosemount and Arrowfield–Mount Arrow make good sparkling wines, Arrowfield in particular producing a delightful 1987 MC (méthode champenoise) Chardonnay Pinot, which I tasted in October 1989. Pale yellow-gold in hue with a fine bead, vigorous mousse and complex nutty yeasty aromas, this wine offered most intricate nutty, smoky, buttery creamy flavours in a superb palate. (18.5 pts)

Victorian sparkling winemakers such as Chateau Remy, Taltarni and Yellowglen have already been mentioned, but there are others such as Brown Brothers at Milawa who also produce excellent sparkling wines by the champagne method from the classic varieties grown high in those north-eastern valleys. The alpine chill of these hills has also attracted makers such as Orlando, which has commissioned the planting of pinot noir and chardonnay in the Buckland Valley for the same reasons.

Elsewhere in Victoria, smaller local makers such as Yarra Burn make a speciality of champenising pinot noir, as do the Cope-Williams family with pinot noir and chardonnay at their Romsey Vineyard in the Macedon region. And at Great Western a sparkling wine subculture based upon the Seppelt tradition has seen the emergence of sparkling wine of excellent standard from Best's and Mount Chalambar.

In South Australia, smaller makers such as Wirra Wirra have a quite commendable wine called 'The Cousins', while the former Krondorf principals, Grant Burge and Ian Wilson, now pursuing their separate wine paths, are each making good champagne-method wine from the classic varieties—in Wilson's case, as he proudly proclaims in his advertisements, to 'keep the frogs on the hop'. Whether those frogs will be seriously impeded by any quick leap in the popularity of upmarket Australian sparkling wine remains to be seen, but there is no doubt that as long as Australian quality continues to rise and the French franc continues to firm, top-of-the-market Australian sparkling wine will be a superbly viable alternative to champagne. Our winemakers have the skill. Do our consumers have the will?

VINTAGE CHART

CHARDONNAY

LEADING AREAS	1986	1987	1988	1989	1990
NEW SOUTH WALES					
HUNTER VALLEY	☆☆☆☆	☆☆☆☆	☆☆☆ – ☆	☆☆☆	☆☆☆
MUDGEE	☆☆☆☆	☆☆☆	☆☆☆☆	☆☆☆☆	☆☆☆☆
VICTORIA					
BENDIGO	☆☆☆☆	☆☆☆	☆☆☆☆	☆☆☆☆	☆☆☆☆
DRUMBORG[1]	☆☆☆ – ☆	☆☆☆	☆☆☆☆	☆☆☆☆ – ☆	☆☆☆☆ – ☆
GEELONG	☆☆☆☆	☆☆☆☆	☆☆☆☆ – ☆	☆☆☆☆	☆☆☆☆
GOULBURN VALLEY	☆☆☆	☆☆☆	☆☆☆☆	☆☆☆☆	☆☆☆☆
GREAT WESTERN[2]	☆☆☆☆	☆☆	☆☆☆☆	☆☆☆	☆☆☆☆ – ☆
MACEDON	☆☆☆☆	☆☆☆☆	☆☆☆☆	☆☆☆	☆☆☆☆☆
MORNINGTON PENINSULA	☆☆☆☆	☆☆☆	☆☆☆☆☆	☆☆☆	☆☆☆☆☆
NE VICTORIA	☆☆☆☆ – ☆	☆☆☆ – ☆	☆☆☆☆ – ☆	☆☆☆☆ – ☆	☆☆☆☆ – ☆
PYRENEES	☆☆☆ – ☆	☆☆☆ – ☆	☆☆☆☆	☆☆☆☆	☆☆☆☆
YARRA VALLEY	☆☆☆☆	☆☆☆ – ☆	☆☆☆☆☆	☆☆☆	☆☆☆☆☆
SOUTH AUSTRALIA					
ADELAIDE HILLS NORTH	☆☆☆☆	☆☆☆☆☆	☆☆☆☆	☆☆☆☆☆	☆☆☆☆
BAROSSA	☆☆☆☆	☆☆☆☆	☆☆☆☆	☆☆☆☆☆	☆☆☆ – ☆
CLARE	☆☆☆☆	☆☆☆	☆☆☆☆☆	☆☆☆☆ – ☆	☆☆☆☆☆
COONAWARRA	☆☆☆☆	☆☆☆	☆☆☆☆	☆☆☆	☆☆☆☆ – ☆
McLAREN VALE	☆☆☆☆	☆☆☆☆	☆☆☆	☆☆☆	☆☆☆☆
PADTHAWAY	☆☆☆☆	☆☆☆	☆☆ (frost)	☆☆☆☆☆	☆☆☆☆
WESTERN AUSTRALIA					
LOWER GREAT SOUTHERN	☆☆☆ – ☆	☆☆☆☆	☆☆☆☆ – ☆	☆☆☆☆ – ☆	☆☆☆☆ – ☆
MARGARET RIVER	☆☆☆	☆☆☆	☆☆☆	☆☆☆☆	☆☆☆☆
SW COASTAL PLAIN	☆☆☆☆	☆☆☆ – ☆	☆☆☆☆☆	☆☆☆☆☆	☆☆☆☆
SWAN VALLEY	☆☆☆☆	☆☆☆	☆☆☆	☆☆☆☆	☆☆☆☆☆
TASMANIA					
PIPERS BROOK	☆☆☆☆	☆☆☆☆	☆☆☆☆	☆☆☆☆	☆☆☆☆☆
HOBART	☆☆☆	☆☆☆☆	☆☆☆☆	☆☆☆☆☆	☆☆☆☆☆
AUSTRALIAN CAPITAL TERRITORY	☆☆☆☆	☆☆☆ – ☆	☆☆☆☆☆	☆☆☆	☆☆☆☆☆

[1] Sparkling wine base only.
[2] Both sparkling base and still wine.

VINTAGE CHART

SEMILLON

LEADING AREAS	1986	1987	1988	1989	1990
NEW SOUTH WALES					
HUNTER VALLEY	☆☆☆☆☆	☆☆☆☆	☆☆☆	☆☆☆	☆☆☆
MIA [3]	☆☆☆☆☆	☆☆☆☆	☆☆☆☆☆	☆☆ – ☆	☆☆☆☆
VICTORIA					
MACEDON	—	☆☆☆	☆☆☆☆	☆☆	☆☆☆☆
SOUTH AUSTRALIA					
BAROSSA [4]	☆☆☆☆	☆☆☆☆	☆☆☆☆☆	☆☆☆☆	☆☆☆☆☆
CLARE [4]	☆☆☆☆	☆☆☆	☆☆☆☆☆	☆☆☆☆	☆☆☆☆☆
WESTERN AUSTRALIA					
LOWER GREAT SOUTHERN	☆☆☆☆	☆☆☆	☆☆☆	☆☆☆☆	☆☆☆☆☆
MARGARET RIVER	☆☆☆☆	☆☆☆	☆☆☆☆	☆☆	☆☆☆☆
QUEENSLAND					
GRANITE BELT	☆☆☆☆ – ☆	☆☆☆☆ – ☆	☆☆☆	☆☆☆☆	☆☆☆☆

[3] Sweet botrytised styles only.
[4] Wood-matured styles.

SAUVIGNON BLANC

LEADING AREAS	1986	1987	1988	1989	1990
VICTORIA					
GEELONG	☆☆☆	☆☆☆☆ – ☆	☆☆☆☆	☆☆☆☆ – ☆	☆☆☆☆
PYRENEES	☆☆☆☆ – ☆	☆☆☆☆	☆☆☆☆ – ☆	☆☆☆☆	☆☆☆☆
YARRA VALLEY	☆☆☆☆	☆☆☆☆	☆☆☆☆☆	☆☆☆☆	☆☆☆☆☆
SOUTH AUSTRALIA					
CLARE	☆☆☆☆☆	☆☆☆☆☆	☆☆☆	☆☆☆☆	☆☆☆ – ☆
COONAWARRA	☆☆☆☆ – ☆	☆☆☆	☆☆☆☆	☆☆☆	☆☆☆☆☆
McLAREN VALE	☆☆☆☆☆	☆☆☆	☆☆☆☆☆	☆☆☆☆	☆☆☆☆
PADTHAWAY	☆☆☆☆	☆☆☆☆	☆☆ (frost)	☆☆☆	☆☆☆
WESTERN AUSTRALIA					
LOWER GREAT SOUTHERN	☆☆☆☆	☆☆☆	☆☆☆☆	☆☆☆☆☆	☆☆☆☆
MARGARET RIVER	☆☆☆☆	☆☆☆	☆☆☆☆	☆☆☆☆	☆☆☆

VINTAGE CHART

MARSANNE

LEADING AREAS	1986	1987	1988	1989	1990
GOULBURN VALLEY	★★★★	★★★★	★★★★	★★★★★	★★★★

VERDELHO

LEADING AREAS	1986	1987	1988	1989	1990
NEW SOUTH WALES					
HUNTER VALLEY	★★★★	★★★★	★★★	★★★	★★★
WESTERN AUSTRALIA					
MARGARET RIVER	★★★★	★★★	★★★★	★★★★★	★★★★
SW COASTAL PLAIN	★★★★	★★★ – ★	★★★★★	★★★★★	★★★★
SWAN VALLEY	★★★	★★★★	★★★★	★★★★★	★★★★

RHINE RIESLING

LEADING AREAS	1986	1987	1988	1989	1990
VICTORIA					
DRUMBORG	★★★	★★	★★★ – ★	★★★★	★
GREAT WESTERN	★★★ – ★	★★	★★★ – ★	★★	★★★★
MACEDON	★★★★★	★★★★	★★★★★	★★★★	★★★★★
SOUTH AUSTRALIA					
ADELAIDE HILLS NORTH	★★★★	★★★★★	★★★	★★★★	★★★
BAROSSA	★★★	★★★	★★★★	★★★	★★★★
CLARE	★★★★	★★★★★	★★★★	★★★★	★★★★★
COONAWARRA	★★★★	★★★	★★★★	★★★★	★★★★
McLAREN VALE	★★★★	★★★ – ★	★★★★	★★★	★★★★
PADTHAWAY	★★★★	★★★★	★★ (frost)	★★★	★★★
WESTERN AUSTRALIA					
LOWER GREAT SOUTHERN	★★★★★	★★★★	★★★★	★★★ – ★	★★★★★
TASMANIA					
PIPERS BROOK	★★★ – ★	★★★	★★★★	★★★★	★★★★★
HOBART	★★	★★★ – ★	★★★★ – ★	★★★★★	★★★★★

VINTAGE CHART

CHENIN BLANC

LEADING AREAS	1986	1987	1988	1989	1990
WESTERN AUSTRALIA					
SW COASTAL PLAIN	★★★★	★★★★ – ★	★★★★★	★★★★★	★★★★
SWAN VALLEY	★★★	★★★★	★★	★★★	★★

PINOT NOIR

LEADING AREAS	1986	1987	1988	1989	1990
NEW SOUTH WALES					
HUNTER VALLEY	★★★★	★★★★	★★★	★★ – ★	★★★
VICTORIA					
BENDIGO	★★★★★	★★★	★★★★	★★★★	★★★★
DRUMBORG[1]	★★★★	★★★	★★★	★★★★★	★★★★ – ★
GEELONG	★★★★	★★★★ – ★	★★★★ – ★	★★★★	★★★★
MACEDON	★★★ – ★	★★★★	★★★★★	★★★★★	★★★★
MORNINGTON PENINSULA	★★★★	★★★	★★★★	★★★★★	★★★★
YARRA VALLEY	★★★★★	★★★★	★★★★★	★★★	★★★★★
SOUTH AUSTRALIA					
COONAWARRA	★★★ – ★	★★★	★★★★	★★★★	★★★★
WESTERN AUSTRALIA					
LOWER GREAT SOUTHERN	★★★★	★★★★	★★★★★	★★★★	★★★★★
MARGARET RIVER	★★★★	★★	★★	★★★★	★★★
TASMANIA					
PIPERS BROOK	★★★★★	★★★	★★★★	★★★	★★★★★
HOBART	★★★★	★★★★	★★★★★	★★★★★	★★★★★

[1] Sparkling wine base only.

VINTAGE CHART

SHIRAZ

LEADING AREAS	1986	1987	1988	1989	1990
NEW SOUTH WALES					
HUNTER VALLEY	☆☆☆☆☆	☆☆☆☆☆	☆☆☆ – ☆	☆☆☆	☆☆☆
MUDGEE	☆☆☆☆	☆☆☆☆	☆☆☆ – ☆	☆☆☆	☆☆☆
VICTORIA					
BENDIGO	☆☆☆☆☆	☆☆☆	☆☆☆☆	☆☆☆☆	☆☆☆☆
GOULBURN VALLEY	☆☆☆☆☆	☆☆☆☆	☆☆☆☆	☆☆☆☆	☆☆☆☆
GREAT WESTERN	☆☆☆☆ – ☆	☆☆☆	☆☆☆☆ – ☆	☆	☆☆☆☆
MACEDON	☆☆☆☆ – ☆	☆☆☆☆	☆☆☆☆☆	☆☆☆	☆☆☆☆☆
NE VICTORIA	☆☆☆☆ – ☆	☆☆☆ – ☆	☆☆☆☆ – ☆	☆☆ – ☆	☆☆☆☆
PYRENEES	☆☆☆☆ – ☆	☆☆☆	☆☆☆☆ – ☆	☆☆☆☆	☆☆☆☆
SOUTH AUSTRALIA					
ADELAIDE HILLS NORTH	☆☆☆☆☆	☆☆☆	☆☆☆☆	☆☆☆	☆☆☆☆☆
BAROSSA	☆☆☆☆☆	☆☆☆☆	☆☆☆	☆☆☆	☆☆☆☆
CLARE	☆☆☆☆	☆☆☆☆	☆☆☆☆☆	☆☆☆☆	☆☆☆☆☆
COONAWARRA	☆☆☆☆	☆☆☆ – ☆	☆☆☆☆	☆☆ – ☆	☆☆☆☆
McLAREN VALE	☆☆☆☆	☆☆☆☆	☆☆☆☆	☆☆☆	☆☆☆☆
WESTERN AUSTRALIA					
LOWER GREAT SOUTHERN	☆☆☆☆ – ☆	☆☆☆☆	☆☆☆☆ – ☆	☆☆☆☆	☆☆☆☆☆
SW COASTAL PLAIN	☆☆☆	☆☆☆ – ☆	☆☆☆☆	☆☆☆ – ☆	☆☆☆☆
SWAN VALLEY	☆☆☆	☆☆☆☆	☆☆☆☆	☆☆☆☆☆	☆☆☆☆☆
QUEENSLAND					
GRANITE BELT	☆☆☆☆☆	☆☆☆☆	☆☆ – ☆	☆☆☆☆	☆☆☆☆

VINTAGE CHART

CABERNET SAUVIGNON AND CABERNET BLENDS

LEADING AREAS	1986	1987	1988	1989	1990
NEW SOUTH WALES					
HUNTER VALLEY	★★★★	★★★★	★★★	★★★	★★ – ★
MUDGEE	★★★★	★★★★	★★★	★★★	★★★
VICTORIA					
BENDIGO	★★★★★	★★★	★★★★	★★★★	★★★★
GEELONG	★★★★ – ★	★★★★	★★★★ – ★	★★★★	★★★★
GOULBURN VALLEY	★★★★★	★★★★	★★★★	★★★★	★★★★
GREAT WESTERN	★★★★★	★★★	★★★★★	★★★★	★★★★
MACEDON	★★★ – ★	★★★★	★★★★★	★★	★★★★★
MORNINGTON PENINSULA	★★★★	★★★	★★★★★	★★★★	★★★★★
PYRENEES	★★★★ – ★	★★★	★★★★★	★★★★	★★★★
YARRA VALLEY	★★★★★	★★★ – ★	★★★★★	★★★	★★★★★
SOUTH AUSTRALIA					
ADELAIDE HILLS NORTH	★★★★★	★★★★	★★★★	★★★	★★★★
BAROSSA	★★★★★	★★★★★	★★★★	★★★★	★★★★★
CLARE	★★★★	★★★	★★★★	★★★★	★★★★★
COONAWARRA	★★★★	★★★★	★★★★★	★★★ – ★	★★★★★
McLAREN VALE	★★★★	★★★★	★★★★	★★★★	★★★★★
WESTERN AUSTRALIA					
LOWER GREAT SOUTHERN	★★★★★	★★★★ – ★	★★★★ – ★	★★★★★	★★★★★
MARGARET RIVER	★★★★	★★★	★★★	★★★★★	★★★★
SW COASTAL PLAIN	★★★	★★★ – ★	★★★★	★★★ – ★	★★★★
SWAN VALLEY	★★★★	★★★	★★★★	★★★★	★★★★★
AUSTRALIAN CAPITAL TERRITORY	★★★★	★★★ – ★	★★★★★	★★★	★★★★

SPARKLING WINES

LEADING AREAS	1986	1987	1988	1989	1990
ADELAIDE HILLS SOUTH	★★★	★★★★	★★★★	★★★	★★★★ – ★

VINTAGE CHART

Notes on the use of the vintage chart

Vintage charts are of necessity generalisations, and the chart set out here is no different. Winemaking skills are of a high standard in Australia. Therefore extremely poor vintages are very rare, and even then good wines may often be found, just as poor wines may sometimes be found in good vintages. The trick is to try and taste before you buy. This is usually quite easy when buying at the cellar-door but more difficult when buying at retail outlets although it may be possible at tastings conducted by good wine merchants.

The evaluations of varieties in the various areas are based on reports given to me by winemakers of long experience in that district, all of whom wish to maintain strict anonymity. I thank them for their assistance.

In the chart, ★★★★★ is of outstanding quality, ★★★★ of good to excellent quality, ★★★ average to good, ★★ fair only, ★ definitely taste first. Where a hyphen (–) is used it indicates a half-star, e.g. ★★★★ - ★ is the intermediate classification 4½ stars.

The chart covers the vintages 1986 to 1990. Whites and reds from all these vintages may be found in good bottle shops, though at time of writing, 1990 reds were still in cask and unlikely to be generally released for sale till 1992 or later.

The choice of 'leading areas' is entirely my own. Thus rhine riesling and shiraz are absent from Margaret River and the Yarra Valley, though the varieties are of course grown there; other varieties are more worthy in those areas. There are no entries for cabernet sauvignon in Tasmania; rarely does the variety ripen properly there. The reader will no doubt notice other omissions, to his or her fury. They are not mere oversights. As I mention often in this book, not all of Australia is suitable for every grape variety.

Traminer has been omitted from the chart after due consideration. It should generally be drunk within one to two years of its vintage, often growing oily and fat after this. Doubtless after reading such a statement, some winemakers will write to me pointing out how fresh and fragrant his or her traminer is after seven or eight years in bottle. Such wines are the exception to the rule.

USING THE SENSES TO ASSESS WINES

By normal use of sight, smell and taste (our precious yet 'common' senses) most wine enthusiasts can gain a very fair impression of the quality of any wine presented to them. Tasting experience certainly helps, but it is not indispensible.

Colour

Visual aspects of wine—colour, condition and clarity—can anticipate much of what one smells and tastes in wine. Almost all good grape juice, with few exceptions, begins life (for wine is a living substance) a healthy green in hue.

As **white grapes** ripen, their colour changes from a vivid green to a much paler and translucent green-yellow. In the flesh and juice of that grape the levels of fruit sugars such as glucose and fructose grow while the levels of acids such as tartaric and malic decrease—pH, that measure of alkalinity and acidity tending to increase also. The grape colour shows in the wine. Thus a good white wine, when young, will usually show hints of green on a pale yellow background.

As **red grapes** ripen, the green bunches change in colour to green-red, to red-purple and finally to purple. The French call the colour changes of both whites and reds *véraison*. The colour of red wines is of course extracted from the skin of the grape, the grape 'must' remaining in contact with the skins after crushing and during most of fermentation, unless the winemaker has another purpose in mind: e.g. in the making of rosé the skins will be removed when the desired colour is obtained; and in the making of sparkling wine base from red varieties such as pinot noir or meunier, when skin contact and consequent pink coloration is not desirable.

In white wine making the juice usually receives as little contact as possible with the skins, unless for an increased flavour effect in varieties to be fermented and/or matured in wood, such as chardonnay or semillon. During crushing, white juices usually receive a small addition of sulphur dioxide to prevent oxidation, being then separated from their solids (particles of skin and pulp) by one of three methods: the addition of enzymes and cold settling, filtration, or centrifuging. Small amounts of sulphur dioxide are also added to red 'musts' for the same purpose prior to fermentation, which for reds usually takes place between 20 and 25°C, whereas whites require a lower range of 10 to 15°C to preserve delicacy of aroma and flavour.

Faults in colour and condition include cloudiness, usually indicative of metallic contamination or bacterial spoilage, or brownness (oxidation). Clarity and hue are important in all wines. Depth of colour is important in younger reds destined for cellar aging. There are four degrees of wine colour: 'brilliant' or 'clear' wines being most desirable, whereas 'dull' and 'cloudy' wines are most certainly to be avoided.

Two more aspects of appearance of white wine deserve attention. The first is the deeper yellow hue of some young whites, which usually results from fermentation and maturation in new small oak barrels which, because of their larger surface area compared to wine content, allow greater air contact with the wine, a tolerated byproduct of oxidation, associated with some chardonnays and semillons.

The other aspect of appearance, rarely seen these days, is the deposit of potassium bitartrate crystals (a natural deposit of tartaric acid, once amusingly called 'wine diamonds') in white wines that have not been cold-stabilised, when such whites are being chilled prior to consumption. This deposit is quite harmless and is avoided in modern winemaking by chilling whites to about 5°C prior to bottling, thereby precipitating the tartrate crystals in the tank rather than later in the bottle.

The final aspect of appearance that needs to be mentioned is the 'crust' of red wines which may be noticeable in wines as young as three to four years old. 'Crust' is a mixture of tartrates and colouring matter no longer required by the wine, as it continues to maturity. It is gritty and unpleasant to the taste but is in fact quite harmless. If the bottle is stood upright for half an hour prior to service it will sink into the punt of the bottle, and thereafter the wine may be safely decanted.

Mention should also be made of the depth of colour in young reds. Often such profundity of hue connotes an equal depth of palate, degree of body and youth. So one should anticipate not only depth of fruit, but also more tannic astringency and acidity. It is all a question of balance, whether such a colour is an indicator of equal quality.

Nose

It is generally acknowledged that about 90 per cent of all taste sensations occur because of our sense of smell. Air breathed in through the nose transports the wine's aroma molecules to the olfactory epithelium at the roof of the nose, where olfactory nerves (aroma receptors) are stimulated. This stimulation transmits the sensation through neurons to the brain.

Air is also inhaled through the mouth, where it passes over the back palate (the back of the tongue), is heated by body temperature, and rises to the back of the nose by way of the respiratory canal and the olfactory receptors. What happens then is that the most complete sensation of smell and taste occurs after you swallow the wine, because swallowing forces a warmer air draught with a concentration of odour molecules to the aroma receptors.

Thus smelling a good wine can tell the taster a great deal about it. With experience the taster can detect grape variety, regional characters and often the method of making (e.g. carbonic maceration), as well as the maker's particular technique with that wine—an emphasis on ripeness and skin contact and type of oak. One can also detect bottle age.

Likewise, smelling a bad wine is most instructive. A discussion of wine faults and factors leading to imbalance in wine is given later.

Although not a practice I follow in this book, it has been customary to divide the smell or 'nose' of wine into three parts: 'aroma' denotes smells derived from the actual grape variety as juice; 'bouquet' denotes smells derived after winemaking from fermentation, wood-aging, or bottle-aging; and 'off odours' are smells derived from faulty winemaking, such as hydrogen sulphide, excessive sulphur dioxide, or volatile acidity.

Taste

The tongue is covered with most important little bumps called papillae. Those contributing most to our sense of taste are called fungiform or circumvallate papillae. The different concentration of these taste buds (epithelial cells) causes what we call the front, middle and end palate ('finish') of a wine. As it is quite difficult to separate these three portions of palate, the most normal sensation of taste is a synthesis of all three in the middle of the tongue.

Taste buds at different areas of the palate perceive different sensations. These differentiations are called the four primary taste sensations: *sweetness* at the tip of the tongue; *saltiness* (hardly ever found in wine) at the front sides of the tongue; *acid* (the zest and life of wine) on the rear sides of the tongue; and *bitterness* (tannin/astringency) at the back of the tongue.

There are also tactile sensations—the tongue can feel the viscosity (thickness or body) of the wine in the mouth. Body is the amount of alcohol and tannic extract a wine has, which softens as the wine ages. 'Weight' is a synonymous wine term, being measured as 'delicate', 'light' 'medium' or 'full'.

Other tactile sensations are the 'drying' of the palate by tannin (both grape and wood); hotness from high alcohol levels; the 'dumbing' of wine that is too cold; softness; and, conversely, hardness.

Harmony of component parts results in wines of good balance. Acid and alcohol should be in balance with fruit, the only factor that may be in excess.

Wine faults

OXIDATION A wine, or indeed grapes, exposed to simply too much air. The results are brownness in colour, 'strawiness' on nose, and dull, stale, flat tastes on palate. A fault that may occur at any stage of the winemaking process if insufficient care is taken.

EXCESSIVE ACIDITY A fault found most often in white wines picked green and unripe, resulting in an excess of malic acid, the 'apple' acid, a raw, tart taste which puckers the mouth and unbalances the palate. It is less common in red wines which undergo a malolactic fermentation, converting malic acid to softer, more palatable lactic acid and giving off carbon dioxide.

Another offensive acidity that must be mentioned is the volatile kind. VA, as it is commonly called, results from the presence of an excess of acetic acid and occurs in all wines to a lesser extent. It is caused by bacterial action, which oxidises alcohol during and after fermentation and, if present in excess in a young wine, finally converts it to a very disagreeable vinegar-like liquid. Volatile acidity within bounds is acceptable only in extremely sweet botrytised whites.

EXCESSIVE RESIDUAL SUGAR A fault, chiefly of whites, though it may occur in rosés or nouveau-style reds, is the retention of unfermented grape sugar in the form of glucose and fructose. Residual sugar is usually detectable by palate at levels over 5–6 grams per litre. When used as a winemaking technique to fill out the middle palate of rhine riesling and other white wines it is acceptable, but the retention of too great an amount leads to a mawkish, cloying palate which seems neither sweet nor dry. Great care is also needed in the making of wines that retain unfermented sugar, as the merest trace of active yeast could lead to the wine refermenting in the bottle.

ALCOHOL In the presence of yeast, grape sugar converts chemically into alcohol and carbon dioxide, so alcohol is a very necessary constituent (in proper proportion) of table wines, which, according to type, may contain any amount of alcohol between 10 and 14 per cent. However, alcohol in excessive amounts in table wine gives a hot, peppery taste. Note that grape sugar measured in degrees Baumé gives an almost exact conversion into percentage of alcohol in the finished wine.

SULPHUR DIOXIDE A preservative used in wine since ancient times as an anti-oxidant. It is still employed today in virtually all wines but to a smaller extent. In excessive amounts it imparts a disagreeable chemical odour, particularly noticeable at the back of the nose, as well as bleaching the colour of a wine and hardening its palate.

OAK The many types of oak impart various smells and tastes to red and white wine during fermentation and maturation. The use of oak vats and casks in the making and maturation of wine has been traditional in Western Europe since the Roman Gauls invented oak cooperage 1700 years ago. The smells and flavours of oak have been multifariously described. Terms such as 'vanillan', 'spicy', 'coconut' and 'smoky' (perhaps an epithet more appropriate to the degree of barrel toasting than to the oak itself) are in common use, but whatever the description, the smell and taste of oak should not intrude too much upon the wine—'oak' being a wine fault if it dominates the fruit character of either white or red wines, throwing it out of balance.

TANNIN An organic constituent of wine derived from the skins, seeds and stalks of red grapes during the fermentation and maturation of red wines, which may also appear in white as a result of fermentation and maturation in new oak, which imparts its own tannins to white wines. Though tannin is important in the self-clearing of young reds and in their proper maturation over a number of years, its appearance in whites is not so highly regarded. Its presence in excess can be perceived on nose and palate: on nose by a powdery woody aroma; on palate as a drying sensation on back of the tongue and gums, often described as 'furry'.

HYDROGEN SULPHIDE Rotten egg gas or the smell of it in wine. Produced as a degradation of sulphur dioxide in the presence of yeasts in fermenting wine—detectable in amounts as low as 1 part per million and removable from young wine if treated swiftly. When bound into red it is manifested on nose as 'meat' or sometimes 'garlic' or 'rubber' with corresponding off-flavours on palate.

CORKINESS The foul chemical smell and taste of cork tainted by the complex chemicals, 2,4,6 trichloroanisole (2,4,6 TCA) and guaiacol. The odour of 2,4,6 TCA is detected on nose as mould or wet hessian, while that of guaiacol is similar to smoke or phenol. 2,4,6 TCA is thought to occur because of the reaction of chlorine on cork lignin consequent upon the washing of corks by calcium hypochlorite, or alternatively because of the spraying of cork oaks by wood preservatives containing chlorophenols which are subsequently degraded by microbial growth. Guaiacol probably occurs as a result of faulty corkwood affected by a streptomyces mould. Similar characters have also been known to occur in oak casks carelessly rinsed with cleansers containing chlorine.

GRAPE VARIETIES AND ACCEPTED SYNONYMS IN AUSTRALIA

ACCEPTED NAME	ACCEPTED SYNONYM
BARBERA	
CABERNET FRANC	
CABERNET SAUVIGNON	
CHAMBOURCIN	
CHARDONNAY	
CHENIN BLANC	
COLOMBARD	
DORADILLO	
FRONTIGNAC, WHITE	MUSCAT À PETITS GRAINS BLANC
GAMAY NOIR À JUS BLANC	
GRENACHE	
MALBEC	
MARSANNE	
MATARO	
MERLOT	
MEUNIER	PINOT MEUNIER
MONDEUSE	REFOSCO
MÜLLER-THURGAU	
MUSCADELLE	
MUSCAT GORDO BLANCO	GORDO, AND MUSCAT OF ALEXANDRIA
NEBBIOLO	
PALOMINO	
PEDRO XIMENES	PEDRO XIMINEZ
PINOT NOIR	
RIESLING	RHINE RIESLING
RUBIRED	
RUBY CABERNET	
SANGIOVESE	
SAUVIGNON BLANC	
SEMILLON	
SHIRAZ	SYRAH
SYLVANER	
TARRANGO	
TRAMINER	GEWÜRZTRAMINER
TREBBIANO	UGNI BLANC
VERDELHO	
VIOGNIER	
ZINFANDEL	

GLOSSARY

ACIDITY A general term describing the acids in table wine. Tartaric, malic and citric are the three major acids, present in total between 5 and 7.5 grams per litre (g/l). Such acidity, which occurs naturally in table wine but may be supplemented when necessary by the winemaker, is fundamental in providing flavour, life and balance in all table wine and in counteracting bacterial spoilage.

ANTI-OXIDANT Any permitted additive such as ascorbic acid (vitamin C) which prevents the oxidation of wine, white wine particularly.

APPELLATION A description or designation, in particular, of a wine-producing area such as Mudgee.

APPELLATION D'ORIGINE CONTRÔLÉE A system of law which defines wine regions and regulates and enforces the types of vines and methods of viticulture and sometimes winemaking that may be employed in such regions. The system originated in France, spreading later to Italy, Germany and Spain, the object being to guarantee the authenticity but not necessarily any particular level of quality of such wines.

AROMA The smell of the grape variety or wine, a term used in this book co-extensively with 'bouquet'.

AUSLESE In German wine law a legally regulated term indicating a certain sugar level (°Oechsle) for wine must, attained usually as a result of attack by *Botrytis cinerea* (noble rot). In Australia an unregulated wine description generally indicating a late-harvested sweet white wine, often but not necessarily affected by noble rot.

BALANCE The harmony between the various components of the flavours and sometimes the aroma of wines. In flavour, between fruit and acid in non-oaked white wine; and between fruit, oak and acid in oak-matured white and red. In aroma, between fruit and oak.

BARREL FERMENTATION The technique of fermenting red or white wine in a barrel, sometimes used in red wine for finishing fermentation, but important these days in fermenting white wines such as chardonnay where the effect of fermentation in barrel is required by the winemaker for complexity on nose and palate.

BARRIQUE A small oak barrel of 225 litre capacity, a term of Bordeaux origin.

BAUMÉ A hydrometer scale for the measurement of grape and other fruit sugars, the Baumé measurement being approximately equal to the alcohol content of the wine if all available sugar is allowed to ferment out.

BEERENAUSLESE A regulated German wine term indicating a greater Oechsle (sugar) level than Auslese. A term not regulated in Australia, but generally descriptive of extremely sweet botrytis-affected white wines.

BERRY SET The success or otherwise of the vine in evolving or 'setting' its fruit in springtime after flowering.

BLANC DE BLANCS A still or sparkling white wine made from white grapes, a term used commonly in Champagne, France, for champagnes made totally from chardonnay.

BLEND Any mixture of red or white grapes or wines used to produce a blended red or white wine. In Australia the winemaker must specify the blend, e.g. cabernet sauvignon–merlot, if using less than 80% of the dominant variety, but need not do so if more than 80% of the dominant variety is used. Therefore a wine consisting of 85% cabernet sauvignon and 15% merlot may be called either cabernet sauvignon or cabernet sauvignon–merlot.

BLIND TASTING A tasting where the identities of the wines tasted are unknown to the tasters.

BLUSH WINE A wine with the merest trace of pink, an American fad of the late 1980s.

BOTRYTIS/*BOTRYTIS CINEREA* a naturally wind-blown mould which attacks the skin and dehydrates the flesh of red or white grapes. Its effect, always undesirable in red grapes and often in white, is to cause oxidation in the colour, nose and palate of resultant wines. In ideal conditions (cool, slightly humid weather or a similarly controlled artificial environment), *Botrytis cinerea* (*pourriture noble* in French, *edelfäule* in German and 'noble rot' in English) concentrates the sugar and acid components of white grapes resulting in intensely sweet wine, much reduced in quantity. Rhine riesling and semillon usually produce the best examples of sweet botrytised whites.

BOTTLE AGE   The controlled and slightly oxidative effects of aging red and white wines in the bottle in favourable cellaring conditions. Also, the changes, usually favourable, resulting in the colour, nose and palate of a wine that has been so cellared.

BOUQUET   *See* Aroma.

BRUT   In sparkling wine parlance, the driest of wines, which usually does contain some sugar (up to 1.5% by volume).

BUTTERY   A term descriptive of the aroma and palate texture of a white wine, usually oak-matured, that has undergone total or partial malolactic fermentation.

CASK-FERMENTED   *See* Barrel fermentation.

CASSIS   The aroma and sometimes the taste of blackcurrants found in top-quality cabernet sauvignon, excellent in moderation.

CHÂTEAU   A common term for a wine estate in Bordeaux and sometimes in other areas of France. Occasionally used in Australia (e.g. Chateau Tahbilk).

CLARET   Traditionally the English term for the red wines of Bordeaux. In Australia any red wine with a dry, slightly astringent finish, only rarely these days used to describe wines of quality. St Henri Claret is one such wine of quality.

CLIMAT   (French) The environment of a particular vineyard: its soil, aspect and microclimate.

CLONE   A group of vines descending from a common parent. Such vines are usually selected for several viticultural purposes, e.g. quality or quantity of fruit, or both, or resistance to disease.

CLOS   A French term denoting an enclosed vineyard, usually quite small and surrounded by a wall, often the subject of a single ownership.

CLOSED   A term applied to young wines subdued in aroma and/or flavour, sometimes resulting from recent bottling.

COOL FERMENTATION   Fermentation carried out usually with the assistance of some refrigeration at a lower than ambient temperature, which will vary from white to red and according to the wine style to be made.

CORKED   The mouldy smell and sour taste of a wine affected by mould spores in corks, thought to be the result of interaction of the residue of cork bark insecticides and chlorinated town water when such bark is washed. A character that can vary from barely noticeable to revoltingly obvious.

CÔTE   (French) Hillside, often where the best (and poorest) vineyard soils are. The most famous is the Côte d'Or of Burgundy, which grows the world-famous pinots and chardonnays of that area.

CRU   (French) Literally 'growth', a term used in the classification of wines, e.g. *grand cru* (great growth), *premier cru* (first growth), applied to many famous French wine areas.

CULTIVAR   A plant variety, e.g. a grape variety, produced and propagated by cultivation.

CUVÉE   (French) Literally the contents of a wine vat, extended to mean all the wine made at a certain time. Also, in Champagne, applied to the free-run juice of the first pressing (from which the best wine is usually made) and also to the blending of base wines which are then bottled, tiraged and set to referment according to the classic champagne method.

DEGREE-DAYS   A method of heat summation originally devised by Professors M. A. Amerine and A. J. Winkler to differentiate Californian wine growing areas according to their suitability for growing certain wine grapes. Heat summation means the total of the mean daily temperatures above 10° Celsius (50° Fahrenheit) during the growing season—a base set because below that temperature there is almost no growth. For example, a mean daily September temperature of 16°C in an Australian vineyard area would result in a summation of 180 degree-days for that month (i.e. 6 × 30). Thus the system can be extended to all wine growing areas throughout the world.

DEMI-SEC   Literally 'half-dry', a term applied both to still and sparkling wines to describe a perceptible level of sweetness in the wine, in champagne usually between 4 and 6% by volume.

EGG WHITE   The albumen of an egg, beaten and added to wine to clarify it and sometimes in red wines to soften tannins.

FERMENTATION   The process of converting grape juice into wine by adding yeast which converts the primary grape sugars (glucose and fructose) into alcohol and carbon dioxide.

GLOSSARY

GRAND CRU *See* Cru.

HYBRID A grape variety produced by cross-pollination of two parent varieties, so as to produce a vine for a certain purpose, e.g. earlier ripening, disease resistance, etc. Such varieties may be bred from two *Vitis vinifera* parents or a cross of *Vitis vinifera* and an American species.

KABINETT (German) A term originally denoting a specially reserved wine, but since 1971 legally defined to mean a wine made from fully matured grapes without added sugar and from a delimited area.

LEES The residue of yeast cells, tartar, skins, seeds, etc., found in vats and casks after a wine has completed its fermentation or after any subsequent racking.

MACERATION, CARBONIC An alternative form of fermentation whereby the juice of whole berries is fermented inside the berry without any prior crushing or with only partial prior crushing. The resultant wines, usually red, are distinctively fruity and forward on nose and palate and are intended to be drunk young.

MADERISED An oxidative change to white wines brought about by storage in excessively hot conditions.

MALOLACTIC A secondary fermentation of wine occurring after the primary fermentation whereby its malic acid component is broken down by bacteria into lactic acid and carbon dioxide. Desirable in red wines and increasingly used in wood-matured whites.

MARC The residue of grape skins, stalks, seeds, etc., left after grapes have been pressed. In France, often distilled to make a spirit (e.g. Marc de Bourgogne).

MERCAPTAN Produced during the fermentation process by the reduction of hydrogen sulphide to ethyl mercaptan and ethyl sulphides, marked by an offensive smell, sometimes described as garlic, rubber, game or boiled cabbage.

MÉTHODE CHAMPENOISE The classical method of making sparkling wine, whereby the secondary fermentation of the wine (to put the bubbles in) takes place in the bottle in which the wine is sold.

MISTELLE A legal grape juice concentrate used to sweeten white wines.

MOUSSE The foam of a sparkling wine, which in younger wines should be vigorous and which, importantly, imparts life and zest to the wine in the mouth.

MUST In white wine making, the unfermented white juice. In red, the greenish-red mixture of juice, pulp, skins and seeds to be fermented.

NOBLE ROT *See* Botrytis.

OAK/OAK COOPERAGE A traditional medium for maturing red and white wine, used since Roman times and invented by the Roman Gauls as a way of transporting wine (as opposed to that other method of ancient times, the amphora). The taste imparted to wine by new oak barrels has become accepted in Western cultures and is part of winemaking skill today. Oaks from all over Europe and the USA are used in the fermentation and maturation of red and white wines, French oaks such as Nevers, Limousin, Tronçais, Allier and Vosges being the most favoured medium for maturation.

OENOLOGY Literally, the study of wine; more appropriately, the science of winemaking.

OIDIUM Powdery mildew, a fungus disease of the vine.

OXIDATION The exposure of wine to too much air, with a consequent browning of colour and the appearance of 'strawy' aromas and flavours.

OXIDATIVE A wine in the process of oxidising.

pH The power of hydrogen. A measure of acidity or alkalinity running on scale from 1 (extremely acid) to 14 (extremely alkaline). Table wine usually has an acidity between pH 3 and 3.6.

PHYLLOXERA The vine louse, a native of North America, which was introduced to Europe in the 1860s by the importation of native vines and proceeded to devastate the vineyards of Europe by eating the roots of *Vitis vinifera* for the next 50 years, until it was effectively controlled by grafting vinifera varieties on to resistant American rootstocks, a practice still necessary today. Australia, especially Victoria, was also badly affected about the same time.

PREMIER CRU *See* Cru.

QUAFFING WINE Any white or red wine designed for immediate drinking.

ROOTSTOCK Types of vine roots on to which are grafted varieties of *Vitis vinifera*. This procedure is followed to protect the vinifera variety from various root-eating insects such as phylloxera and nematodes. Provided all watershoots are pruned off, the vine above the graft will faithfully reproduce its vinifera variety.

ROSÉ A pink wine usually made by crushing red grapes and allowing the resultant juice a few hours' skin contact (for colour extraction) before the skins are removed. Vinification then proceeds as for white wine.

SEC (French) Literally 'dry'. In reality, slightly sweet, especially when appearing on a champagne label, where such a wine will contain between 2 and 4% of sweetness by volume.

SECONDARY FERMENTATION In still wines red or white, *see* 'Malolactic'. In bottle-fermented sparkling wines, it is the fermentation taking place in the bottle, which creates carbon dioxide (the bubbles), after the addition of the liqueur de tirage (a mixture of sugar and yeast).

SEKT A German term for sparkling wine.

SMOKY-OAK The smell and taste of oak that has been charred or 'toasted'. New small oak barrels may be ordered with various degrees of 'toast', light, medium or heavy.

SPÄTLESE (German) Literally 'late-picked', usually indicative of a degree of sweetness between Kabinett and Auslese.

SPUMANTE An Italian term to describe a sparkling wine.

STAINLESS STEEL A hard steel alloyed with a high percentage of chromium with a high resistance to rust and other corrosive agents. Widely used in wineries in any tanks and equipment where wine or juice is likely to come into contact with metal. Because it is virtually inert it imparts no taste to wine, nor do stainless steel tanks have, like oak casks, any 'pores' through which air may affect wine. It is also very easy to keep clean.

STALKY The bitter green taste of grape stalks, sometimes present in poorly made red wines.

SULPHUR DIOXIDE (SO_2) An anti-oxidant and preservative added to must at fermentation and also in small amounts to wines during maturation in tank or cask. In excess it imparts an unpleasant chemical odour which scours the nostrils and delays the natural development of colour, nose and palate. Of very ancient use in connection with wine, it is referred to in Homer's *Iliad*.

TABLE WINE Any wine intended to be used at table as an accompaniment to food, but in some European countries a wine of lesser quality or low classification, e.g. in German, *Tafelwein*, in Italian, *vino da tavola*.

TANNIN A complex component of wine, drawn from the skins, seeds and stalks of grapes. Because of red winemaking methods, it is present in greater quantities in red than whites. Plays an important part in clarifying young red wines after primary fermentation and thereafter during maturation, helping to create a proper structure for longevity. Easily perceived during tasting as the drying sensation on the sides and back of the tongue.

TERRA ROSSA Literally 'red earth'. A reddish soil above a limestone base. In particular, the soil found in Coonawarra in a north–south strip, about 15 kilometres long varying in width from a few hundred metres to about 2 kilometres. Produces cabernet sauvignon and shiraz grapes of superb quality and in good quantity, but should not be overcropped.

TROCKENBEERENAUSLESE (German) Literally 'selected dried berries'. The sweetest category of all botrytis-affected German whites. A term strictly defined in Germany, but not in Australia.

VANILLIN A sweet aroma, often detected in wines that have been matured in American oak.

VARIETY, VARIETAL A term describing the various kinds of wine grapes, e.g. the chardonnay variety or simply 'chardonnay' and, by extension, the wines made from such varieties. Australian wine law prescribes that a varietal wine so labelled must contain at least 80% of that variety.

VÉRAISON The point in time when grapes begin to change colour from green to translucent green–yellow in the case of white grapes, and from green to red–purple in the case of red grapes.

VIGNERON (French) A winegrower and winemaker.

VIGNOBLE (French) A vineyard.

VINIFICATION The process of making wine.

VINTAGE The wine of a particular year and also the time when grapes are picked for winemaking. A great wine from a memorable year.

VITIS VINIFERA The vine species, native to Europe and the Middle East, from which most of the world's wines are produced.

WOOD-MATURED Red or white wines matured in oak, rarely in other timbers.

YEAST Single-celled organisms found naturally on the skins of grapes and capable of being cultured. Importantly, the catalyst responsible for transforming grape sugar into alcohol and carbon dioxide.

YEASTY The aroma of yeast in newly made white or red wine. Usually passes off after a few weeks.

INDEX

A

Abbey Vineyard, 143
Adams, Tim, 55, 81, 133
Adelaide, 39, 69, 145
Adelaide Hills, 4, 34, 35-38, 60, 128, 145, 179-180
Adelaide Plains, 39, 69, 181
Albany, 64, 111, 156
Alcorso, Julian, 41, 111
Alexanders, 173-174
Alkoomi, 46, 56, 64, 83, 156-157, 185-186
Allandale, 117
Allanmere, 14, 117
Allied Vintners, 116
Allier (oak), 6, 10, 11, 12, 15, 18, 21, 22, 25, 26, 99
Aloxe-Corton, 2
Alsace, 70, 90
Alto Adige, 90
Amberton, 62
American (oak), 11, 31, 35, 54, 99, 113, 116
Anderson, Stuart, 24, 25, 109, 120, 150, 151
Angle Vale, 39
Angove's, 39, 69
'Anne', 50
Antcliff, Alan, 71, 94
Apulia, 3
Ardèche, 3
Argentina, 57, 112, 165
Arrowfield (Mount Arrow), 14, 16, 52, 113, 160, 166, 193
Ashbrook, 45
Ashmans, 114
Auburn, 40
Auld, Patrick, 116

Australian Capital Territory, 17, 89
Austria, 71, 90
Avoca, 25, 120, 122, 153, 192

B

Bailey's, 29, 62, 125
Baldivis Estate, 186
Baldwin, Gary, 118
Balgownie Estate, 24-25, 109, 120, 150, 163
Balkans, the, 163
Ballandean Estate, 57
Balnarring, 88
Bannockburn, 22, 62, 106-108, 120, 123, 150
Barbera, 187
Barooga, 4, 30
Barossa Ranges, 60, 146
Barossa Valley, 38-39, 53, 57, 60, 69, 74, 78, 109, 146, 162, 180, 192
Barossa Valley Estate, 39
Barry, Brian, 82, 148, 183
Barry, Jim, 61, 81, 133, 148, 183
Barsac, 47
Baruzzi, John, 159
Barwang Estate, 120
Basedow, 38, 53-54, 78, 130, 146
Bear, John Pinney, 139
Beaujolais, 2, 165, 187
Beechworth, 30
Bellarine Peninsula, 22
Ben Ean Vineyard, 50
Bendigo, 23, 25, 53, 66, 85, 91, 109, 120, 150-151, 171
Beresford, 35, 60, 178
Berriedale, 88

Berri-Renmano, 39 (*see also* Renmano)
Bertranges (oak), 24
Bertuch, Dr Graeme, 172
Bianchet, 123, 169
Bidure, la, 137
Biturica, 137
Bituriges, 137
Blanche Barkly, 151
Blass, Wolf, 38, 54, 55, 81, 82, 130, 161, 180, 191
Blaxland, Gregory, 95
Bleasdale, 127
Blewitt Springs, 54
Blue Pyrenees Estate, 172
Bordeaux, 47, 48, 50, 57, 69, 137, 163, 165, 167, 168
Botobolar, 119, 161, 167
Botrytis, 36, 47, 48, 50, 52, 65, 71, 73, 76-77, 80, 143, 177
Bourgeuil, 163, 165
Bowen, 73, 127, 143, 177
Brady, Tony, 133
Brand, 32, 73, 127, 143, 177
Bremer Wines, 74
Bridgewater Mill, 61, 182, 191
Broke, 11, 115, 117, 119
Brokenwood, 14, 51-52, 116-117, 159, 161, 166
Brown Brothers, 27, 29, 30, 62, 87, 124-125, 152, 153, 172, 173, 187, 193
Brown, John Charles, 87
Buckland Valley, 193
Bulgaria, 163
Buller, 87, 125
Bunbury, 42, 56, 134
Bungendore, 17, 167
Burdigala (Bordeaux), 137

INDEX

Burge & Wilson, 162
Burge, Grant, 53, 60, 180
Burgundy, 2, 7, 9, 95, 98, 99, 100, 101, 102, 103, 105, 106, 107, 110, 187
Buring, Leo, 72, 75, 76
Burnbrae, 119
Busby, James, 3, 48, 57, 95, 112, 137, 164, 165
Busselton, 42

C

Cabernet Franc, 163, 165
Cabernet Sauvignon, 137 *et seq.*
Cadillac, 47
Cahors, 165
Calais Estate, 52
California, 3, 8, 57, 71, 95, 112, 137, 164, 165
Callatoota, 160
Campbell, 87, 125
Canada, 3
Canberra, 17, 30, 89, 167
Cape Clairault, 56, 63, 155-156
Capel Vale, 42, 64, 84, 134, 186
Cape Mentelle, 45, 56, 134, 153, 155-156, 186, 187
Carmody family, 23
Carrodus, Dr Bailey, 106
Cartwright, Bob, 68
Cashmore, Mark, 8, 9
Cassegrain, 17, 53, 120, 161, 164, 167
Cassegrain, John, 17, 53, 62
Castlemaine, 121, 151
Castle Rock, 83, 158
Cathcart Ridge, 27, 123, 172
Central District (South Australia), 95
Central Highlands (Victoria), 27, 120, 121, 150
Chablis, 2, 30, 57
Chais Clarendon, 34
Chambers, 87
Chambertin, Le, 100
Chambourcin, 187
Champagne, 21, 95, 192

Chandon, Domaine, 2, 96, 191
Chardonnay, 2 *et seq.*, 63, 190-193
Chardonnay (village), 2
Chassagne-Montrachet, 2
Chatsfield, 83, 185
Chenin blanc, 56, 64 *et seq.*
Chianti, 138
Chile, 48, 57, 137, 164
Chinon, 163, 165
Chittering Estate, 42, 183
Cimicky, Charles, 180
Clare, 31, 33, 36, 37, 39, 40, 48, 54, 55, 61, 71, 73, 78-82, 132-133, 146-148, 163, 181-183
Clare Estate (Penfold's), 40, 181-182
Clarke, Jeff, 28, 152, 171
Clos Colline (Cassegrain), 17
Coghill Vineyard, 22
Coldstream, 96
Coldstream Hills, 19, 20, 53, 62, 106, 111, 149, 169
Colombard, 68 *et seq.*
Condrieu, 68
Conti, Paul, 42, 65, 133
Coolawin, 145
Coonawarra, 4, 31-32, 35, 36, 45, 58, 59, 61, 71-73, 90, 97, 101, 125-127, 139-144, 146, 162, 173-177
Coonawarra Machinery Company, 72, 142
Cope-Williams, 23, 108, 193
Corino, Carlo, 160, 187
Coriole, 35, 128, 145
Corowa, 29
Corton-Charlemagne, 24
Côte de Beaune, 101
Côte d'Or, 2, 98, 100
Cowra, 3, 4, 15, 16, 35, 36
Cowra Wines, 16
Craiglee, 23, 121-122
Craigmoor, 119, 167
Crawford River, 85
Croser, Brian, 5, 35, 37, 97, 191
'Croser', 191
CSIRO, 164
Cullen, 44, 63, 111, 155, 162, 184

Cullen, Diana, 44, 155, 184
Cullen, Vanya, 44, 184
Currency Creek, 35, 59

D

'D', 192
Dalwhinnie, 25, 122
Dalwood, 133
Daringa, 35, 60, 145
Darling Ranges (Perth Hills), 42, 183
Darlington Vineyard, 183
Dead Man's Hill, 91
de Bortoli, 52
de Castella, Hubert, 29, 139
Delatite, 27, 28-29, 86-87, 91, 169, 170
Denmark (Western Australia), 45, 156, 157
Diamond Valley, 19, 88, 168
Dimethyl sulphide, 140
Donnybrook, 134
Donovan, 85
Doonkuna, 17, 89
Drayton, 13, 51, 66, 89, 114, 115, 160, 166
Drayton, Trevor, 13
Dromana Estate, 22, 108, 169
Drumborg, 84-85, 150
Dundon, Rob, 178
Duval, John, 131

E

Eaglehawk Estate, 55, 81
East Gippsland, 23, 170
Echuca, 30
Eckersley, Ken, 23, 150
Eden Valley, 4, 37, 38, 40, 48, 73, 74-78, 82, 90, 129, 146, 163
Egan, Reg, 108, 150
Elderton, 78, 130, 180
Elgee Park, 22, 68, 88, 169
'Elizabeth', 50, 51
Elizabeth (South Australia), 148
Elliot, 12, 13

INDEX

Ellis, John, 23, 27-28, 121, 154
Elsewhere Vineyard, 39
Erudgere, 119, 167
Evans & Tate, 44, 63, 133, 155, 156, 184
Evans family, 13, 73
Evans, Len, 13

F

Farmer Brothers Trophy, 30
Farr, Gary, 22, 106-107
Fearn Hyll, 85
Fermoy, 45
Fernhill—*see* Thomas Fernhill
Fiumara, Robert, 91
Flaxman's Valley, 90-91
Fletcher, Brian, 20
Florita Vineyard, 81
Fordwich, 119
Forest Hill, 46, 82-83, 157
France, 2, 3, 47, 57, 68, 95, 112, 137, 163, 187
Francois, Château, 52
Frankland River, 5, 45, 46, 64, 82, 84, 120, 133, 134, 135, 156, 157, 158, 186
Fraser, 14, 52, 117
Fratin Brothers, 26
French oak, 10, 15, 31, 99, 116
Freycinet (Tasmania), 41
Freycinet (Western Australia), 56, 63, 185
Frontignac, white, 92
Fyffe, David, 19, 104-105, 149

G

Galafrey, 156
Gamay noir à jus blanc, 187
Gault-Millau, 103
Geelong, 4, 22-23, 62, 96, 101, 108, 109, 120, 123, 150, 169
German oak, 8, 9, 19, 31
Germany, 70-71, 84, 89, 90, 91, 95
Gherardi, Peter, 185

Giaconda Vineyard, 30, 173
Gilbert, Joseph, 76, 139
Gilbert, Simon, 118
Gilbey's, 116
Gin Gin, 42, 67, 158
Gippsland, 4, 23, 150, 170
Gironde, 164
Glenrowan, 62
Gnangara, 133
Goodwin, Steve, 62
Goonawarra, 23
Goulburn River and Valley, 27, 61, 124, 151
Goundrey, 45, 64, 83, 135, 157
Gramp's, 39
Grand Cru, 37, 129
Grange, 126, 131-132, 192
Graves, 47, 137, 164
Graveyard Vineyard, 14, 118, 159
Great Dividing Range, 27, 96, 150
Great Western, 25, 26, 27, 39, 46, 84, 85, 120, 122-123, 154, 172, 190, 192
Grillet, Chateau, 68
Grilli, Joe, 39, 181
Grinbergs, Martin, 21
Grosset, Jeffrey, 41, 82, 148, 183
Great Southern, Lower, 45, 82, 156, 185
Grenache, 134, 187

H

Hainault, 183
Halliday, James, 19-20, 106, 169
Hanging Rock, 23, 121
Hanlin Hill, 79
Happ, Erland, 45, 134, 184-185
Hapsburgs, 70
Hardy, Thomas & Sons, 32-33, 34, 39, 59, 73-74, 79, 110, 128, 144-145, 178, 179
Haselgrove, 143
Hastings Valley, 17
Hawkes Bay, 155, 164
Heathcote, 24, 121
Heathcote Winery, 24, 66, 91, 121

Heemskerk, 41, 192
Heggies, 38, 39, 76, 77, 179
Heidsieck, Charles, 192
Heidsieck, Piper, 192
Heinz, 79
Henschke, 37, 54, 74, 77, 129, 146, 179
Hickinbotham, Stephen, 22
Hickinbotham Winemakers, 22, 108, 150
Hill of Grace, 129
Hillside Vineyard, 135
Hill-Smith Estate, 37, 39, 54, 60
Hilltops, 120, 135, 161
HJT Vineyards, 30
Hobart, 111
Hoey, Alan, 76
Hohenzollerns, 70
Hohnen, David, 153, 155
Hollick, 32, 72, 110, 143, 177
Hollydene, 12, 13
Holmes, 129
Holmes à Court, Robert, 46, 83
Home, Ian, 191
Hope Valley, 39, 91
Hooper, Rodney, 157
Hordern's Wybong Estate, 118
Horseshoe Vineyard, 52
Houghton, 42, 46, 65, 66, 83, 157-158
Howard Park, 83, 157
Howard Vineyard, 115
Hugo, 33, 74, 128
Hungerford Hill, 10, 51, 73, 115, 143, 166, 192
Hunter Estate, 12, 13
Hunter, Lower, 13, 49, 50, 51, 114, 118, 120, 160, 166, 167, 192
Hunter, Upper, 52, 89, 118, 160, 166, 193
Hunter Valley, 3, 4, 8, 9, 10, 11, 12, 13, 14, 15, 48, 49, 50, 71, 95, 101, 102, 103, 104, 112, 113, 114, 116, 117, 138, 158, 166, 167
Huntington Estate, 16, 52, 119, 160, 161, 166-167
Huon Valley, 89

INDEX

I

Idyll Vineyard, 169
Ingoldby, 35, 60, 145
Iran, 112
Italy, 3, 48, 70, 95, 137, 138, 143, 165

J

Jacaranda Ridge, 142
Jamieson's Run, 173, 175
Jane Brook, 42, 65
Jasper Hill, 121
Jesuit Brotherhood, 182
Jimmy Watson Trophy, 127, 139, 141, 144, 155, 156, 176
Johannisberg riesling, 71
John, Philip, 49
Jolimont, 87
Jordan, Dr Tony, 99
Jud's Hill, 82, 183
Jura, 3, 95

K

Kaiser Stuhl, 38, 130, 131, 146
Kalimna, 130, 146
Katnook, 32, 59, 72, 127, 142, 176
Kaval, Roland, 29, 125
Karina, 88
Kelly, Dr Alexander, 144
Keyneton, 37, 179
Kies Estate, 38
Killeen, Chris, 173
Killerby, Dr Barry, 42
King River Valley (Victoria), 17, 29, 62, 87, 91, 153, 172
King River (Western Australia), 64
Kinzbrunner, Rick, 30
Kirri Billi, 143, 177
Klevner, 95
Knappstein, Tim, 40, 58, 61, 74, 79-80, 147-148, 162
Knight Granite Hills, 85, 121
Kominos, 57
Koombahla, 29, 62

Krondorf, 39, 78, 162, 193
Krug, 192
Kyneton, 171

L

Laira, 127, 143
Lake, Max, 114, 138, 158
Lake's Folly, 13, 138, 158
Lakewood, 180
Lance, David and Cathy, 19, 105, 168
Landragin, Dominique, 190, 191-192
Lange, Merv, 185
Langhorne Creek, 74, 127, 178
Langton, 45, 64, 135
Lark Hill, 17, 89, 167
Latour, Louis, 3
Launceston, 41
Lauriston, 39, 181
Le Amon, Chateau, 53, 120, 151
Leasingham, 40, 55, 78, 79, 133, 148, 183
Lebanon, 2
Lebrina, 5
Leconfield, 143
Leeuwin Estate, 43, 63, 96, 111, 155, 162
Lehmann, Peter, 38, 53, 130, 146
Lenswood, 77
Leonay, Chateau, 75
Leschenault, 42, 56, 134
Lillydale Vineyards, 21, 87
Lillypilly Estate, 89, 91
Limousin (oak), 6, 9, 11, 35, 36
Limestone Ridge, 32, 127, 174
Lindeman's, 11, 31, 32, 49, 50, 58, 59, 66, 72, 87, 110, 127, 140-141, 142, 144, 146, 173-174
Little's, 52, 160
Loire, 57, 64, 65, 156, 163, 165
Long Gully, 21
Longleat, 124, 173
Loupiac, 47
Lynch, Ken and Joyce, 135
Lyndoch, 78

M

McAlister Vineyard, 170
Macarthur, Sir William, 70, 165
Macedon, 4, 23-24, 27, 84, 85, 96, 108, 121, 151, 193
McLaren Vale, 4, 33, 34, 54, 57, 59, 74, 95, 127-128, 144-145, 162, 166, 178-179, 187
McMahon, Peter, 17, 18, 107, 149
Mâcon, 2
McWilliam's, 11, 17, 52, 89, 113, 114, 120, 158-159
Magill Estate, 126, 130-131
Main Ridge Estate, 22
Malbec, 165 *et seq.*
Mandurah, 43, 186
Margaret River, 5, 43-45, 46, 47, 55-56, 58, 63, 67, 83, 84, 96, 111, 134, 155-156, 158, 183-185, 186-187
Marienberg, 145
Mariginiup, 133
Marion's Vineyard, 41
'Marmite', 97
Marrowbone Road, 53, 114
Marsanne, 67-68
Marseille, 112
Marsh Estate, 52
Mast, Trevor, 26, 172
Mataro, 187
May, Brother John, 182
Mazure, Edmond, 192
Meadowbank, 89
Meadow Creek, 153
Medoc, 137, 155, 164, 165, 174
Melbourne, 23, 108, 121
Menetou-Salon, 57
Merlot, 163 *et seq.*
Merrick's, Stoniers, 22, 108
Merrill, Geoff, 34, 57, 158
Methoxypyrazine, 57
Meursault, 2, 8, 24, 26, 37
Middle East, 2, 112
Middleton, Dr John, 17, 18, 101, 107, 149-150, 168
Milawa, 29, 87, 124, 152-153, 187, 193

Mildara, 31, 39, 72, 126, 140, 173-175, 191
Mildura, 4, 31
Mintaro Cellars, 82
Miramar, 16, 52, 119, 161
Miranda, 17, 53
Mitchell, Jane, 80-81, 147-148
Mitchell, Thomas, 86, 173
Mitchelton, 67, 68, 86, 124, 152, 161, 173
Moët, 5
Mokoan, Lake, 30
Mondavi, Robert, 57
Mondeuse, 172, 187
Monichino, 30
Montara, 27, 85
Montrose, 15-16, 52, 62, 119, 160-161, 167, 187
Moondah Brook, 42, 65, 67, 158
Moorilla Estate, 4, 41, 88
Morey St Denis, 106
Mornington, 4, 17, 21-22, 88, 96, 108, 109, 120, 150, 155, 168, 169, 170
Mosel, 70
Moss Wood, 5, 43, 55, 96, 111, 155
Mountadam, 37, 77, 145
Mount Arrow—*see* Arrowfield
Mount Avoca, 25, 61, 122, 154
Mount Barker, 5, 45, 46, 55-56, 58, 64, 82, 84, 111, 120, 134, 152, 156-157, 163, 185-186
Mount Bingar, 53
Mount Buller, 27, 86, 170
Mount Chalambar, 26
Mount Edelstone, 129
Mount Helen, 27-28, 30, 58, 61, 86, 152, 170-171
Mount Hurtle, 60, 145
Mount Ida, 121
Mount Langi Ghiran, 26, 85, 123, 154, 172
Mount Lofty Ranges, 34, 35, 145
Mount Mary, 17, 107
Mount Pleasant, 10, 11-12, 49, 50-51, 89, 114, 115, 160
Mount Pleasant (South Australia), 37

Mourvedre—*see* Mataro
Mouton, 176
Mudgee, 3, 4, 52, 62, 119, 160-161, 163, 166-167
Murray River, 4, 29, 30, 96
Murrumbidgee Irrigation Area (MIA), 4, 16, 48, 50, 52, 62, 91, 96, 119, 167
Muscadelle, 65, 69
Muscat, 92
Muscat Gordo Blanco, 69
Musigny, le, 100

N

Nagambie, 67, 124
Nebbiolo, 187
Netley Brook, 46, 157
Nevers (oak), 7, 8, 11, 12, 25, 26, 35, 36, 99, 110
New South Wales, 3, 4, 7, 17, 48, 49, 62, 89, 95-96, 138, 153, 161, 166-167
New (Wine) World, 3, 57, 70, 90, 163, 165
New Zealand, 3, 95, 137, 155
Nicholson River, 23, 170
Norman's, 34, 74, 145
Nursery Vineyard, 72

O

Oakridge Estate, 168
Oakvale, 52, 117
Old Block Vineyard (St Hallett), 130
Olive Farm, 42
Orange (New South Wales), 161
Oregon, 3, 95
Original Vineyard (Brand's), 127
Orlando, 38, 39, 46, 77, 90, 162, 193
Osicka, 173

P

Padthaway, 4, 31, 32-33, 58-59, 71, 73, 74, 90, 95, 97, 110, 127, 144, 177, 179
Palmer, Château, 141
Partalunga, 78
Passing Clouds, 151
Paterson, David, 117
Pato, Chateau, 117
Paulett, Neil, 82, 133, 183
Peaches Trophy, 105
Pearse family, 83
Pedare, 60, 78, 91, 110
Peel Estate, 43, 134
Pemberton, 46
Penedès, 138
Penfold's, 3, 13, 38, 39, 40, 79, 82, 116, 126, 130-132, 162, 176-177, 180, 181, 192
Penola, 143
Perth, 28, 43, 65, 133
Perth Hills, 42, 183 (*see also* Darling Ranges)
Petaluma, 3, 35-37, 73, 79, 82, 143, 175-176
Peterkin, Dr Mike, 44
Peterson's, 52, 117
Petrus, Château, 163
Pettavell, 108
Pewsey Vale, 76-77, 139, 145, 179
Pfeiffer, Chris, 29, 87
Phillip, Governor, 137
Phoenicians, 112
Piccadilly, 35-37, 97, 191
Pierro, 44, 63, 111
Pike, Andrew and Neil, 41, 82, 133, 148, 183
Pinot noir, 94 *et seq.*
Pinot nero, 95
Pipers Brook, 4, 5, 41, 88, 91, 111
Pirie, Dr Andrew, 91, 111
Pirramimma, 33, 74, 145
Plantagenet, 45, 83, 111, 135, 157, 158
Poitou, 57
Pokolbin, 11, 17, 49, 89, 115, 117, 120, 143, 161
Polish Hill River, 39, 41, 82
Pomerol, 163, 164
Porongorups, 83, 158

INDEX

Porphyry, 50
Portet, Dominique, 122, 153, 192
Port Macquarie, 17, 53, 62, 96, 120, 161, 167, 187
Port Phillip, 22, 169
Pouilly-Fuissé, 2
Pouilly-Fumé, 57
Pratten, Dr Peter and Mrs Diana, 64, 134, 186
Preece, Colin, 122, 153
Primo Estate, 39, 69, 181
Prince Albert Vineyard, 108
Provence, 137
Pyrenees, 25, 61, 85, 122, 153, 172
Pyrus, 32, 173-174

Q

Qualco, 46
Queen Adelaide, 46
Quelltaler, 55, 81
Quincy, 57

R

Randall, Warren, 97, 190
Redbank, 122, 154
Redbrook Vineyard, 155, 184-185
Redgate, 63, 185
Redman, Bill, 127
Redman Winery, 143
Reed International, 113
Remy, Chateau, 172, 192, 193
Renmano, 39, 60, 74, 178, 181
Reuilly, 57
Reynell, John, 95
Reynella, Chateau, 33, 34, 95, 126, 145, 178
Reynolds Yarraman, 52, 118
RF, 39, 162
Rheingau, 70, 75
Rhine riesling, 27, 39, 47, 70 *et seq.*
Rhone, 67, 112, 173, 187
Ribbon Vale, 56, 63, 185
Richmond (Tasmania), 5
Richmond Grove, 3, 12, 13
Riddoch Estate, 72, 127, 176

Riddoch, John, 141-142, 176, 192
'Riesling', 50, 71
Riggs, Iain, 51
Rising Vineyard, 106
Ritchie family, 109
Riverland, 39, 60, 69, 74, 89, 111, 178
Roberts, Bob, 119, 160, 166
Robertson, Rick, 81
Robson, Murray, 117
Robson Vineyard, 117, 160
Rochford, 85
Rockford, 78, 146
Roederer, Louis, 4, 192
Rosbercon Vineyard, 30
Rose Hill Vineyard, 114, 115
Rosemount Estate, 14-15, 52, 89, 118, 143, 161, 177, 193
Roseworthy College, 17, 148, 181
Rossetto, 17, 53
Rothbury Estate, 9-10, 13, 16, 49, 50, 51, 95, 103-104
Rouge Homme, 31, 32, 110, 127, 142
Roupnel, Gaston, 100
Roxburgh, 14-15
Royal Sydney Wine Show, 39, 40
R2 (yeast), 6, 19
Rubired, 187
Ruby cabernet, 187
Rumania, 48
Rumbalara, 57
Rutherglen, 120, 125, 152
Ryan, Phil, 115, 159
Ryde, 95
Ryecroft, 34, 54, 60, 128

S

St Emilion, 164, 165
St Gilbert, 167
St George Vineyard, 140-141, 142
St Hallett, 38, 53, 69, 78, 130, 180
St Helga, 77
St Henri, 130, 132
St Hilary, 39
St Hubert's, 20, 106, 123, 168

St Hugo, 142
St Leonards, 29, 125, 152, 173
St Matthias, 41, 89
St Véran, 2
Salinger, 190, 192
Saltram, 130
Sancerre, 57, 95
Sandalford, 67, 134
Sangiovese, 187
'Sauternes', 52
Sauternes, 47, 50
Sauvignon Blanc, 57 *et seq.*
Savagnin, 3
Savoie, 95
Saxonvale, 3, 8-9, 10, 12, 51, 117-119, 159
Scarpantoni, 33, 34, 59, 74, 128, 179
Seaview, 144, 162, 192
Sefton, Daryl and Nini, 169
Semillon, 47 *et seq.*
Seppelt, 10, 30, 33, 39, 46, 73, 78, 84-85, 97, 122, 150, 154, 161, 163, 177-178, 181, 190, 191, 192, 193
Seppelt, Karl, 37, 77, 129
Serenella Estate, 52
Sevenhill, 82, 133, 148, 182
Seville Estate, 17, 18, 88, 107, 123, 149
Shapira, Steven, 42, 183
Shaw, Philip, 15, 143
Shiraz, 112 *et seq.*
Shottesbrooke, 179
Simon, Andrew, 14
Simon Whitlam, 14, 52, 117, 118, 160
Sissingh, Gerry, 49, 51, 115
Skillogalee, 81, 182-183
Smith, Dr Bob, 118
South Africa, 48, 137
South America, 3, 70
South Australia, 4, 48, 57, 65, 66, 69, 90, 95, 109, 125, 127, 132, 138, 139, 148, 173, 191
Southern Vales (Winery), 54
South West Slopes (New South Wales), 135

INDEX

Soviet Union, 48
Spain, 3, 137, 138
Spatburgunder, 95
Stafford Ridge, 37, 60, 77
Stanley Wine Co, 39, 40, 55, 79, 146, 181
Stanthorpe, 41, 62, 89, 135
Stanton & Killeen, 173
Steingarten, 77
Stockhausen, Karl, 49, 75, 115
Stoney Vineyard, 89
Stonier's—*see* Merrick's
Strathbogie Ranges, 27, 86, 152, 170
Sunraysia, 17, 69, 87, 125
Sunshine Vineyard, 50
Sutherland, Alasdair, 9, 118, 159
Sutherland, Neil, 14, 117
Swan Hill, 66
Swan Valley, 42, 83, 133, 158, 163
Switzerland, 95
Sydney International Smallmakers Competition 1989, 82, 122

T

Tablelands, Central (New South Wales), 161
Tahbilk, Chateau, 53, 67, 68, 86, 124, 125, 139, 151-152
Taltarni, 51, 85, 122, 153, 163, 172, 192, 193
Tamburlaine, 52, 117, 160
Tarrawarra, 20-21
Tasmania, 4-5, 41, 48, 88, 91, 135, 154, 163, 191, 192
Taylor's, 39, 40, 81, 148
Terrace Vale, 14, 52, 117, 160
Thalgara, 117
Thistle Hill, 161, 167
Thomas Fernhill, 35, 60, 74, 128, 145, 179
Thomson, Viv, 25
Tisdall, 27, 28, 30, 86, 152, 170-171
Tinson, Harry, 29, 30
Tocaciu, Pat, 72
Tollana, 33, 60, 72, 77, 78, 129, 145, 146

Tolley Pty Ltd, Douglas A., 39, 60, 78
Tooma, 4
Traminer (Gewurztraminer), 3, 90, 91
Trentham Estate, 62
Tronçais (oak), 15, 18, 22, 26, 99
Tucker Trophy, 39
Tulloch, 13, 51, 113, 116, 160
Tulloch, Hector, 116
Tulloch, Jay, 116
Tulloch, Keith, 115
Tumbarumba, 4, 96
Tyrrell, Murray, 166
Tyrrell's, 3, 7-8, 10, 13, 49, 51, 53, 95, 96, 101, 102-103, 113, 114, 192

U

Umbria, 3
United States, 70

V

Vasse Felix, 83, 185
Verdelho, 66-67
Vickery, John, 75
Victoria, 4, 17, 27, 29, 31, 61, 65, 66, 68, 69, 84, 85, 87, 89, 96, 104, 108, 109, 113, 120, 125, 126, 138, 139, 148, 149, 154, 163, 167, 170, 171, 172, 173, 191, 192, 193
Victoria, Cuvée, 96, 191
Viognier, 68
Virginia (South Australia), 60
Virgin Hills, 171-172
Vollrads, Schloss, 75
Vosges (oak), 6, 10, 12, 15, 18, 21, 22, 23, 25, 36, 37, 99
Vougeot, Clos, 3

W

Wade, John, 45, 83, 157

Wahgunyah, 29, 87, 125, 152
Walkershire, 124, 173
Wangaratta, 30, 173
Wanneroo, 65, 133, 134
Wantirna South, 108, 150
Warby Ranges, 29
Warrenmang, 122, 154
Washington State, 3, 164
Watervale, 75, 78, 81
Watervale Cellars, 82
'Wattles', the, 54
Weaver, Geoff, 37, 74
Wendouree, 133, 148, 183
Wentworth, 62
Western Australia, 3, 5, 41, 45, 46, 48, 55, 56, 63, 64, 65, 66, 82, 84, 111, 133, 134, 138, 155, 158, 183, 186, 187
White, Alex, 21, 87
Whitlam, Nicholas, 14
Whitlands Plateau, 27, 29, 30, 153
Wignall, 45, 64, 111
Willespie, 66, 156
Willyabrup, 155, 184
Wilson, Ian, 193
Wilson, Dr John, 82
Wilson Vineyard, 82, 183
Windy Hill, 64, 135
Winery, Old, 166
Winewood, 57
Wirra Wirra, 33, 54, 59, 74, 145, 178, 193
Wolf Blass—*see* Blass, Wolf
Woodbury Estate, 78, 146
Woodley, 46
Woodstock, 60, 128, 145
Wyangan Estate, 53
Wyndham Estate, 12, 13, 51, 66, 116, 119, 160
Wynn, Adam, 37, 110
Wynn's, 31, 45, 71, 72, 97, 110, 126, 141, 142, 176, 192

X

Xanadu, Chateau, 45, 56

Y

Yalumba, 38, 76, 179, 192
Yarra Burn, 19, 104, 105, 149, 193
Yarra Glen, 21
Yarra Ridge, 21, 62, 169
Yarra Valley, 4, 17, 18, 19, 20, 21, 22, 47, 53, 62, 87, 88, 96, 101, 104, 105, 108, 120, 123, 147, 150, 162, 167, 168, 191
Yarra Yering, 106, 107, 169
Yarrinya, 21
Yellowglen, 190, 191, 193
Yeringberg, 21
Young (New South Wales), 120
Yugoslavia, 71, 163

Z

Zambelli, 150
Zema Estate, 73
Zinfandel, 187
Zuber Estate, 121